2442 STEPS TO CRAZY

—THE BEGINNING

D1500681

2442 STEPS TO CRAZY
—THE BEGINNING

This story is based on real events

By

D. Paul Fleming

ISBN: 979-8-9876396-1-0

The will to never quit, to never give up, to keep fighting when everyone around you surrenders...That is the power of faith.

Without hope, you only have faith. Without faith, there is little need for hope.

Together, hope and faith will carry you through all of life's battles.

Dedicated to all who suffer from abuse, physical or mental. You are the reason this book was written.

Tell me your story so the beastly grip of cruelty is wiped clean from your life: www.blackhawkbooks.com.

OPENING CHAPTER

Don't breathe, or Crazy will hear you. Don't move, and we'll be safe…for now, or at least I could hope. Hiding seemed to be a perfect defense, the only defense against what was sure to happen if I didn't crawl into small spaces and worm away from the madness swirling around every second of my life.

God, how I hated him. How I hated the sight of him, the anger of his presence, and the meanness that came with his every look. His dark, sunken eyes and that breath of his. It smelled like the dead chickens we'd find in the coop. The ones with the small white worms stacked on top of one another. That smell, that putrid musk that seemed to cling to the inside of your nose. His breath smelled of food gone bad, like when you refused to eat dinner and it was waiting for you in the morning, covered in those multicolored flies.

Why won't someone help me, hide me, or take us away from this life of misery? I've tried to hide before, but Crazy would find me and drag me out of the protective shell I thought would keep me safe. His anger was so visible on his face. I'd scream with all my might as he ripped me away from my hiding place. Grabbing hold of my arm with those hands of fury, those fists of power. Knowing

1

if he found me, a beating was certain, by his hands or by that wooden stick.

Hiding was the only thing I had, the only weapon I could use to fight back. He found me last time in the wooden box with the white balls that made me gag. It was the place where Mother stored the winter blankets. The old chest she said came from her grandmother. He found me when I hid under the stairs with all the spiderwebs. He found me when I tried to hide at the neighbors' small apartment. They told Crazy where I was. If only they'd known what their betrayal would cost me.

I kept searching for places to hide, to run to when Crazy's face started to contort into that terrifying shape. The way it looked when he would go past rage and into his fits of screaming and throwing anything and everything within reach, including Mother, my brother, or me. We were cared for just like all the objects—a lamp, a table—to be tossed about in his powerful spiraling anger. Running and hiding was the only option to avoid, or maybe delay, a beating.

Tucked away in my newest hiding place, I prayed—begged, really—for God to take us back to the time before Crazy entered our lives. Those were the happy times. It was just Mother, my older brother by two years, and me. No beatings, no hitting, and Mother always protected me against anything scary, like a dream or a person I didn't know or like. She'd hold me with such love and warmth, it felt like everything in my life was in place, perfect in a way only a child could understand.

Mother never yelled at me or my brother. She never raised her voice or let anyone yell at us or harm us. She was soft and pretty, with the best smile in the world. She gave us everything we wanted and made sure we were never hungry. Happiness was a real thing, a real feeling that was always with us. Life was so much fun before Crazy.

I didn't know fear, real fear, until Crazy came into our lives. To me, he was like the story about the wolf in sheep's clothing Mother would read to my brother and me before tucking our blankets tightly around us with that mother's love. That love that only exists from that single special person. It's a unique gift that's impossible to explain, but it's real. A mother's love is a magical feeling, like an invisible cloak of warmth, joy, and safety that somehow radiates from the arms and the smile of a mother. The only proven magic to heal your hurts and mend a bump or a cut or to make everything right again. My mother's love could fix anything...before Crazy.

No one else in the world can offer that feeling, which is impossible to describe. Like telling Mother about the shadows I would see. Sometimes I could feel Crazy before he entered a room. Mother would tell me the shadow people were real, that they were there to protect me. She said they were my own private guardian angels. The type who helped us move forward in life and stayed with us no matter what happened. She told me they were spirits of goodness sent by God to watch over us. They were there to keep me safe when she wasn't close by so nothing in the world could harm me. Mother would sit beside the bed before we would close our eyes and talk to those spirits. We'd ask them to watch over me, watch over my brother, and protect us from any darkness that could steal our souls or lead us in a bad way. She had us talk to them with her so we'd believe they were real.

Sometimes I could see and hear the shadows, but my brother never could. I always felt safe in their presence. I was never afraid of them, and I felt comforted by them like a secondary mother feeling, the kind that makes the sickness so much better, the kind that makes the hurt of scraping your knee stop hurting, like a gentle kiss from Mother. That magical way that can only be understood as a mother's love, yet a sense of it resided in those shadows.

We were in the park when I first remember Crazy and Mother talking. Later that day, he was in our apartment. He was at our table, eating our food. He had slicked-back hair, smelled like burnt toast, and was always lighting those sticks that created a smell that stuck to everything and lingered like a dumpster in the heat of summer. His smell was changing the comfortable and familiar odor of our home and quickly turning it into something else. It was becoming something less loving, with hints of fear tied behind the plumes of billowing smoke as Crazy tipped his head back and blew the stench toward the ceiling like he was trying to keep it away from us as he sat on the small sofa next to Mother. She laughed, and they poked fingers into each other's sides when he wasn't sucking on those smoke sticks or drinking from those brown bottles. He had a rhythm as he moved his hands, one to his mouth with the brown bottle, and with the other following, he'd suck the stick of fire held between his fingers. He'd take in deep breaths, and with a loud popping sound, he'd pull the burning stick from his lips. He'd take another deep breath and hold it for a second before pushing the light-colored smoke toward the ceiling, making a face like that of a wolf with its nose pointing at the moon as it howls.

I didn't like Crazy one bit, and he knew it. I made sure he knew of my displeasure for him, for the smoky mess he made, and for getting in the way of my mother and me. His face would change when I would push my way in between him and my mother. He'd get a look that wasn't nice. There was a scheming behind that face.

Maybe a planning of things to come, and then it would wash away. Back to that false smile to hide his true feelings, his true intentions. I could sense it coming off him, and it felt painful inside my chest. There was something very wrong with him.

A dark shadow followed close to him, but it wasn't a shadow you played with on the ground. It kind of floated and moved around like the breeze was pushing it in different directions. It would spiral and circle with different tones of blackness, dark gray at times but mostly shades of black. Sometimes you couldn't see it, and then it would reappear in the blink of an eye as if it had walked out of him.

I would stare at the flowing blackness around Crazy and watch it move about like it was its own person. Mother would tell him I could see an imaginary playmate as he scowled and told her that wasn't a real thing and she should stop me from believing in those old wives' tales. You could see the darkness growing when he would get upset, like when Mother told him of such things as guardian angels. It was like an early warning signal, a signal I'd come to learn so much more about as Crazy spent more and more time around Mother, my brother, and our home.

My brother, on the other hand, was open to Crazy's invasion. My brother and I were very different kids, and we both knew it, even at this early stage of life. He was always seeing the good side of things, regardless of how bad they got. He always found the good in people no matter how bad or evil they were. There was something about him, a way of just wanting to "go with the flow." To be part of the group. He was a friendly kid who could get along with everyone, no matter who they were. He didn't care much about yesterday and was always talking about tomorrow as the better days ahead.

My brother welcomed Crazy into his life. He wanted to share Mother with him, and he was happy Mother had someone in her life. Maybe it was because he was with her for a couple of years before I came along, or maybe it was just his way. Crazy never paid much attention to my brother, as if he was there but not really seen. To Crazy, my brother had a presence, like those shadows I could see. There but never really seen.

I told my brother there was something about Crazy that wasn't right. In fact, there was something really wrong with him. I'd try to explain what I could see and what it felt like, but my brother would just laugh it off as if I were making it all up. My brother wanted nothing to do with the feelings I'd get or the things I saw. I grew to believe he was afraid of what he couldn't see. Of course he would never let me know he was afraid of anything, not as the big brother.

I wanted to regain Mother's attention and stop what was fast becoming an everyday thing, having Crazy in our lives all the time. One day I found him asleep in our bed. I stood beside the bed looking at his sleeping face, wondering why he was in my spot. His big fat head, greasy hair, and smelly mouth were crushing my pillow. He made a lot of noise when he slept, growling sounds that rolled in and out of his throat. He made gurgling bubbles that popped inside him and echoed out of his mouth and into the air. Sweat beads ran down his forehead, down his cheek, and onto my pillow. As I watched, more sweat collected on my pillow. I became angry and thought of ways to make him get out of my bed, get off my pillow, and get out of our lives. Most of all, he needed to get his face off my pillow.

As my anger built, I started to breathe with a bit of authority.

nose. Crazy put on his shoes and walked out the door, saying he was going to the store and would be back soon.

That was the first time Crazy terrified me, and it was only the starting point of what was to come. My wish of him vacating our lives wasn't coming true. It wasn't long before we were packing up and moving to a place where Mother, Crazy, my brother, and I would live. It was not the last time I'd have a bloody nose…

—ɷ—

A few months earlier, the city park was the place for hide-and-seek, but in a fun way. In this real-life hiding spot, tucked deep into the corner under the bed, I held my breath as Crazy walked past. The sheet and square-pattern quilt covering hung close to the floor, only allowing a few inches of opening to see his feet walking past again and again as he looked at my prior hiding places without success. I could feel his anger growing each time he passed by, but I didn't dare move a muscle. I kept asking for help from anything to make the fear go away and stop the hurt. Please, God, help me!

Why hasn't God sent his angels or his warriors to stop this never-ending nightmare or even tried to help me? Surely he would send help, right? He wouldn't let this continue; that's not how God works; he's here to help us, to take care of us, right? At least that was what Mother would tell us before we moved to this house in the woods, before we had a sister. I was losing trust quickly that there was anything out there except the evil that came along with Crazy and this new life, which I was hating more and more with each passing day.

Okay, I thought, stop thinking so loudly, or you'll forget to watch for Crazy. Use your ears and be quiet; don't breathe. Oh my God, he's coming this way...He's at the door, he's coming back toward the bed, and this time he's not going to walk past the bed. I couldn't breathe; I couldn't move a muscle. Crazy stopped, his bony white feet with their witchlike claw toenails at the edge of the bed coverings. He put his hand on the bed as if to slap it to see what would happen. I saw his knee as he bent down, the entire bed shaking as I was. I saw his hand grabbing at the soft, comforting covers hanging as a protective shield to hide me. He pulled them back and stuck his entire head under the aged wooden board that held up the stale-smelling mattress. As he looked over and under every inch of the underside of the bed, his putrid breath kicked up the dust bunnies scattered about.

Oh no, I thought, don't let him see the dust trail leading directly to me. The dust path had cleared away when I slithered across the dirty floor to this spot of safety. Please, God, don't let him see me. My lungs burned from holding my breath. I held my hand over my mouth and nose in a fisted grip to ensure I wouldn't make a sound. My chest began to throb, heave, and ache, and I knew if I didn't inhale soon, it would be all over, one way or another. Death at the hands of Crazy or by my hand over my mouth...Where was that help I was begging for!

Maybe death wasn't a bad thing. Surely getting ripped from this seemingly safe hiding place would result in the worst beating yet. The one that would finally kill me and bring an end to all the beatings. Maybe I would find peace in death. At least it was a hope—or was it a wish? It had to be better than the beatings!

It wasn't the first time I'd thought of dying, of death. In fact, it was coming to be more and more on my mind as the only escape from the terror and fear that had become my existence, my common way, that daily grind that had no ending point except maybe death. I closed my eyes as tightly as possible as Crazy pushed his hairy limbs as far under the bed as he could reach.

Maybe dying was the answer—that was what filled my head as I squeezed my eyes shut, as if locking myself into another space and time. If God wasn't here now and I died, where would I go? Would I be stuck here hiding from Crazy forever? Well, dying has to be better than this life, I thought. Why do I seem to be calming down when I think about death? Has Crazy already rubbed off on me? Will I be just like him? No way. I'll be the best dad ever, and my kids will love life and never be afraid—at least that was the hope, the prayer enlisted in my mind, and I wished to be invisible so Crazy wouldn't see me.

If Crazy had had a flashlight, he would have found me with ease. As he clawed and grabbed under the bed in a frantic scramble, a calm started to take hold of me. I could see a shape forming inside my eyelids. It was a woman, or at least it felt like a woman. She was in the distance, so I forced my eyes to look harder. She had a white glow flowing around her like a mist, a foggy mist. It was like looking at steam coming out of the freezer on a hot summer's day. My chest stopped hurting as I worked to focus on the wispy lady. The fear faded away, and quiet took hold in my mind.

As I concentrated and focused, she moved closer, and I felt the fear completely release. Crazy was just inches away and clawing to find me. Just as the thought of Crazy returned, it just as quickly faded. My focus went back to the image of this lady. She was in a white flowing dress like nothing I'd ever seen before. It was beautiful; she was beautiful. I could see her feet below the dress and her hands reaching out to me as the dress danced like it was gently blowing in the wind. My face cooled, and my lungs stopped hurting as everything went silent. I could hear nothing, not a sound, not even my heart, which had been beating a path out of my chest and throbbing in my ears. It all stopped in quiet, peaceful calm. It was almost like the lady wouldn't let me return my thoughts to Crazy or the fear I was hiding from. It was as if someone had heard my prayers and sent this graceful lady to me. Her hands reached toward me. Her arm followed as she leaned forward, inching closer. She appeared to be offering me something. In her hand she held something—what was it? I couldn't see, but it felt like it was something good. I wanted to know what it was, but at the same time, it was like I already knew and just couldn't recall, like knowing you ate breakfast but not remembering what it was. As her face became more visible, I could see she had a cloth over her head. It was see-through material of the same white fabric but a different shade. Some of the covering was darker, and some was lighter as it stopped along her hairline just at the start of her forehead. Her bright-blue eyes were as warm as anything I could ever remember. Who was she? What was she doing? How could I see her so clearly and still not know who she was? Yet deep inside me, I knew her. It was confusing and calmingly real at the same time. She was trying to tell me something as she smiled without moving her lips, her mouth, or her face. It was as if she could smile without smiling, yet I knew her smile; somehow I knew that smile. That smile made me feel safe. It made me feel as if I was going to be all right. Her silky white figure was just beginning to fully take shape. Her outstretched hand was so close I almost started to reach back to her, and then she stopped. She quickly began to drift backward in the direction she came from. She descended a shaft of pulling waves of light with darkness just on her outsides until she completely disappeared into a speck of light. She disappeared into my eyelids. I wanted her to take me with her, but somewhere inside me, I knew I needed to stay. I had no idea where that feeling came from, yet it was fast becoming a part of my being. It was as if this lady had inserted something inside my core that caused me to know I was here for a reason. A reason that could not be understood but a reason all the same.

As the last bits of her feeling left me, I returned to the house of fear and pain. Just as quickly as that feeling had gone away, it returned, and I was back under the bed with my hand over my mouth and my nose. The pounding in my ears and my chest returned, but it wasn't quite the same. Something inside me was different.

A clunk shook the bed, and I was fully back to that place before the white shadow lady came to visit me.

That stench from Crazy's mouth quickly faded as he pulled his head out from under the bed. In doing so, he bonked the back of his greased ducktail on the old wooden board. *"Damn it!"* he yelled as he withdrew from my hiding place without finding me. Was the white misty lady responsible for keeping me safe and keeping Crazy from finding me? His hands had been only inches away from the clothes I used to conceal my body parts and prevent him from seeing where I was. I thought he'd see me once he pulled those dirty clothes away. How come he stopped? How did he hit his head on that board at the exact moment he was reaching to pull back the last thing keeping me safely hidden? Was that wispy lady an angel? Was that possible? Did God hear my prayers and send that lady to keep me calm and concealed!

As Crazy stood up, I could feel his anger growing as he screamed, "Where are you, you son of a bitch?" That wasn't all he said. "When I find you, you'll be sorry I had to look for you. You're going to be punished for this, so you might as well get it over with."

And with that, I was certain the lesson I was going to get would be very painful, even more than if I'd just come out before he had to search for me. For now, I wasn't giving up my safety spot. Maybe the angels put a cloud over me so he couldn't see me. I was safe for now. As he moved away from the side of the bed, I saw his feet pacing back across the room as he headed into the next place where he thought I might be hiding. Finally, I could breathe again, but only enough to stop the pain and not give away my hiding place. The dust was tickling my nose. Not sneezing became my newest worry as the dust crept into my burning throat. Exercising my mouth, my cheeks, and my tongue to make enough saliva to stop the dryness was an effort, but it worked, and I could breathe. But don't sneeze or it's over, I told myself.

The flood of emotions overwhelmed me—relief, fear—and I knew when he found me, I would pay the price even more than before. But for the moment, I was safe. Freedom from beatings, if only for the moment, had become my goal in life, even when I knew it would be worse when he found me.

I had won, for the moment, by finding a secret hiding spot, but I couldn't think about the future; I just had to live in the moment. While this round was mine, if only this once, living in the moment would become my mantra. It became an approach to survival I didn't even know I was creating—or maybe it came from another source. Is that possible? As the relief washed away and calm began to enter, I could feel the energy pulsing all around me start to let go, like a light breeze pushing it someplace else. The sweat that had been running down my face evaporated, and the sweat that had soaked into my shirt felt so relieving, so cooling, and so comforting. As the calm took hold, I wanted to close my eyes and find that peaceful place for just a few minutes. I thought: If I'm ever so quiet without falling asleep, I should be okay. I wanted to savor the moment so I could remember it when I needed it most, which would surely be coming soon enough. Don't fall asleep, I kept saying over and over again in my head. You can't fall asleep; keep your guard up and stay on full alert. But I couldn't fight the need to sleep, and as the moments of calm and relief took over, my eyes began to close on their own.

I gave in to the exhaustion and felt the release that comes with finding peace within and forgetting about the worries at hand. I saw the darkness behind my eyelids, followed by colors, stars, and faces flashing past my eyes. I pictured a man on a horse. It felt like he was smiling at me. I got a sense of complete safety as I looked at the man and then noticed his long black hair was braided with a tan shoelace running from his head past his shoulders to his belly. The calm seemed real, like I'd known this feeling before. It was as if the man was telling me something, but no words were coming from his mouth. There was no movement of his lips, like he was whispering in my ear, but I didn't hear him; rather, I just knew what he was telling me. Much like the wispy lady I'd experienced just a short time before. How was this possible, again? What was happening to me? Why was I seeing these people, these images?

While it wasn't the first time I could remember seeing people behind my eyelids, it was the first time I had seen the person on the horse and the wispy lady. Were those blows to my head from Crazy causing me to see things, to imagine things that weren't there, or was I dreaming these happy, warm feelings like they were real? It had felt real, and I caught myself thinking inside my presleep, wondering if I was awake or asleep.

Before I could go further down this rabbit hole, I got an overpowering sense to let go and follow the man on the horse as he turned and started walking toward a stream. I could feel the coolness of the water, and my throat stopped hurting as I got the drink I so badly needed. As I looked up from the brook, I saw the man sitting on a rock looking off into the distance. I looked where he was looking and saw a skyline of such deep-blue color that it almost stopped my breath, but in a good way this time. I wanted to look back at him, toward the flowing brook, yet I couldn't stop looking at the shade of perfect blue. It changed from light to a darker blue just below the mesmerizing skyline. A bright white light started coming toward me. I wasn't afraid, and I could feel myself wondering what it was. It was as if my question was answered without hearing a word. "The pain will end" is what it was whispering. The pain in the back of my head, in my legs, and in my neck was gone. All those stars that twinkled throughout my eyesight faded away as if they had never been there. All of it was the handiwork of Crazy's beatings. My entire body started to feel better, as if I were a brand-new canvas and the colors behind my eyes had reset my existence, ready for a new painting to be created.

I looked back toward the brook, toward the man on a horse, just in time to see him disappearing in a soft glow of fading light.

His hand lifted, and he pointed to me with an outstretched arm. His index finger pointed with intention, with purpose, but as I watched his image fade away, I sensed I was falling into a deep, deep sleep.

—◊—

Why am I so cold? I'm shivering; it's so cold. Those were my first thoughts as I started to return to reality. I was curled into the fetal position, trying to stay warm. It was so cold and dark. I didn't remember where I was. I could feel my back up against something hard while my feet were pressed against another hard surface that wouldn't move. I picked up my head only to bonk it on something else that was apparently another solid surface, and this one hurt. I checked to see if there was blood only to find a different spot that hurt just the same. I was covered in clothes. They didn't smell nice, and they were wrapped around me like mini blankets. Everything was starting to come back to me, but where was I? Why was I here, and where was here? What was that noise, and who were those people talking some distance away? As I gathered my thoughts and tried to understand what was happening—or what had happened—it started rushing back to me, and just like that, I was back in the world of fear.

Was I hiding once again, or did I finally run away as I'd been planning? Was this the chicken coop in the backyard, or maybe the hay barn across the street, the one owned by the friendly old farmer family? They used the barn for their cow food and hay-making machine. I loved that haymaking machine. It was so cool to watch it pick up the grass and spit out a chunk of hay in a perfect box that magically glued it all together. I thought the farmer's son who drove the giant green tractor must be having so much fun. I wanted to do what he did. I wanted to experience the freedom of being in the open fields with no one watching over you as you pulled a huge lawn mower around with a tractor that had tires taller than the guy driving it. The tractor sat in that old barn the farmer filled with hay until there was no room left for anything else.

That old red wooden barn with white trim board along the roof line and around the windows always made me smile. I used to sit across the street dreaming of a place to hide from Crazy as I watched the farmers stack the hay inside. They used a rope to pull the hay to the second floor. It had a huge metal double hook that stuck into the bales so they wouldn't slip and fall to pieces. The farmers looked like they were having so much fun. I imagined I could make a hidden room at the top by the door they pulled the hay in through. Surely no one would think to look up there, right?

Of course, the old farmhouse we moved into was better than the apartment in the city we were born in. That apartment was hot in the summer and cold in the winter. We had to walk up the long stairs to get to our door. Mother would drag my brother and me when she couldn't carry us. This old house made strange sounds, and I was sure I could see a little girl in a nightgown with bare feet and sandbox-colored blond hair. Her hair was just past her shoulders. She walked around at night when it got quiet. The house was so big, with a storefront-sized picture window in the kitchen looking out into the yard. The dogs were tied up, and you could see all of them through the picture window.

In the backyard were the old chicken coops, which smelled so bad you had to hold your nose when you opened the door. When the wind was right, it made the entire house smell like the chickens. Looking out the picture window, you could see apple trees growing in rows of eight. There were so many rows, I couldn't count them all. Sometimes the cows would get over the rock wall and eat the green apples without the farmer knowing, which would make the cows act really strange. They would be stumbling around and mooing at the cars as they passed, like they knew the drivers or where they were going. I didn't know why green apples made the cows act funny, but when they did, they would get out of their fields and venture all over the place. Then everyone in the area would gather around to collect them back to their proper fields.

One time, a cow was just outside our side door that led from the dirt driveway into the small room next to the kitchen. My mother had spent her entire life living within a one-block radius (her "neighborhood," as she called it). She lived in the "big city," or at least that was what the farmers would say about the city made famous by Samuel Colt and the author of *Huckleberry Finn*.

Our house was all white on the outside, and the inside had dark-colored wood floors with big wide boards that made tripping a common occurrence. It had the odor of a very old place. I used to wonder how it had gotten that way. Who had built such a big house, and why didn't they have running water or a bathroom that worked? There was an old hand-dug well in the front with a big flat stone covering the opening. The well had run out of water, so we would use metal cans the farmer used for milk deliveries. We had to be careful not to spill them when we tried to get a drink, which was an adventure in and of itself. Mother and Crazy would fight about the mean German shepherd, Duke. We had gotten him from someone for "protection"; at least that was what they said. He stayed chained up in the yard, and you didn't want to go near him.

The rest of our house was like any other, or so I thought. There were three rooms that were off limits, and the second floor was rented to someone else. I didn't learn until sometime later that Crazy had bought the house with plans to rent out half to help pay for the bills. He'd gotten it for a really cheap price, as the late 1960s would go. There must have been a good reason the house was so cheap. Maybe because no one wanted an old, run-down farmhouse in the middle of nowhere.

At that time, Mother didn't drive, and we only had one car. That was normal in those days. However, there was more to the cheap price than was visible. After a while, the renter just left without taking their stuff. They left screaming about something that had happened in the middle of the night—something that scared them pretty badly. Mother and Crazy tried to stop them and talk, but they were having none of it. They just wanted to get out of that house and drive somewhere, anywhere. This left a hole in the income stream and led to more fights, which became another ongoing battle we'd get to enjoy as dinner entertainment.

One night while Mother and Crazy were having one of their R-rated verbal assaults between the two prizefighters, something happened that changed everything. I have to say, I'd never seen Crazy afraid before—and honestly, only a couple of other times after that—but what happened in those three rooms shook him to his core. It made me smile to see him enjoying that same level of fear he worked me over with so often. What exactly happened is a story for another time, but that little girl with bare feet and sandbox-colored blond hair in a nightgown had friends—or maybe not friends but definitely people closer to her world than the one I was living in. From that day on, those three rooms stayed bolted shut, and to reinforce the serious nature behind Crazy's fears, he nailed a big stick across the doors at the top and bottom for extra protection. That was the first chink in the seemingly unbreakable armor of Crazy and his horrifically abusive ways. Maybe God was helping me.

The house was surrounded by farmland, which had either hay-fields or cows fenced in with electrically charged wires. You didn't have to learn twice not to touch those wires—unless you were a cow with a belly full of green apples, and then it only seemed to make them happier, because it didn't stop them from getting to the other field full of those special treats. My brother and I shared a room in the front of the house, and my younger sister stayed in Mother's room with our newborn sister.

Overall, it was a house in the country with land and a lot of room to play, but there was always something there that made you think you were being watched. I'm not sure I minded since I saw so many faces and people when I closed my eyes anyway, but boy, it bothered my brother an awful lot. Not long after the three rooms were locked down, the second-floor renters left as well. Maybe they didn't like the nightlife, compliments of the owners at no charge. The loving way they addressed each other or the method of child raising could have chased them off. Maybe it was because the animals kept disappearing. I never did get an answer as to what caused the first renters to vacate so quickly or what scared Crazy. Once the other tenants left the house, it really got rough. Without those two renters, we had to listen to a daily fight about paying bills.

One night, the old farmer who owned the fields came to talk to

Crazy about the house. The two of them sat at the kitchen table for a long time. Mother was listening but left from time to time, as if she didn't want to hear the story. At one point she shouted, "That's it; we are moving!" She fled the kitchen and paced about like she was searching for answers to a problem. She talked to herself and then to God. She went back into the kitchen to hear more or ask a few questions, only to resume her pacing back at the front of the house. The old farmer seemed to want to help, but Crazy said he'd done enough. As the old farmer left, he gave a warning. I didn't hear much of it, but it sure as hell frightened the two grown-ups in the house.

By the time the two of them were left alone, Crazy was rather deep into one of his brown bottles he enjoyed so much. I crept from my bed to the door to listen, watch, and get what I could. The two of them sat at the kitchen table. Mother started to cry, saying, "We are leaving this house." Crazy had a different view, which was the one that ended up ruling the day. I know they were worried, and while I didn't know all the matters, I would learn more the longer we stayed in that historic farmhouse.

It turned out it was one of the very first houses ever built in the area. It dated back to well before the Revolutionary War. That land, as the story goes, had a history that caused the natives to "walk around" the area and warn others to stay clear. The troubling history was the reason it was so cheap and why people didn't stay long.

Mother and Crazy kept talking long into the night. I went back to bed and left the matter for another day. One that was going to make everyone sit up in their beds and wish they never lived there.

—◊—

I could hear voices in the distance as the play rewound in my mind. The flashes of terror rekindled the fear that seemed to disappear as I slept tucked away in my den of temporary safety. My chest started to tighten, and I felt my breathing start to labor as those flashes kept replaying. Crazy reaching under the bed as he searched in vain and with false intentions. I closed my eyes again and pressed the mental film projector like a stop button so the images would no longer loop in a constant rerun.

The room was completely dark except for the light coming from under the doorway. It was time to decide what to do. Should I stay under the bed forever, or should I simply walk into the kitchen, where the faint voices were coming from? Should I surrender myself to Crazy? Should I surrender to my fate and another beating? My stomach growled and snapped with its disapproval of not being filled in a very long time. The groaning sent cramps across my belly, curling me tighter into a ball until the pain faded. I knew hunger pangs all too well. They had come to visit more and more since we began life with Crazy. I was not sure which was more painful, beatings or hunger…or was it mental cruelty!

I drew a few deep breaths and counted the steps in my mind. Each step would bring me closer to pain, but each step also would give me time before the pending body blows. I started to focus on the steps, each step, and how many steps—twelve or maybe fifteen—wait, it was four steps from the bed to the door. How many to the kitchen table? I couldn't remember, but I thought it was six steps. So fourteen was the number. Yes, fourteen. The decision made, I scurried along the floorboards using my hands and forearms to pull myself from under the bed.

Pushing the dirty clothes in front of me, I advanced toward the light coming from the bottom of the door. The voices were getting louder. One seemed upset, but someone else was with Mother and Crazy. Who was it? The farmer? No, that wasn't his voice. I'd never heard that voice before.

I stood up with a sigh, wiped my face, and shook off the dust from my shirt. My socks were covered in animal hair and dust bunnies from my rabbit hole.

I reached for the doorknob with one last sigh, an exhale in preparation for what was to come. Pull the door open. Fourteen steps. I forced myself to take the first step—the hardest of them all—that first one that would lead to a destiny of fear and hate, pain and bruises. I pushed myself to take that step and head toward my fate and make my way across the living room and into the opening leading to the sounds in the next room. I heard tears in the voice of Mother, who was now arguing with someone whose voice I still didn't know.

When I walked into the kitchen after hiding for, for…What time was it? So, it was dark, but I felt awake. Before I left the safety under the bed, I could see there was light coming from under the door, which I saw shining across the floor but stopping a foot or so under the bed. Was that sunlight or light from the broken lamp? I turned to look out the picture window only to see darkness with a couple of red and blue flashing lights reflecting off the plate-glass window. Where were those lights coming from?

I stood at the threshold between the old farmhouse kitchen and living room wondering how long I had been hiding. The darkness outside, my stomach growling…I had no idea how long it had been. The hunger cramps turned my attention away from the colored lights. Remembering the gooey oatmeal from that morning, I thought, *Boy, I'll bet it would actually taste good right now.*

I was so hungry it chased the fear right out of me, almost like something had used my hunger to mask what I was walking into. A distraction of sorts. Or maybe it was a mental way of hiding from what was surely to come at any moment. A beating, a switch across the backs of my legs, my calves, my thighs, my back. The hunger was doing its job, as the fear was gone, replaced by cramps in my belly as hunger took charge over what was coming.

As I stood at the threshold, a silence fell over the entire area, as if a clap of thunder had pierced the air with the deafening quiet that falls just before the storm clouds release their torrential rains. Maybe if I pretended like I didn't know anything was wrong, things might be fine. Maybe Crazy had forgotten all about his planned beating before I ran to hide. That beating to teach me not to leave the milk on the table—that's right, the beating was over leaving the milk on the table instead of putting it in the fridge. If you leave the milk on the table, the world will end, children in Africa will starve, and the family will go bankrupt, according to Crazy. I was the worst child ever, with no understanding of how things worked or how much they cost. Of course, I thought we were getting milk from the farmer, who had hundreds of cows and plenty of milk. So how much could it cost to walk outside with a cup and start squeezing those udders under the cows' black and white spots? It was easy. At least that was what the old farmer told us, and since they hung so close to the ground, even Crazy could do it, right? What I didn't realize was who the voices belonged to. The voices that overtook the kitchen as I stood in the doorway thinking about the milk.

The sounds changed to silence that woke me to the people staring at me from the table just four steps from where I was and fourteen steps from my hiding den. I had been right—fourteen steps. Man, I was getting good at counting how far things were, but that thought quickly faded as I felt the eyes staring at me. I felt relief, worry, hate, and confusion all at once in a wave of energy that washed over me. Where were these feelings coming from? I crossed the wide opening into the kitchen, still puzzled by all the strange voices. Who were they, and why were they here? Crazy didn't like people in the house, period! Or maybe Crazy didn't like kids to have people in the house. Or did we never have people in the house because of Crazy? Now, that one was going to take some thinking.

Stepping past the threshold and into the kitchen, I saw my brother sitting at the table, then Mother, followed by Crazy standing with a guy in a heck of a nice suit. Wait—he had a big black belt and a gun on his hip with nicely pressed pants and shiny shoes. Oh no...the cops were there, and Crazy did not like the cops. Now I was done for.

I saw more people, but before I could figure out who they were, Mother started screaming and running at me. I wasn't sure if it was a good scream or a bad scream. It was quickly followed by her bursting into tears and screaming words I couldn't understand. I felt the rush of emotions flooding off her, hitting me like a gust of wind as she closed the distance between us. So now I thought it was bad screaming, but at least she would be between me and Crazy. I prepared for the impact from Mother as she bull-rushed across the room, turning my face to the side and closing my eyes, ready for the first blow and knowing if I had anything in my bladder, it was surely going to make a puddle in short order.

Up in the air I went as Mother wrapped both arms around me

and started kissing my cheek and thanking God for "returning my baby to me."

I was confused, and she was crying in happiness and thanking God. This couldn't be an answer from God. I was trying to get him to protect me, so how could she be thanking him?

The other people in the room were all around me, touching me as if to see if I was real or not. Before I knew it, a policeman was looking me square in the face, just over my mother's shoulder. He asked where I'd been and what had happened to me. He wanted to know how I had gotten home and if I was all right. Strange—the cop was the first one to ask if I was all right. I don't remember anyone else asking.

The cop, a Connecticut state trooper from the Colchester barracks, said he needed to look me over and asked Mother to put me down. He needed to see if I was hurt in any way. "Hurt in any way"…That was why I was hiding, was my thought, but best to keep that to myself. I was starting to believe I wasn't in real trouble, at least for the time being. The cop, who was the only policeman in the small farming community, said he'd been looking for me since yesterday. *Yesterday*…How could that be? What time was it? What day was it?

It seemed it was well after midnight, and my mother had called the state trooper, who, in turn, called the chief of the all-volunteer fire department. That call started an all-out search for a lost boy.

The cop started talking into his black handheld walkie-talkie. He was letting everyone know "the boy is safe and in the home." He followed by asking for "a medic" to come "look over the boy." Several men rushed into the kitchen through the side door with big smiles on their faces. It felt good that someone was happy to see me. At the same time, I was wondering where all these people had come from.

"We've been looking for you all day, little boy. Where were you?" called out a tall, large man wearing a white firefighter helmet. He wore a thick tan jacket with yellow stripes and patches on the front.

Two other men dressed in blue shirts burst through the door with smiles beaming across their mouths. One let out a "Thank God" so loud it started to bring the fear back inside my chest.

As Mother danced and swung me in her arms, making circles in the room, I could see more people gathering in the kitchen. Everyone was smiling with joy and relief, with one exception: Crazy. He had that look of anger in his eyes. His mouth was trying to show a smile while his eyes, the wrinkles in his forehead, and the crow's feet on each side of his dark, bitter eyes showed me he was not happy. He looked so stern, with such a glare, as if to say, "Just wait until these people leave, and I'll show you what happens next." His expression and his pumping, angry veins told me all I needed to know.

The trooper must have seen it, too, as he looked at Crazy, then at me, and back at Crazy. The trooper turned his head slightly to the side and asked, "Are you all right, sir?"

Crazy broke his glare with a short, terse response to the trooper: "I'm fine." Nothing in his two words offered comfort, only anger and hatred toward a little boy who had successfully hidden for more than half a day and avoided Crazy's wrath.

"I'm the fire chief. We've been looking all over for you, son. Where were you?" he asked in both a demanding and concerned voice.

I didn't want to say, so I just closed my eyes and squeezed Mother's neck to avoid answering.

"We have dozens of people out looking for you. Can you tell us what happened to you?" asked the trooper.

I clung to Mother's neck, looking outside. The blue and red lights flashing, reflected in the window, revealed a number of fire trucks, cars, and police in the driveway and on the grass.

"A kid could get lost for days or weeks and freeze to death out here," said one of the men entering the house.

Another yelled out the door, "*We found him*, and he's safe!"

Mother started demanding I tell her what happened. Where was I? Did someone take me? There were people everywhere, coming inside, going back outside, talking, shaking hands, and even hugging one another. The demands to relinquish my hiding place grew louder, from many people, all of them strangers to me.

I refused to say a word and hid my face, again, in Mother's shoulder. Finally, the crowd began to clear out of the kitchen. The cars and trucks began leaving the old farmhouse. The fire chief and trooper became sterner in asking my whereabouts: "Where were you?" "Were you hiding in the woods or in the house?" "Son, was anyone else involved? Was someone helping you hide?" "Were you afraid of something, or did you just get lost?" The questions kept coming without response.

Thinking I was in even more trouble than ever, I completely shut down and started crying. Mother gave me a firm hug, then pulled me off her and onto my feet. "You need to tell us where you were," she demanded in a soft, comforting voice that ended with "You won't be in trouble if you just tell the truth."

"He must be thirsty," called out someone from behind the fire chief.

After a few minutes and a big glass of milk, of all things, the fire chief and state trooper figured out I could not have come from outside since there were people all over, so I must have been inside. With that said and a few more prods from the chief, I said I had fallen asleep under the bed and just woke up. I didn't say why or if I was afraid of something despite their repeated asks. They couldn't believe I was under the bed the entire time. They had me show them where I was, to reenact where I had hidden for so long and so well.

Crazy raised his voice in protest with his claims: "I looked under that bed a couple times, and he wasn't there."

The trooper asked me to show him "exactly" where I was and how I'd managed to hide so well.

I slithered back under the bed, dragging the dirty clothes with me. I curled up into the den like a fox under a rock, pulling the dirty shirts close to me so no one could see my body. While Crazy continued to claim it had not been my hiding place, the trooper and fire chief believed me but asked why I was hiding.

Crazy's face lit up with panic. A powerful rage washed over him as the questioning started to sound like an "interrogation," according to Crazy, the trooper staring him dead in the eye without blinking for the longest time.

I was wondering what would happen if I told the truth. Would they arrest Crazy? Would they put him in jail for hurting me? For hurting my brother and Mother? It was a question that would enter my mind many times in the coming years, but for this night, it was only a first thought, the first time I'd considered what would happen if I told the police what was going on in our world. Crazy worked hard to threaten us about what would happen if we "talked outside the family." This was the first time his warnings played out in real life. The first time I considered telling someone about my fear and the abuse; the beatings; the punches to the face, the head; and the wooden stick whipping my legs, my back. Telling someone where all the bruises really came from. It was terrifying to weigh these thoughts, to think of making a decision. Do I say something, or do I remain silent?

"The kid fell asleep under the bed. It's over. So thank you for the help, but it's time to leave," explained Crazy.

There was nothing more the trooper or chief could do, so they turned and headed out of the house.

To that end, the siege was over, and my first brush with the law had taken shape. After things settled down, Mother put my brother and me to bed. The rest of the people engaged in the search went about their way, and the house went quiet.

As I lay in the bed thinking about the day's events, I smiled and thanked God for helping me avoid Crazy's "lesson." I'd won my first round against him, so I knew evil had a weakness. But I also knew that the morning, not far from coming, would be another story.

For now, I was in bed, warm and with a full belly. Mother had made me a grilled cheese sandwich with another glass of milk. The milk bottle was put back into the fridge quickly once the glass was filled. The dangers of forgetting to put the milk bottle into the fridge was etched into our memories, forever!

Lying in the darkness, my brother asked me if I had really been hiding under the bed. I told him I had been and that Crazy had come close to finding me. He told me how mad Crazy had been and that Mother had said it was his fault I ran away, as she'd thought I did. He told me how they argued and how Crazy threatened

Mother if she told the police anything about the family. "I'll kill you and your bastards if you say one word." Not the first time Crazy had said he'd kill Mother or us—it was becoming rather commonplace.

We talked for a while like we always did. Talked about what we thought would happen in the morning. My brother said, "Stop worrying about it and get to sleep."

It took some time, but finally I drifted off. As I did, I started to dream and saw that man with the long braid. He was standing a long distance away, but it felt like he was close. Something about him made me feel safe, but I couldn't figure it out. A calming comfort fell over me, both as a dream and in my bed. That quiet calm that seemed to show up just before an explosion erupted in my life, a warning of things to come.

The deep, quiet calm was shattered by the smashing of the bedroom door and yelling from Crazy. *"Get your asses out of bed!"* Crazy was shaking my brother and me from our dreams and quickly back to reality. "I want to see you both in the kitchen. Get dressed," came the orders in a manner normally reserved for a drill sergeant.

With that, the new day was upon me, and new fears raced over me like water falling over the hills of Niagara. And just like that, it all started over again—fourteen steps to the kitchen!

CHAPTER 2

Pulling ourselves quickly out of the warm comforts of quiet slumber, my brother and I jumped to our feet as we'd been ordered. We knew if we didn't make our beds before anything else, it would lead to a crack from the whip stick or a slap to the back of the head when we least expected it. We hurried ourselves straightening up the sheets, pillows, and bed coverings as quickly as we could. Trying not to focus on the need to pee so badly, my brother said the same thing I was thinking: "Make the bed first, or else." He either had to use the bathroom as desperately as I did, or he was reading my mind...Was he? I always wondered what made my brother think the way he did. I would spend hours sitting in punishment thinking about what he was thinking. Imagining how he thought about things and how he managed to appease Crazy when all I could think about was the hate I felt from him.

Did my brother feel that hate, that vile force flowing off Crazy? Could my brother feel his evil power hovering around him, like cigarette smoke drifting, spinning in circles around him, creating a cloud of choking misery that refused to leave. Was I the only one who could see his dark colors pulsating like a blob of tar in a heated pit ready to be pumped onto an asphalt roof? When I'd ask my brother what he saw…"I don't see anything." He didn't see colors or bubbles. Not even the tar-like heat signature boiling off Crazy… He saw nothing! What was wrong with me? I wondered as I fluffed the slim remains of my old pillow and watched feathers puff out of the holes and slip away from the stained pillowcase. There wasn't much of the pillow left, but it felt like my only friend. Almost like those who visited in my dreams.

I grabbed the feathers and stuffed them back into the case, pushing them deep into the bottom so they would stay put. I turned to my brother, who was standing almost at attention, waiting for me to finish my work and knowing the game we were about to step into. A game of "who goes first" into Crazy's lion den. Whoever finished making their bed, cleaning the room, and getting to the door first got to go second down the pathway to meet our morning's rendezvous with the day's lesson—or lessons.

My brother stood firm just to the right of the door handle, knowing I would be leading the way once again. I knew he was afraid, very afraid, although he'd never admit it. He looked different when he was scared and had a buzz about him much like a bunch of bees when you upset their hiding place. The only time my brother worked fast at chores was when he needed to beat me so I would have to go first; otherwise, he was as slow as the melting snow on our front stairs in January.

My brother never liked to do chores or manual labor. He liked finer things and would tell me how he'd live in a big house overlooking the water someday, and I could come live with him anytime. He was going to be rich and have all the things we talked about, from toys to spaceships. For now, my brother was just afraid, and somehow it made me feel like I was helping by leading the way. I never did make the bed faster than my brother. I always let him win.

I reached up to grab the doorknob, glancing at my brother just over my right shoulder. He was holding his breath. I pulled open the door, and we headed toward the kitchen.

Just as we took that first step, a booming thunder of anger filled the air, demanding to know where we were and telling us, "You'd better get your asses over here, and I mean quickly."

Without stopping at the bathroom, almost wetting myself, we scurried forward taking two steps at a time and losing count. With my brother close behind me, I faced Crazy from a distance as he started to shout at me about the "events" of yesterday. Seeing my brother in discomfort and me pushing my knees together, Crazy barked, "Go to the bathroom, and you'd better not piss on my floor."

We stood shoulder to shoulder as we relieved ourselves with perfect aim, thus saving us from either a bathroom scrubbing or the prized leather belt he had sitting on the table within arm's reach. Returning to "front and center" as ordered, we stood frozen once again as we waited for the lesson to begin. Crazy toyed with the thick leather strap, playing a slapping-sound game as he prepared himself for the lecture we were to receive.

Was he planning on using that strap again today, this very morning, or was it just one of his mental games to loosen us up for his verbal assault? We were about to find out. I found myself wondering again, What is my brother thinking right now? Is he wishing Crazy was dead, like I am? Is he wishing Crazy would just leave and never come back? Is he asking God to strike him with lightning and fry him like a fish in a pan of boiling Crisco until he melts into the fat and bubbles so there is nothing left? Is that what my brother is thinking? Probably not!

—⚏—

Crazy saw I wasn't focused on him, so he demanded I pay attention by pushing that dark, smelly leather strap up under my chin. "What are you thinking about?" he demanded.

Oh, crap. What do I tell him? Boiling Crisco…fried fish into bubbles…Maybe not just now. "I don't know" was the best I could think of, and I heard my brother sound off a short sigh of "Oh, crap."

"I don't know" were three words you didn't use as an answer to Crazy. They always led to a beating and sometimes to beatings after a beating when you were sent to bed without any food for the day and he decided the lesson needed more flavoring, so he'd come visit you with his friend Mr. Leather for a bit more educational experience.

Frozen in fear as I tried to come up with a response, Mother popped into my mind. "I was wondering where my mother was. That was what I was thinking. I don't know why I said 'I don't know.'"

Oh, great. I had just said those beating words again and again. Crazy was surely going to make me turn around so he could put Mr. Leather to work. I heard my brother wincing beside me, hoping he wouldn't become a part of the growing rage that was filling the air with that thick, sickening taste of bitter pain that was about to explode any second.

Then something very strange, something different, happened. Just when Crazy would normally explode and shift into swinging like Babe Ruth for the fences, a smirk took over his face as he drew his head back like a chicken, changing his thoughts. The fear was in full control inside my stomach and chest, but just for a second, it released a bit as I tried to figure out what Crazy was thinking.

He sat down in his favorite spot at the head of the table, the master of his house. He put his right arm on the back of the chair as he leaned back against the faded-green chair with its wooden back. The chair did its customary creaking and moaning noises, as the tired old seat was well past its prime. Crazy shifted around a bit as he prepared to start in on what would normally be a barrage of verbal insults. But this morning, something was different. Looking over at the other seats around the table, I saw there were two bowls with spoons in them. You could smell cold oatmeal in what must have been yesterday's breakfast, saved from the pot a day earlier. What was he waiting for? I wondered. Crazy's mouth opened. "The cops are coming back in a little while, and we need to discuss yesterday before they get here. Sit down, both of you."

My brother and I took our usual seats. Mine was within striking reach, just short of arm's length from Crazy's hairy knuckles with those dirt-encrusted fingernails. We quickly saw it was yesterday's oatmeal, still in the bowls, just as they'd been left from the day before, the bowls of gelled oatmeal fixed to the spoons like Elmer's Glue from an elementary class project. It wasn't the first time Crazy had saved the leftovers. It was a lesson we had become very accustomed to over the years: if you didn't finish your plate completely, it would be with you until you were hungry enough to finish what you had started.

"Eat your breakfast, and don't even think about getting more milk or brown sugar. Just eat it as you left it," ordered Crazy.

We began to chew on the sticky oats at the same time Crazy started in on how we'd act when the cops came back to talk to me.

Talk to me? What for? I wondered far too loudly. I'd thought it was just a whisper. Crazy went into detail about how I'd embarrassed him by hiding. How his wife had been mortified, shamed, disrespected, and treated like a whore by her son. I'd made the entire family look as if we were trash. Crazy went on. "You are good for nothing. You'll never amount to anything in your pathetic, worthless life." He said I was too "sensitive" to be a boy; in fact, I must be a girl, the way I cried and carried on like a baby, a little girl baby, good for *nothing*...

As Crazy lashed out with a torrent of all things nasty, directed at my heart, I felt a new kind of pain taking hold and growing. This pain was far worse than beatings. Beatings seemed to heal in time, but his verbal cannonade was like a beating drum hammering at the soft tissue of my insides. Ripping, pulling, and tearing at all the places that could possibly cause true hurt, true pain. My throat had a lump growing so big it started to hurt inside my ears. I fought to swallow it. To keep it down below the back of my teeth so it wouldn't come out as crying or weakness. It was a miserable set of feelings.

The avalanche of hateful words kept coming and coming. A

sea of darkness flooded my chest and cut off my breath. I sat there barely hearing his never-ending stream of painfulness as I tried to block out as much as possible. I was no longer hungry. Before, I would have eaten rocklike remains just to fill my growling belly, but now my stomach was in knots and spinning like a metal top defying gravity. I thought I was going to puke.

My brother, on the other hand, was digging deep into the day-old pasty globs of goo without hearing a single word Crazy was spotlighting. It was as if he had no signal, no sounding board or receiver. The hate was just floating past my brother like water down a drain. What was he thinking, and how come it hurt me so much and not him? Was it because the drivel wasn't directed at him, even though it was intended for both of us? How did my brother zone out Crazy, and more importantly, how did he get away with it? What was wrong with me!

I turned my look back to Crazy. I felt my eyes start to close ever so slightly as I focused on his hellish face while his yellow-and-black teeth appeared and disappeared behind his lips. He was still pouring out a fire of sounds so mean I started to feel myself changing from hurt to anger. As the feelings changed and morphed into reverse hate, the pain started to dull a bit, helping me recover while finding an internal hiding place for the mental battering ram that Crazy kept pouring across the breakfast table and onto me with an eagerness behind his eyes that could only be witnessed to be believed. My brother, of course, never looked at Crazy. Instead, I could hear him clean his bowl by the sounds of the spoon repeatedly clanking on the inside of the cheaply made container.

"You're a nasty little pig that should eat with the chickens, so if you hide on me again, that's exactly where you'll be sleeping, permanently!" Crazy said with a spitting touch as he leaned forward to emphasize his intent.

It did little to shake my convergence from fear to anger as I wiped the spittle from my nose and my upper lip. I glared back at him, wishing to all that was holy for him to be butchered in a million painfully slow ways. Praying that what was behind that locked, nailed-shut door that scared him so badly would break free and find him while he was sleeping and I'd get to watch them do the ghostly work.

He must have seen my change from fear to fight. My eyes must have given it away. It must have been the powerful rage pumping from my body like a racehorse in full stride with its head and nose outstretched in sheer defiance of his devilish alliance. He raised his smacking hand, but I didn't flinch, not in the slightest. Almost daring him to hit me. I kept my face pressed forward as he debated his next move. "I dare you" poured from my eyes.

You see, knowing the cops were coming back told me he would not be willing to put a mark on me, out of self-preservation. The fear of having to face the law or someone tougher than him changed the colors around Crazy. I had learned this game a long time ago. The first time I grasped this understanding was when someone showed up at the door during one of his rampages. An unknown source banging on the door with authority and demanding it be opened broke the trapped air that surrounded that battle. Mother had been punched in the face, between her cheekbone and her right ear. She took a left hook from Crazy after she dared him to punch her. "You don't have the balls," she would taunt and tempt during many of their heated love fests. Mother lost that day, and it was brutal to witness, but once authority poked its head into his world, Crazy would retreat like any other gutless bully.

In the distance, the sound of slippers quickly shuffling, scratching the floor, added to the growing tension at the breakfast table. Mother was on her way. She charged through the door opening and straight into the face of Crazy. Her charge was led by her right finger, with her chin closely following. Her outstretched arm gained ground on Crazy's nose as he reluctantly diverted his menacing glare from me to the approaching bear. Mother would keep up her chin wagging, pushing her chin closer and closer as if inching up to that invisible line. The one that would push Crazy's button to the point of no return. Her mouth was flapping away with the same vile sewage he had cast upon my heart. It was as if she truly intended to protect her favorite child. Her mouth kept wagging away with the same demeaning statement: "*Leave my son alone...*" Mother's pointing finger, flipping to and fro, was ever so close to touching his face as she stuck her butt in the opposite direction. It was comical and tragic at the same time. Her behind was retreating while her front continued the charge of the light brigade until neither side could back down. Was I rescued or creating a far worse outcome?

I had followed Mother's example a few times before, with mixed results. My nose sticking out as far as I could push it, daring Crazy to take a shot as Mother was doing the same. So I tried a little harder, hoping he would strike so the cops could take him away as they had done once, before we'd moved to this isolated house in the woods. My chin was tempting fate and Mother was teasing his temper when my brother piped up. "Do we have more milk?"

—⁓—

Crazy jumped straight up and out of his seat. The chair flew back, tipping over a few feet away. His sudden jolt caused Mother to pull her face in the same direction as her behind, her hands and arms instantly surrounding her face, her head. Her eyes pointed toward the floor, closing tightly as she awaited the onslaught. The pause that followed was as intense as any I'd experienced. Dead air hung like thick summer humidity just before a thunderstorm cracks to life.

It's a unique feeling to go from total fear to its absolute reverse in mere seconds. That surge coursing through your veins, pumping, jerking your body from one end of the emotional spectrum to another. It leaves you with a focus, a clarity, as if your entire world has opened wider than anyone can possibly imagine. You see more than just what's in front of you. It's like having limitless peripheral vision that expands in all directions. You can see with perfect vision what's above, below, and around you without changing your focal point or concentration. It's like everything slows down, giving you time to track, to follow, and it allows your mind to comprehend what's playing out and what's going to happen. Time to figure out your next move, how to defend yourself. An internal quiet that works your ears to the point where you feel the same as a hunted animal. Its ears perk up, turning in directions of danger, searching while its instincts plan, manage the escape, or formulate an offense. You feel in all directions, just like seeing or hearing. This powerfully intense emotional ride triggers a sense of knowing. One that filters out everything except what's needed to survive. You move in more dimensions than you live in when life is "just a normal day."

What's wrong with me? I wondered, almost out loud. How do I turn this on and off without having to engage in the fear Crazy puts me through? Can I learn to shift into "nonfear mode" without having to be assaulted by him, or anyone? What makes me think of these things? Maybe Crazy was right; maybe I was the problem!

Crazy smirked as he turned away from Mother, stepping away from the table. "Pick up that chair and finish your oatmeal," he commanded.

Just like a hot spoon through soft Crisco, the tension was broken. Crazy had flipped that switch back into the pretend stepfather role as if nothing had happened. We all were expected to follow his lead and turn the emotional corner the second he so ordered, without saying a word. We all fell in line as expected and awaited his next set of orders.

"Get outside, feed the animals starting with the chickens, and get your chores done before the cops get here," commanded the master.

Yesterday's oatmeal was pulled from in front of me. The spoon ripped from my finger and flipped onto the counter. "It'll be here for dinner; don't worry about that. Now, get moving."

My empty belly followed my feet, two steps behind my brother, like marching soldiers heading to our next assignment.

"When you finish your chores, get back in here…You need to be taught a lesson for hiding on me."

My hopes of avoiding a "lesson" were dashed by his parting joust.

Chickens weren't the only farm animals Mother and Crazy had invested in. They picked up geese, ducks, dogs, rabbits, cats, and an old goat that would eat anything. It was becoming a small farm but was tended by city slickers without a single day's training or understanding of how best to manage livestock. More importantly, they had no understanding about how to pay for all the feed while trying to earn money selling eggs, unlike other farmers, who had generations of kin and connections. They failed to understand there was an old Yankee network of trading and bartering and a subculture of currency that never allowed the revenuers to trace the hayfields of crops to cash. Trading eggs for other items was something I watched the old farmers doing. I quickly figured out, if you wanted something done, you needed to find out what the other person needed and how to make it happen without cash changing hands. Crazy and Mother didn't seem to grasp the old Yankee economic engine. They demanded cash as if they still lived in the city. The learning curve was fast outpacing the cost to feed the animals.

When the well stopped working shortly after we moved into the old farmhouse, the oldest farm family in the area came to help. It was a hand-dug well and the only source of water for the family and the animals. The pump and water line needed replacing. The farmer said he'd replace the line in trade for tending fields and using Crazy's land to feed cows, but that barter was refused. Crazy offered cash but needed time to pay. I could see it wasn't the method the old farmer favored. The well got fixed, but Crazy never paid the farmer. So when there were no hay bales left to use as bedding for the foul, one of us needed to ask Crazy what to do. The barn across the street was filled with hay. Little did we know how much trouble a bale of hay would bring!

—m—

One of us had to ask Crazy what to do about the hay! Rock, paper, scissors, best out of three. My brother and I decided the loser had to go back inside and ask about the hay. My brother threw twice, and with a low grunt and a "crap," he turned and headed back into the lion's den. He barely had time to ask before popping back outside and calling to me, "You need to get back inside. He wants us at the table."

Now it was my turn. "Oh, crap!"

Settling into the infamous assigned seating, Crazy launched into a fit of verbal lesson teaching. The ways of the world and how Mother didn't believe his punishments were needed. He could talk for hours, and we'd just have to sit here and listen, or at least pretend to. He rambled on about his ideas for new punishments and how lucky we were, how hard he had it growing up compared to our "easy lives." Crazy dove into his childhood. Getting up at 4:00 a.m. to shovel coal into the furnace so his five sisters, mother, and brother wouldn't be cold when they woke up. His ten-mile paper route before heading to school, walking uphill both ways in the snow with no socks and holes in his shoes. He just stopped talking at some point, but it wasn't necessarily a good thing. The silence became very eerie—ominous, even. After twenty minutes or so, it became outright creepy. The air was broken when my brother fell asleep and hit his face on the table. How did he do it?

"*Ducks!* That's the answer—*ducks!*" That fiendish glow fluttered above his head, like heat broiling off the pavement on a mid-August afternoon. He had a smile reserved only for the criminally insane, and when he sported that look, buckle up! A look so odd that no matter how hard you would think, how much work you would put into figuring out what was behind the evil that made up his thoughts, it was just not possible to understand. Not his world.

"Ducks! Ducks! Ducks!" He carried on about ducks. His smile grew as he looked out the picture window at the geese and ducks milling about, quacking at their limited breakfast and asking for the water buckets to be filled. In the reflection, I could see his unabashed look bouncing off the plate glass. It was a view into his soul as he beamed with his thoughts without sharing more than *"Ducks...ducks!"* Crazy didn't realize I could see his reflection, or maybe he didn't care if anyone could see his face light up with his unsettling thoughts. He must have formed a plan, a new method of punishment. Why else would we be sitting back at the table, waiting, while he plotted? Was he getting enjoyment watching over unkempt livestock calling for help, locked in a pen or on a chain? No water! Only the old goat was able to search for food; at least the goat wasn't suffering. *"Duck walk! It shall be duck walk!"*

He looked directly into my eyes with his black cut-out holes for eyes. *"Duck walk!"* What the heck is "duck walk"? I thought.

Mother looked at him and said, "The animals need to be fed. They need water."

Crazy ordered Mother to feed them; he had a punishment to manage. "On your feet, you little shithead, and get up against the wall," he demanded. Then he proceeded to explain how I was to walk like a duck for the next hour without stopping. Walk across the kitchen, back and forth, until he said to stop. "Hands on your hips, not on the floor. Walk like a duck," he bellowed. "Your ass should be an inch off the floor, thumbs in your armpits," he demanded. Away I waddled—without pain at first, but that quickly changed.

My brother let out a hearty laugh as I tried to balance on the fronts of my feet waddling across the kitchen floor. Making every effort to act like a bird, I let out a few quacks, which simply pissed off the master. "You think this is a game, do you?" he questioned as he headed toward the cupboard, searching for my ammunition. Each time he turned his head, I'd place my thumbs under my armpits and flap like a duck. His intent to humiliate was taking its toll. My knees began to ache, with the stabbing pain growing in depth and strength. The longer I duckwalked, the more my knees hurt. After a while, I couldn't move very well, and this game, this punishment, was becoming brutal. The silliness that caused my brother's laugh, his playful smile, vanished after the second or third lap.

Mother was outside tending to my counterparts. There was little hope of her rescuing me, not in the near future. Where is that state trooper? flashed through my mind. I could only duckwalk in short sprints before my legs no longer worked. My hips locked so badly it felt like knife points jabbing deeper and deeper into my joints. My muscles were cramping in fist-sized knots. My hips locked in place until I finally fell over in agony, fighting the urge to cry. Crazy was barking away: "If you can't complete the lesson, I have another one planned."

I tried again and again to keep walking like a duck, but each surge became shorter and shorter. The pain grew, spreading across my entire lower body. Cramps crippled my legs and hips until I could no longer go on. I wasn't even close to the one-hour guideline, the time that was the key to learning the lesson.

I lay on the kitchen floor, the pain racing up and down my legs, my back, my hips. The pain started to withdraw just as the cramps reemerged and grabbed hold. My muscles locked up, causing even more pain. My right calf formed a knot so tight it looked like a baseball had replaced what was the back of my lower leg. I was so thirsty the sweat dripping off my face offered some relief as it slid past my lips and onto my tongue. The salty taste wasn't the most pleasant, but somehow it sent a wave of relief, as if it were a full glass of cold water being dumped into my mouth.

Crazy was seated in his spot at the table holding something in his hand, tapping it on the table like a calling card. "Are you through? You done?" were his only words directed at me.

I tried to stretch out my legs, with little success. At least I'm not hungry anymore, I thought as my tongue searched for more liquid, any liquid.

Crazy started barking about how I had brought this on myself by hiding from him and causing him so much embarrassment. I wasn't listening; it was just more of the same.

Instead I was asking God to stop the pain, to help me, but I must have said it out loud, because Crazy shouted, "He can't help you—only I can, and you need to be taught to respect me and my house!"

I repeated my request using that secret voice we all use when we don't want anyone else to know what we're doing. The pain came and went in waves. The cramps and muscle locks faded in and out. There was so much pain, my mind started to fade away, heading to that place where no one could find me. It must have been working, as my mind started to calm, like when the wind stops blowing and the ripples on the water settle down to form that perfect reflection. "It will be okay," I heard whispered in my ear, as if someone was lying right next to me. My ear was pinned to the floor, so where did it come from? It caught my attention so much that I forgot about the pain and the misery, and a more quiet calm passed over me like a cool summer breeze on a warm day. The sounds of Crazy disappeared into the background, and I sensed something was with me. It felt like an old friend stopping by unexpectedly, and it warms your heart to see them. It changed the air, the sting from my body, and relieved so much of the pain it felt like I had fallen asleep, dreaming perhaps, but with my eyes open.

I still heard some of Crazy's ramblings, but overriding his horrifying tone was a sense of peaceful bliss. A taste of honey filled my mouth. I was no longer thirsty for some reason. I couldn't see anything other than the floor, the underside of the kitchen table, and the bony sticks with dark-black hair. It was the wizard of pain, preparing to conduct the newest in child-teaching techniques from his version of *Animal Farm*. I was starting to catch my breath, almost as if something was pushing back against the evil one. Pushing just long enough for me to regain my strength for the next round of fun and games. "We are with you," I heard in the same ear as moments ago but with a different message.

"Who is that?" I asked out loud but just under my breath.

No response. Was it the ones who lived in the rooms Crazy kept locked, nailed shut? Were they there?

As those thoughts walked across my mind, I started to see another pair of legs just behind Crazy, who was still sitting in his chair. Whose legs are those? I wondered. As I tried to train all my focus on those legs, I realized the feet were wearing soft slippers. I could see the bottom of a dress as the skinny white legs moved closer to the table. Sweat dripped into my eyes, forcing me to close them and wipe away the stinging drips. When I looked back to find those legs, they were gone, and so was my pain, at least for now.

A tapping began to sound off, louder and louder. My mind trained on the sound—*tap, tap, tap*. What is that? took hold as I regained some of my bodily control. *Tap, tap, tap*...It was getting louder and more dedicated. *Tap, tap, tap* went the beat in its rhythmic tone, calling to me as if a type of Morse code was sending its warning...*tap, tap, tap*. My body was releasing many of the cramps; the pain evaporated into small, pulsing waves of manageable levels. *Tap, tap, tap*...until I had to get up and see what it was, see what was calling to me, egging my curiosity to a point of no return. *Tap...tap...tap* instructed me to sit up and find the source. My body was recovering from the foul-feathered flapping masterpiece of step-parenting by Beelzebub.

As I strained to stand, forcing joints and muscles back to their normal positions, the tapping continued. Standing with a last menacing stretch, I was now staring at him and the tapping. A bottle was in his grip. Not his normal brown, the ones filled with his happy juice, but a really small one with a red cap. A thin neck and some green writing. I'd seen this bottle before but couldn't remember what it was. The red cap reminded me of something, but I couldn't quite place it. As my legs regained their stamina and the shaking was replaced with soreness, I wiped away the remaining sweat as a bitterness washed over me once again. I could feel his hatred of me growing. Crazy sat quietly, confident with that determined look that had gotten me into this duckwalking mess, *tap, tap, tapping* away with his red-capped bottle.

He wasn't done! This wasn't over, this lesson! Thoughts of what was next overtook the body ache as the tapping continued, echoing off the walls and surrounding both ears like a heartbeat gone bad. He flicked the ash from his cigarette onto the floor. He brought it to his scornful mouth and pulled at a deep, long inhale. He was calculating his next moves. He held it for a bit before releasing gray clouds into the air. It worked its way in my direction. His next puff was intentionally blown at me as if to say, "You have more coming," and with that, the tapping of the red-capped bottle was so violent, I was sure it would break.

What was the next torture? The next test of wills—would it be a test of faith? How much worse could my life become! How much pain could I possibly survive? That grinch-like smirk rolled his cheeks high into his sunken eyes. His eyes fixated on me as he started to open his clenched fist concealing most of that bottle... And then he turned the bottle so I could see the label, the full label. My heart sank deeper than I thought possible. Oh, God, please, *no*!

The tapping stopped with one final commanding smash of the table, his fist doing the honors, the red-capped bottle bouncing in the air, landing on its side. The fisting bang was intended to set the stage for another round of "punishment," but it unintentionally knocked over his coffee, the milk Crazy had left on the table, and a glass pitcher from his mother. That glass pitcher had been a gift of sorts, and a really nice one. Mother only used it on special occasions. She called it "the nicest serving dish we own." She must have brought it out to serve iced tea to the volunteers searching for me. Well, it was closer to the table edge than it should have been. With his last hammering for effect, it tipped over just enough to cling to the lip of the table. But once the second blow bounced it so close to the edge of the rocking tabletop, it decided enough was enough and jumped to its death, shattering into a thousand pieces and scattering in all directions. The actual smash as it hit the floor was louder than Crazy's fist bump. Maybe someone wanted to show him up a bit. Either way, Crazy would be sure I received all the blame, as if I had reached out, picked up the priceless pitcher, and tossed it with my very own hands.

Inside I was shaking, knowing I'd be getting extra lashes for his actions. Of course, that state trooper was still coming to revisit our loving domain, right? I was hoping so, as it remained the only reason I wasn't tied to the yardarm already. Crazy's face was awash with even more anger than normal, knowing he'd have to explain the glass pitcher. He didn't explain himself to anyone, so having to explain the pitcher should be an adventure to watch and painful to feel, at least for my backside.

He took a heavy inhale, and an even heavier, slower exhale followed as he collected himself. He was readying his next move, but he was unsure of the process with the glass spread across the kitchen floor. His bare feet sparkled with specks of glittering glass fragments dusting his smelly feet. He peered under the table to see where to step next. Unsure and uneasy, he lifted his feet off the floor and demanded that I "get the broom and sweep up this mess before I cut my foot and really get pissed off!"

Well, getting him pissed off would be a sight to see, since I thought I'd seen all his rage points. I didn't think he had another level, another gear, but maybe pissed off was a downshift for him. Let's not figure that one out today and just get the broom.

My bare feet surely wouldn't collect broken glass nor cut into my flesh the same as Crazy's. Of course his toes mattered, and mine, well, mine didn't. I quickly crossed the room, grabbed the broom, and used it with the efficiency of a professional cleaning service.

I cleaned up most of the glass just in time for Mother's reentry into the ongoing day's saga in the kitchen. She stopped just short of the table. "What happened?" she cried out with a bit of fake exasperation. "Was that my best pitcher? The one your mother gave me?" she asked with limited humph behind her words.

"Your kid did it," Crazy sounded off, and without waiting for a response, he added, "He pissed me off, and I banged the table—but you should have taken care of it yesterday and put it away. If you had, this would not have happened."

So there you have it: it was both my fault and Mother's. The blame spread to all parties except the one who hit the table.

Mother pressed back with a short "You didn't need to blame everyone else…" and quickly cut off her finish, knowing it was a mistake.

Crazy lit up like a Christmas tree with inflating rage boiling over the top. "How dare you question me!" And the game was in full swing.

The two went at it while I cleaned up the rest of the mess. The wood plank flooring was so old and had many hiding places for dirt, let alone broken shards of glass. As I was about to finish, dumping the dustpan into the garbage, a stinging pain rifled up my leg from the bottom of my foot. Jumping out of instinct, I flung the pan of glass chips and dirt into the air with a yelp. The action stopped the pair from their battle of wits and put their attention on the flying chips. I dropped to one knee, blood pooling around my foot.

Mother took the broom and dustpan to finish as Crazy ordered me to sit down so he could look at my bleeding foot. He made quick work of removing the glass and stuck a cloth on the wound with some tape to hold it in place. "Don't think this will get you out of the rest of your lesson, little boy," he said without the slightest hint of compassion.

The broken glass pitcher collected at the bottom of the garbage bag, Mother stewed and sputtered over the loss. Crazy was back in his favorite seat. The red-capped bottle was standing close to his hand, proudly displaying its successful marketing logo. "Stand up and come over here," he commanded. "Open your mouth." He started shaking the red sauce into a foamy mixture while holding his finger over the red cap. *"Open your mouth, dammit!"*

You're going to have to work for this one, was all I could think. I'm not going through this again, not this one.

"Open your fucking mouth, or I'll kick your teeth down your throat!"

Crazy grabbed my jaw, the thumb on his right hand just under my ear, his fingers in the same spot on the other side of my face He squeezed to force my mouth open. I fought with all my might to keep my mouth shut, but he applied so much force I couldn't hold out any longer. My mouth popped open. I fought to close my lips. I couldn't get my teeth to come together, but I still had control over my lips. I tried to shake my head, but he was too strong, and I couldn't break free. Saliva built up and overflowed from the slight opening Crazy had created with his pointing finger. Ripping the corner of my mouth with his heavy fingernail, he created enough space for the saliva to leak out, which gave him the opening he needed. He shoved the open bottle of fire past all my efforts to resist, the opening not much bigger than the shaft of the bottle.

He dumped the contents into my mouth and shook the bottle back and forth. He shook my face, my head, and the bottle until he had the perfect rhythm he needed to empty most of the red liquid into my mouth. I wiggled, shook, and jerked to break free. He trapped me between his knees, which he used like a vise to hold me, and then he shook my body along with my head, ensuring he would get full coverage and plenty of sauce from that bottle into every corner, onto every single taste bud, and down the back of my throat until I started to hack, dry heaving with nausea. The ungodly powerful hot sauce burned like fire throughout my entire mouth and throat and raced its way up my nose until it felt like my entire head was a burning mass of flowing lava. The dry heaves had little effect to curb the inferno as it spread down my throat and into my stomach.

The bottle empty, he released his murderous grip as the blaze expanded into my eyes and my lungs. The pain was unbelievably insane. I crumpled to the floor, begging for relief. Each breath was more painful than the last. My tongue was awash in spit, but that offered no help. My eyes were half-blind in tears. Snot bubbled from each nostril. I was hacking, heaving, gagging!

"Put your face against that wall!" shouted Crazy, pointing to the wall separating the kitchen from the living room. *"Get up. Get off my floor, you little shit. Get your nose on that wall, and you'd better not spit anything out, or you'll get the rest dumped down your throat!"* With one hand, he lifted me off the floor and threw me against the base of the wall like tossing a rag doll across a room. Tears poured

down my face in an uncontrollable stream, still offering little to relieve the agony. A snot bubble grew and popped, sending stinging fragments to burn my cheeks, my skin. My chin took on that dotted, dimpled formation that happens when your mouth produces the saddest face ever possible. Why me? I asked God. Why me?

The pain and anguish are so intense you lose control of your ability to breathe. Your lungs shudder for protection, then demand to be filled, one as tortured as the other. You fight for short, quick inhales amid the bursting exhales filled with spit and bits of stomach acid. Your tongue feels like a colony of fire ants biting away with no end in sight. You can't feel anything except that pain. If you swallow, you know it will sting more, and if you spit, well, Crazy will just add more of his secret recipe, and the game will start all over again.

The conflagration throughout my upper body was overwhelming. Fear diverted to anger. Anger swelled like my throat, my tongue. Rage started taking shape. I had to do something, but what? *Tap, tap, tap* replayed in my head. *Tap, tap, tap!* I began to bang my forehead into the wall. At first it was to fight back, but after a few thumps, a bit of relief entered the game. The more I smashed my head into the wall, the less the fire ants stung. My show of defiance was having an effect I didn't foresee. "You better not dent my wall!" shouted Crazy. One last whack of my forehead into the wall sent a ringing into my ears, and a lot of stars filled my eyes.

The ringing in my ears slowly dissipated. The stars were still twinkling inside my eyelids. I heard Mother behind me. Her hand was on my neck and then the back of my head, a bit of comfort that was deeply needed. She whispered into my ear, "Everything will be okay. You are going to be okay." The pitch of her voice was off; the sound was different. It was the hand of Mother's love, and while it was late in coming, it eased the emptiness within.

I could hear Crazy shuffling about just to my left. He was still in his chair, and while I couldn't see him, I knew he had that smirk across his face. A thrill of satisfaction over the sniveling snot cluster still dangling from my face. I could feel how proud he was of his handiwork, his imagination and inventiveness. I wanted to wipe away the tangled mess but knew better, so I just kept my hands to my side, nose pressed against the wall, and blinked my eyes to clear my field of vision and start to regain some of my abilities.

Mother's hand stayed firm, more comforting as the burning finally started to fade. At least the intense pain was retreating. The longer-term effect, I knew, would last for days, weeks even. The last time Crazy played this game, it took several days for my tongue, throat, and mouth to stop hurting, but they never returned to normal. Maybe if I didn't try so hard to use my teeth to scrape off the fire from the second it hit my tongue, it wouldn't last so long, but that was the only thing I could do—work my teeth to scrape off the sauce as best I could, forcing it to drip out of my mouth. I knew I scraped so hard the surface of my tongue ripped apart, causing more damage, blood. It was the only defense I could muster.

As my eyes cleared, I felt the warm hand and Mother's love still behind me, and I could see what was on both sides of me. Then I heard something that just wasn't right coming into the kitchen. It was Mother, and she was demanding Crazy let me wash out my mouth! How could that be? She was behind me, right?

The loving hand lifted its gentle touch. The feeling of warmth weakened as a cooling breeze drifted across my face.

—∽∾—

"This is *wrong*" hit my ears. Mother's voice bellowed from the threshold on the other side of the kitchen. Then, like a flash, I saw her passing from the kitchen into the living room. I turned my head to get a clear view, and sure enough, Mother was across the room and was now moving out of sight. The hand on my shoulder puzzled me as I realized it couldn't have been Mother. Who was it? I quickly rolled my head around to the right and looked over my shoulder. Nothing, no one. But the feeling within remained, just not as strong.

Mother's love! It was there, and now it was going away. The calm remained, but the loving feeling left with the hand on my back. It left me in deep thought, taking me to a place far away from here and the hell I was living. I rolled my head back to center, nose once again pressed into the wall as silence overtook the room, but only for the briefest time. Who was behind me recaptured my focus. What was that touching me?

Just as I felt like I would recover, there was a scream from the other end of the farmhouse, a shriek of sorts coming from Mother. Maybe she had just realized our two sisters hadn't been fed either and they had decided to run away or hide in protest.

"*The cops are here!*" was the repeated message.

Instantly, Crazy was on his feet, spinning me around to face his grizzly look. "Go clean yourself up, and you make sure you don't talk about our family, or you'll have *hot* sauce for your lunch and dinner. *You hear me, boy?*"

As I stared into his dark, lifeless eyes, a pit of hollow heartlessness was all I could see. Time was limited, but if I just stared at him, delaying, maybe the trooper would see what was happening here. Crazy shook me with his hand on the top of my head. God, make me big enough to fight back. Please, God, make me grow so big I can stop him. Please make me so big and strong I can stomp on him like the creepy crawler he is. Hear me, God—make me a man so huge I can pay Crazy back for all he has done.

Crazy must have known what I was thinking, as he shook me even harder, demanding, "*You hear me, boy?*"

With that, I nodded my response as he pushed me toward the bathroom.

A final "*Not a word!*" trailed my backside, and I could feel the cool water even before I reached the tap. I had survived another round of Crazy!

—◆◆◆—

I hate him with all I have—those words were now cemented into my mind. I kept repeating my godly request as the water soothed my face, my mouth, my being. I kept thinking, Make me so big, so strong that I can kill him. My mission was to survive and kill Crazy! It would become my life's work if only God would make me strong enough, big enough…If he did his part, I would do mine.

From that moment forward, it changed from a thought and a wish and became a focus, just like counting steps. I had to kill him.

Bang, bang, bang, rattled the side door, a not-so-polite way of announcing the arrival of the gun-carrying authority. Mother knew better than to open the door. It was Crazy who would handle the police. *Bang, bang, bang,* sounded off again, this time with even more petition.

Mother called to Crazy, "There are two of them. Are you going to let them in or what?"

Crazy was sitting in his spot at the table, holding his coffee and staring out the picture window. Mother made a quick pass at cleaning the dishes and organizing the kitchen to look a bit more presentable. My sisters were now in the living room, one in an old wooden playpen and the other on the floor fussing with some toys, a bottle by her side.

Bang, bang, bang—but this time it was followed by a sharp command. "This is Sergeant Haines, supervisor, Troop K of the Connecticut State Police. I'm with Trooper Daniels, who was on-site commander yesterday overseeing the reported missing child. We're here to follow up, as Trooper Daniels informed you before leaving the scene late last night."

With my face cleaned up, I stood behind Crazy as he sat in his chair. I wondered what he'd do. Why didn't he just open the door? What was he planning? I was the one who had hidden, so why was he so afraid of the troopers? Was he scared someone would tell them what was going on inside the walls of this lesson factory?

"Sir, you need to open the door. We need to talk to you and your family. *Sir, I know you hear me. Sir!" Bang, bang, bang!* "We know you're in there. Trooper Daniels has been parked on the street for several hours now, so open the door and let us in. We're not looking to escalate this matter. We need to follow up on what happened here." *Bang, bang, bang!*

The trooper was out on the street? Did he know what had been going on all morning?

"Sir, if you don't open this door, we're going to assume people are in distress and make entry on a welfare check. *Sir, do you understand what I am saying to you?*" Bang, bang, bang, bang, bang...

Finally, Mother opened the door, albeit just enough to peek out and stop the repeated hammering and shouting, which at this point had my two sisters crying and starting to scream in panic.

"Ma'am, we need to talk with you and your husband. Can we come in?" asked one of the troopers.

What Mother didn't know was that Crazy had also gotten off his butt and was heading toward the side door just as she began to turn the handle to stop what was about to be a forced entry.

"I'll handle this..." said Crazy, but in a tone opposite the entire morning's proceedings. His "lesson voice," a term I would coin in the not-so-distinct future, was reserved for the tortured ones.

"Sir, we need to come inside and talk with you, so—"

But the trooper was cut off. "You're not coming inside without a warrant. You got one of them?" Crazy leveled his position.

"No, sir. We're here to follow up on the missing child and the search that went on most of yesterday evening. Is there a problem we need to know about?" asked the trooper. "Why can't we enter, sit down, and follow up? We need to complete our report." A reasonable ask considering there had been dozens of volunteers, state troopers, and others engaged in a response to "your phone calls," as the trooper stated several times.

Crazy wanted nothing to do with law enforcement of any kind, for any reason. Now, I don't know why, but one thing that turned his colors was a cop or even a police car behind his car or even parked along the roadside. "Why did you have a trooper stationed outside our house without our knowing about it?" Crazy asked the sergeant.

"Sir, can we come in or not? I'm not conducting this investigation between a door and half your face. Are you letting us in or not?" The trooper was clearly getting agitated.

"*No!*" barked the reply. "You're not stepping foot inside this house. Never again!"

As I watched through the picture window, only feet away from the stone steps leading up to the side door, I could see the exasperated expressions on both troopers' faces. One hung his head for a moment, then looked back up. "Sir, either come outside this instant, or we'll pull you outside for obstructing an investigation."

The tactic worked. After a very short pause, Crazy opened the door and slithered through the opening. He pulled the door shut behind him. The troopers, one on each side of him, walked him down the steps toward the cruisers. The red and blue balls of light slowly rolled in circles on the tops of the massive 1970 police vehicles. Each of the two patrol cars was bigger than the beat-up old two-door Chevy and the faded-green two-seat International truck Crazy used to get to work, depending on which one would start in the morning.

Watching the troopers manhandle Crazy had my heart pounding, but in a good way. Their crisp uniforms, military-style haircuts beneath perfectly rounded hats, and polished shoes that made the sun bounce in all directions were a wonderful sight to my bloodshot eyes. Maybe they'd take Crazy with them and we'd never have to see him again.

Wishful thinking. Once Crazy was outside, he didn't have

any of the swagger he displayed around those who couldn't defend themselves. In fact, from the moment the banging started, I could see the air around him change. It was as if all that power he generated, all the dusty-colored darkness that floated around him was sucked away, as if Mother had used that old Hoover to vacuum his dust cloud out of sight. It was like his authority was grounded, was discharged, or maybe had slipped into hiding. I studied his body language as he was flanked by the two hulking servants of the law. He wasn't the same man as the one who had been serving up lessons a few brutal minutes ago.

Crazy was smaller, so much smaller, standing between those two well-dressed state troopers. Straight lines were pressed into their pants like they had just come off the shelf. They had perfectly pressed blouses, a dull gray with bright-blue piping and flashes of yellow tossed about, giving an even more impressive profile as they stood with one hand just inches from their holsters. If Crazy made a move, they would be ready—guns loaded for just the right moment when he made a move to take control of their authority or tried to run away. If only he'd make the move!

Seeing Crazy cower under their impressive stature was worth the price of admission, so to speak. Crazy had his head down, hands by his sides, his torn leather slippers covering most of his feet. His oil-stained shirt and unwashed pants spoke volumes about the man. Watching him have to look up to authority was a real treat. It was like they could reach out and spank him any second they wanted to, and oh, how I wished they would.

I noticed something move off to my left. I saw my brother come out of the chicken coop and stand half in and half out of the old sliding wooden door. He was watching the goings-on of the police and Crazy. As I looked back, I saw the bigger trooper start to wave his arms, shake his head, and generate a few different stern, scolding looks directed at Crazy. He never moved, didn't twitch. He just stood there, looking up and then back down. He kicked a stone or two with his soft-soled house slippers as if to say, "I'm bored with you," but his body told another story. He was scared. He was worried, and it was growing.

It seemed the senior trooper kept increasing his tone. I couldn't hear what he was saying, but he was clearly getting angry. Not the Crazy kind of angry, an authority kind of angry. Like in school when the principal would ask me where the bruises came from, and I would just look at the floor without saying a word. I could tell the principal was getting angry, but not the beating kind. More of a sympathetic kind, but still it was anger.

At one point, the trooper leaned in close to Crazy's face, almost nose to nose, and let him know about something—maybe something he knew, and he wanted Crazy to be fully aware of the lengths of his "investigation." Of course, I could only guess—wish, really. No one could hear what was being discussed, although Crazy was getting more and more animated as his colors were changing yet again. Red was becoming more apparent as yellow disappeared a bit. Now he was flicking rocks from the undersides of his leather slippers like the start of a bullfight, dusting up the ground in preparation for what was to come. All three shuffled their bodies a bit as if to ready for a fight.

Please, God, make the troopers take him away with them. I

wanted Crazy to do something, anything to get those guns a-blazing, but despite my best wishes, it wasn't going to happen. One trooper pointed deep into Crazy's chest, a sight I thoroughly enjoyed. You could see the warning he was giving to Crazy. Pointing to several positions at and around the house, the trooper continued his version of *Who's the Boss?* until he felt he had made his point and stepped back a bit.

It must have been a while in the making, as the troopers had a lot to say to him. It took so long I didn't even remember Mother feeding my sisters, who at this point had finished their lunch and were sitting contentedly in their seats in the kitchen. The troopers gave one final stern head shot at Crazy before moving back to their cruisers.

Crazy headed for the door and, without a word, went right for his favorite brown bottle. He also opened the cupboard and pulled out his second favorite, a clear longneck glass bottle with a white juice inside. He headed to his favorite chair and ordered everyone to *"leave me be!"* That warning meant we were all to scatter and disappear until otherwise notified. We all scattered to the corners of the old farmhouse or the barn or the yard, each of us retreating to our sanctuary for some peaceful time away from Crazy.

The next few months were rather quiet. No beatings, no lessons, no bruises. Crazy didn't really say much of anything, especially to me. While I have no idea what those troopers said to him, it must have put the fear of jail into him because he was a different person, at least in that Crazy kind of way. The hatred was still obvious to me, but all that darkness that normally surrounded him was tucked away somewhere. Somewhere close, but for now it was in hiding.

From time to time, we'd see the trooper sitting along the roadside very close to our old farmhouse. I'd wave, and the trooper would give a short point with his finger and offer a warming heartfelt smile. One of almost knowing or sensing he was making a difference.

After the snow melted for the final time that winter, I no longer saw the state trooper or any police cruisers along our road. The school bus made its normal rounds, and I'd look for the trooper each day, but once the snow was gone and until the final school day that year, no more trooper. Crazy must have seen the same thing, because I could see the darkness creeping back into play. Little by little it returned until on a fateful day it all exploded into a bloody, hellish mess of flashing lights, horns, sirens, and people all over the old farmhouse. The fear would fully return, and with it came a mighty grip taking hold deep within my stomach. It was all Crazy could do to cover his tracks as the troopers were back, this time inside the house, without need of a warrant. It was a bloody mess!

CHAPTER 3

The sun shone through the window and onto my face with its radiating warmth. The light hit my eyes as I took a deep breath, inhaling the soft morning rays from heaven. The wind gently rustled the lush green leaves of another warm summer morning. I felt my brother's feet touching mine, but I didn't mind. I smiled and felt happiness flowing across my chest. A happiness that for weeks had greeted me with the sun's early wake-up call. The sound of roosters becoming louder as the dew reflected and bounced the sun's rays off the bushes just outside the open window. A small screen held up the old glass frame with chipping white paint. It was a beautiful sight.

I heard a car in the distance. Its motor faded away, returned, and faded again before returning even louder. It barreled down the two-lane road only a strong rock's throw from the window. The nights had been perfect, quiet, and without worry, for the most part. The major exception being the fire station across the street, an old redbrick building sitting close to the old church with a box steeple, green door, and shutters. It had huge stone stairs and fluted columns running all the way up to the section where the bell rang when they wanted you to come to church and sometimes for other reasons, but I hadn't figured that part out just yet. The big red horn on top of the fire station made such a whining noise when it wanted the firemen to come get the trucks and race them somewhere else. Everyone came running when that horn blew—on foot, in cars, or in trucks, racing to get into the big, long red-and-silver fire trucks. It was so exciting to watch, but the noise from that horn hurt my ears and made my insides react like before we got here.

The park was on the other side of the house and across the street. Not the same street as the two-lane main road but another road. My window overlooked the intersection of the two roads. The other kids made fun of me for calling it a park. They called it a green. They were always correcting me when I called it "the park." Not making fun of me, more like having a laugh at one another in fun. There was a huge cannon right in the middle of the park...uh, the green. They said it was from the Civil War and was used in some battle that people from these parts fought in. Down the road was another old house, where the boys I played with said the family was part of the first to sign the Declaration of Independence. Someone still lived in the house who was kin to those people. There was a horse in the barn behind the house, and the family that owned everything lived on the other side of the three rooms we now called home.

It was an old farmhouse, but not scary like the one we ran away from, the one Crazy moved us into. It was warm, happy, and without fear or hate. I was so happy there. I looked over at Mother in her bed with my two sisters. She was snoring a bit, like she did when she was really tired. She worked for the family that owned the property and Fisher's Market across from the green.

The best way to describe the scene is Walton's Mountain. Picture John Boy and Mary Ellen running down the dirt road and into Ike Godsey's general store and post office. Jars of sweets on the counter—a penny would get you a small fistful of goodies, and a nickel would last a couple of visits. Everyone knew everyone else, and they didn't stick their noses in other people's problems. No one ever asked me about Crazy or why we were there. They just wanted to know "Where you from?" We told them, "The big city," to which they always replied, "Oh, Willimantic." We didn't correct them, as it was best to let it be.

It was the best time of my life. We ate and had plenty of water or milk to drink. We didn't have much, but there was always plenty of what was needed, so we were never hungry anymore. Going to bed was like the old days—Mother reading to us, tucking us into our covers. My brother and me talking until we fell asleep. Only now we had two sisters in the bed on the other side of the room, so we talked in whispers so as not to wake the baby, as Mother would repeat time and again.

The summer flew by, and it was time for a new school year to start. My brother and I were allowed to walk to school with the other boys, but Mother wanted us to get used to taking the bus, so for the first days we climbed on board the big yellow adventure and watched the woods, fields, cows, and other farmers working their land as we rumbled down the old roads to the schoolhouse. We'd have a packed lunch in our sacks, a sandwich wrapped in wax paper, folded neatly into a cared-for package. Milk from the school and a snack on a tray kept us filled as the day played out. We made more friends in an environment that was so respectful. "Yes, sir" or "No, ma'am" was expected to lead or trail each response or before you asked a question. There was no yelling, no fighting...It was as close to heaven as I'd been imagining in my requests to save us.

While the path was terrifying and I wished it upon no one, it got us here and made me appreciate every second of this good life. After school we played with the kids from other families, cowboys and Indians with sticks and real bows and arrows. We would help bale hay and ride on tractors. We got rides on the hay wagons as we helped stack the bales and learned to cross-lay them so they wouldn't fall over. Feeding the horse and other farmyard animals was such a delight. I enjoyed collecting eggs from the chickens' hiding places, which I was very good at since I would think like the chicken and figure out where the best places would be, something I had to learn myself. It was the happiest time and most fun I can ever remember. No fear, no pain, no bruises, and Mother had returned to singing at the table and showing her beautiful smile as she held me in her arms and gave me a huge, soft kiss on the head, producing the unique flavor that comes only from a mother's love! God how I loved that feeling from her.

She had promised Crazy was never coming back and that we'd be a family forever. The days melted into one after the other, a seemingly never-ending place full of joy and quiet excitement. At times it was hard to sleep, as I couldn't wait for the next morning. I couldn't wait to find new adventures, new things like fishing in the brook just past the school or the one just past the trees behind the barn with the horse. That brook was next to the neighbors' house, and we'd need permission to fish in the running stream.

We learned to catch worms just after sunset using flashlights and how to dig them out of the piles of smelly stacks of "compost," as they called it. The worms in the compost were so fat, I knew they'd catch a monster fish. I so loved the time in this perfect little town called Scotland, Connecticut. It was tucked halfway between two major cities, but it was a long ride to either. It was heaven, and my prayers had been answered.

As fall crept closer and the rains became more frequent, my brother and I would take the bus home. It took longer than walking, but we didn't get wet, and the rhythm of the wheels, the motor, and the vibrations made me sleepy. I dozed off so many times the other kids had to wake me up at my stop. It was a sleep with dreams of riding bikes and playing with my friends. Dreams of peaceful fishing and laughter at every meal. I sat in the back, but my brother was more of an up-front kind of rider. Getting off the bus, I'd run to see Mother and show her my work for the day, knowing she'd be so happy with what I'd done. Her hugs greeted us in the driveway or just inside the door, as if she'd missed me and I was returning from a long venture from some faraway place.

One day I had a special drawing just for Mother. Flowers painted in a field with her and me holding hands on one side, my brother and sisters on her other side. There were yellow beams of sun shining on all of us, just like it did on those summer mornings through my window. Picture in hand, I would take a short jump off the last bus step and onto the pavement. With growing speed I'd move my legs as fast as they would move along the dirt driveway and into the kitchen, where Mother surely would have zucchini bread, pumpkin cookies, or other baked goodies. A glass of milk, that hug of warmth, and overflowing pride for my family portrait. That was the plan I scratched out when I was making the work of art. As the bus drew closer to our stop, I saw a man standing in the park. The same man I had seen at the red barn. He was standing by the cannon, looking at me through the bus window. His eyes locked onto mine, contact never breaking as the bus ground to a halt. An ache started to collect in my stomach... Something was wrong!

As I stepped off the bus and walked down the driveway, portrait in hand, my senses were on alert. Turning toward the stone stairs with the rusty metal rail, I stopped dead in my tracks. Whose old car was that, and why was it parked where the man who owned the house usually parked his truck? Mr. Sorrels had asked us to keep our toys away from his parking place, so who was taking up his spot? The screen door was slightly open, which meant whoever had gone inside didn't know you had to pull hard and lift up to get it to latch. If you didn't, the flies and bugs came inside or the wind would take it off its hinges, and it would need to be fixed— a lesson we learned as the owner told us, "Make sure you close it tightly so this doesn't happen anymore." He was always polite, never raised his voice or got mad when we broke stuff. He would show my brother and me how to use the tools and make repairs. He was such a nice man, and his wife was always bringing over food. "We have too much, and it would just go to the animals if you don't help us eat the rest" were words she'd used many times when knocking on the door with the warm plates. She'd bake pies and leave them by the door with a note for Mother. She was such a good cook, and we never wasted an ounce of her food—Mother made sure of that.

I stared at the old car, trying to figure out who it might be. It must have been there awhile, as leaves were starting to cover the hood and windshield, but it hadn't been there when we left for school. Walking up the stairs and into the kitchen, just inside the doorway, I started to feel that thickness I hadn't felt in a long time. I saw the air swirling in the room like smoky gray clouds without a smell. It was more like fog, but I had learned that no one else could see it.

My stomach started to tighten as I called out for Mother. No answer. I walked past the table and looked into the bathroom before heading into the living room. No one was there. I looked back into the kitchen as my brother put his stuff on the table and sat down without paying any attention to the worries that were slowly growing in my mind, my stomach, and my chest. That old tightness was starting to gather, something I had almost forgotten about.

The door to the bedroom was closed, so I headed across the small living room, calling out, "Mom, are you in there?" Nothing, just silence. No sisters running around, no radio playing in the background, just silence.

I crept to the door and peered in just enough to see a lump in the bed. Mother always made her bed in the morning, so why were there lumps and blankets tossed about? As I pushed a little more and stepped through with one foot, I heard a shuffle followed by what sounded like breathing. Was Mother in the bed? Was she sick?

There was a soft snore followed by a gasp for air, as if something was cutting off the flow. It must be Mother, I concluded and let out a short sigh, an exhale of relief as I let my mind take me places that didn't exist—or so I thought.

As I headed toward the side of the bed, I realized the noise coming from under the covers didn't sound like Mother. There was a feeling of darkness about the room, an old feeling returning after a long hiatus. The blanket was over her shoulder and covering her face. The pillow was wrapped around her head. Her mouth pointed in the other direction as she moved slightly, rolling toward me. Her face started to emerge, looking toward the ceiling. As the pillow folded down to the side and away from her head, her thin black hair started to show at the same time her foot kicked the sheet and blanket down toward the bottom of the bed, uncovering her entire face and head.

I took a deep inhale, as if taking in that first morning's wake-up call as I pressed my arms over my head, my mind opening for the start of a new day. A flash in the window by my bed caught my attention. It was that blond lady who visited me in her white lace dress, reflected in the glass as if to warn me something was coming. Slowly, I looked back to see Mother's face and started to reach out to shake her, but my entire being was stopped as I was met with that face, those open eyes staring back at me without me knowing...I was being watched. Instantly I was gripped with all that old fear, anguish, and horror.

Staring at me from only a foot or two away, eyes wide open, was Crazy. And with that, my entire world shattered as I was instantaneously returned to that life of constant fear. I froze solid where I stood, not knowing what to do next. I tried to run, but my legs wouldn't move. I tried to scream, but my lungs wouldn't take air in or out. My body started to shake uncontrollably. I saw a tunnel coming at me. Darkness closed around my eyes. A pinprick of light was all that remained, and then complete darkness. I felt myself hitting the floor, and then nothing.

—⁕—

Was I dreaming? Was it happening again?...Or was I remembering? "Boys, put your clothes in those bags, and grab some toys. Put them in the box I put on your bed." Mother was setting the path for a very happy day. We were moving away from Crazy, or maybe running away and hiding would be a better understanding. The shooting was the breaking point for Mother. One that left my sisters screaming for hours. Afterward, they wouldn't even allow him to touch them. They recoiled and ran or crawled away anytime Crazy approached. The baby would crawl like an army ant, a scout racing back to warn the rest of the village of the danger that was coming. She could move so fast on her hands and knees—it looked like a cartoon of Baby Huey trying to return to the crib of safety.

Mother was busy packing what she could with no real plan, just a hurried collection of items for an unknown destination. She had a desperate grasp of confused thoughts with little effort or planning of the escape. The troopers waited outside along with Mother's childhood friend. She was my godmother and the closest person Mother had to anyone willing to help, willing to step into the wolf's den of insanity to help extract us from this nightmarish existence.

The second Mother told us we were leaving, you couldn't wipe the smile from my face. The excitement inside my chest instantly replaced the pain, worry, and fear. I raced about, collecting everything

I thought we needed and ordering my brother to "hurry up, so we can get out of here," which I repeated many times. Needless to say, it was a blessing that we were leaving. Maybe we'd go back to the city and see the park again, see those people Mother knew so well. All those people who warned her, "That man will be the death of you one day." Well, that one day almost happened earlier today.

We weren't running from the Scotland house; this was the Columbia house. You see, for a time things settled down. The trooper would park his cruiser on our road, and somehow Crazy refrained from his lessons. At least the kinds that break bones. He worked out a new lesson plan. One that kept us at the table for hours on end, listening to his lectures, his rants on how tough his life was, how easy we had it. He'd filter through brown bottle after brown bottle until his words made no sense at all. Sometimes, when we were lucky, he'd put his face into his forearm and start snoring. That was when we knew we could leave or go to bed. That all changed in one shattering exchange of insanity.

Crazy had found renters to take over where others had run away. These renters, two girls and one man, said they were doing research for college and needed a place to study, a quiet place. The advertisement listing the house for rent sounded perfect to them. They said they had another couple that would be living with them as well, and they wanted to use the rooms that he kept locked and nailed shut. Crazy and Mother talked about it, loudly at times, but the money was too good for them to pass up. The renters paid in cash, up front. Crazy removed the boards and nails, opening the access to the other rooms, but refused to enter himself. Mother wanted nothing to do with that part of the house. For me, I could feel something similar to Crazy drifting about, just behind the closed door. Almost taunting you to open the door and come in with an invite that appeared friendly, but if you waited, if you studied the door, you could feel it was up to no good.

Whenever I was near that door, I could sense someone standing behind me, but not in a bad way. More like a protector of sorts. It felt like a really tall person with big muscles. It gave me the sense—a feeling, really—and it looked like a picture of an angel from the church Mother attended. That was the picture I was getting in my mind. When Crazy unbolted the door's security system, the three dogs outside began to bark wildly, snapping away at the ends of their chains and running back and forth in a quarter curve using every inch they could gain. The chains strained to hold, tethered to the old doghouses.

Duke, a superlarge German shepherd with wolflike teeth, would jump up and down on all four legs, as if he were on a trampoline. He kept his head down as he hit the ground and pressed up to the sky as he used every bit of his force to propel him as high as he could, his nose pointing so straight in the air it looked like a statue of sorts. He kept doing the same thing over and over until he was so exhausted he had to lie down, panting like a greyhound after winning a mile-and-a-half-long race.

The smaller, gentle dog, named Ginger, tried to protect us from Crazy. Ginger didn't need to be chained; she was a house dog and came in and out as she liked, for the most part. She did get hit with the same stick, a switch as Crazy called it, as I was until she cowered into a corner, hiding to avoid further abuse. She did almost the same thing when Crazy opened the bolted door.

Ginger had her head down as she stared at that door opening. Her back fur stood on end as she slowly let out a deep, guttural sound of rolling effervescence. A faint bark attached to the end of the cautionary tale. I could see she was trying to figure out what was there. She was pacing across the hallway several feet from the door, refusing to take her eyes off the dark-brown wooden door. Ginger kept her nose pointed close to the floorboards, ears perked high, her eyes darting left and right. Then, as if a bolt of lightning had struck her, she jumped into the air and nipped at her backside as if something had taken hold of her. She'd had enough and ran out of sight, into the kitchen most likely.

Crazy stood there trying to figure out what was going on before picking up his tools and walking in the same direction as Ginger. I followed a short time later, but not before hearing what I swear was two or three people talking on the other side of that door. A laugh seemed to close their conversation, yet it didn't feel funny.

There had been a rather quiet period of time, no beatings or hurtful words, but I could tell it was going to end. Between the troopers no longer sitting on the road by the house and the renters who would make noise at all hours of the night, I could see Crazy was getting more and more agitated. It was building up inside him like lava under your feet. Once enough lava gathered, it was only time before the explosion would happen.

The renters had a lot of people coming and going all the time. Some wore funny clothing, and a lot of them wore black pants and black shirts. They made Mother nervous, but they paid the rent, so

Crazy and Mother decided to let them do what they wanted. They really didn't bother us, and we didn't see them all that much. We just knew they were in the house.

A few times, there were a lot of cars and people gathered together. We could hear faint singing—nothing I'd heard before, but I really couldn't make out any words. My brother and I would try to spy on them, but there always seemed to be an invisible shield keeping us from hearing, seeing, and understanding anything they were doing. They didn't stay overnight, because they were rarely there in the mornings. In my mind, their presence helped keep Crazy from returning to his beatings. I'm not saying he changed, but it wasn't the same. Mother said he "promised" not to hit us ever again or force fire sauce down my throat. I didn't hold much stock in anything he said, but Mother worked hard to sell the fable.

At night, the dogs would bark away when they heard the renters singing. They must have been dancing as well. The floorboards were creaking and popping as if a dozen kids were bouncing about. Duke was getting worse, and he looked like he was losing his fur, with spots missing on different places along his strong, heavy body. We were becoming afraid of Duke. He circled at times as if following something only he could see. Mother wanted him gone, but Crazy insisted he remain. She had become terrified of Duke, and rightly so.

After a few months passed with the new renters, Crazy became abnormally quiet. He would focus on something outside his normal gaze. He didn't talk much, didn't lecture us much, and looked like he was in a place other than the house. He'd stopped going to work and sat in the kitchen staring out the picture window. Duke would be barking away as Crazy stared at him from the table.

A foreboding air descended over the old farmhouse. It seemed to encapsulate everything and everyone except Crazy. It was as if it centered on him, or maybe he was its entry point, the focus of its terrifying presence. I could feel a separation of sorts, an "us and them" feeling. Good and evil coming out to play a game of life or death. There was no real way to explain it, and who would listen anyway? I was just a kid.

The barking became more and more fanatic until it suddenly stopped—and at that moment everything changed...everything!

—⁓—

Mother crashed through the side door and across the threshold into the kitchen, screaming bloody murder, yet no one could understand what she was saying. Her pitch was so high it was hard to listen to her. I put my hands over my ears to muffle the screeching sound emanating from her. Short of breath and panting like an overheated dog, she finally got a few words collected so we could follow what she was trying to say. At the same time, she was pointing outside toward Duke. "Cat being ripped apart" was what I could make out.

Shaking Crazy with both hands, Mother fought to get a response. She kept shaking him, screaming at him, pointing outside, and demanding he do something. Looking out that big window, we could see Duke with a doll in his mouth, but only a piece of the doll. Its red stuffing flapped in the air as he shook his head with the might of a diesel engine determined to make it up a steep hill. We watched as Duke used his paws to pin the doll under his considerable force. He ripped and tore it apart with such power and strength it might as well have been made of tissue paper.

Duke's nose, his mouth, his head, and parts of his body were covered in red stuffing. A piece flew high into the air as Duke snapped his jaws back and forth, left and right, with the force of a jackhammer pounding away at its workload. As I watched, I started to realize it was not a doll. It was a cat, one that had wandered too close to his chain's run. Duke was tearing the cat apart; which cat it was, nobody would ever know. He had created such a chewed mess of blood, guts, and matted fur—if not for the head flipping into the air, it would have remained unknown.

Suddenly Duke's eye caught sight of something that changed his interest—the ducks and geese in the pen just past the end of the kitchen wall to my left. With the unbridled force of sheer will, Duke charged time after time until he broke free of the chain limiting his spree. Now free, he charged at the fowl in the wire pen. All the birds were racing, running in circles to find an escape path, but none existed. Without hesitation, Duke smashed through the small wire coop and pounced on one duck with his front paw while grabbing another with his mouth. The shaking was far worse than for the cat. I could see the feathers flinging about, creating a whirlwind of blood splatters like rain droplets. Feathers floated in midair only to drop to the dirt as others replaced them in this violent cycle of horrifying repetitiveness.

Footsteps from the second floor, just above the kitchen, made a panicked-sounding scurry. The feet from the formerly secured rooms must have been watching the same bloodbath we were. People were scurrying around like I'd never heard before. It sounded like there were a dozen sets of legs dancing about, moving back and forth indecisively. A faint scream, a cutoff yell…arguing, and a laugh. A laugh so clear it changed the tone of everything that was happening, and then silence—dead silence.

—◊◊◊—

Finally, Crazy snapped out of his funk and looked at Mother briefly before standing. He paused as if to think out his next move and then turned toward the gun kept above the upper kitchen cabinets. Gun in one hand, a box of bullets in the other, he slid the bolt slightly back to see if a round was chambered and slammed it back into firing position.

Duke was making quick work of the fowl, with their clipped wings and limited escape route. Some battled to stand on one another. Others ducked and dove like a mole, fighting to dig under the frenzied pile of moving pillow stock. All were trying to avoid the jaws of the manic mongrel, who, until this point, had never hurt anyone or anything. His hardened look and deep bark had been his former menacing vice.

Something had changed him; something had happened to cause the formally docile canine to shred our egg-laying suppliers. It was like two kids having a pillow fight while their sisters shot at the floating feathers with squirt guns full of red dye number 7. A strange image to hold in such a nightmarish scene. Duke was becoming soaked from the slingshots of splattering liquids. His formerly tan, brown, and black pelt was now a mess of blood, dirt, and feathers sticking to him like a seventeenth-century tax collector standing at the gangplank of the famed Boston Tea Party while demanding payment to board but only gaining a hot-tar coating and a bucket of feathers.

The other two dogs were still securely chained to their boxes, also barking with sounds never before heard. It was so much to witness it almost became overwhelming; I wondered why it didn't!

A new sense of fear hit my chest and captured my attention, like someone had slapped me with an open hand. It felt like a firecracker had exploded just inches from my fingers, cascading the bubble of energy onto my flesh and bone, knocking the wind from my lungs. It was a new kind of fear. My vision, which had widened in the past when faced with such new levels of fear, narrowed like a tube closing in around me before returning to some form of normalcy. A unique ringing in my ears introduced other avenues to analyze. A pressure wave popping my ears and dissipating the tunnel vision fully awakened all my senses, and I could feel things with much greater sensitivity, as if the hairs standing on end all over my body were receptacles or antennae tuned into some special signal that was trying to relay a message.

Everything was in slow motion. Even the air was moving much slower, as if time itself was working to control events, control the next steps, if you will. My ears were hearing sounds I'd never heard before. My ears were tasting something utterly unique as they tried to share and parallel with my other senses.

Crazy slid past me and went out the door, down the antique stone steps, and onto the worn dirt pathway leading to the killing pen. Duke never slowed down, not in the slightest. Crazy raised the long gun, pointing with care down, its iron sights matching the target. He had the shot he wanted, but in an airy twist, Duke froze as if he knew what was coming. Duke slowly turned his duck-filled mouth toward the barrel. His jaws locked around the bird as it finally stopped fighting. Slow motion crept to a near-perfect still setting, the rifle just feet from Duke's head as both his eyes glared back at Crazy. Duke squinted as a slight wrinkle curled his lips just below his pointing ears. The picture froze, as if someone had paused the world to savor every second of chaos, until the ear-piercing sound reset the proper movement of time.

Kaa-boom filled the air. Without hesitation, Crazy cycled the rifle's bolt to chamber another missile. The plate-glass viewing station vibrated like someone had tossed a rock into a perfectly still pond. I'd never seen glass ripple like waves before. It held my attention for a moment, but the yelp from Duke brought my eyes back to the bloody pen. It looked like a biblical painting depicting hell on earth.

The bullet had grazed his upper shoulder. Duke nipped at the hole as if a bee had stung him, not knowing another stinger was about to find him. A second *boom* filled the air. The glass did its dance, and Duke was on the ground. After a few twitches, he moved no more. I could see the life lifting above his bloody remains, separating from the physical and floating just above what had been a powerful creature. A sense of relief floated in the air, and then in the blink of an eye, it was gone.

Crazy didn't stop there. The other two dogs, who had been barking nonstop, became silent after the first shot was fired. They both retreated as far as their chains would allow. They must have known what was coming. They cowered into balls, their tails wrapped around their backsides as their noses completed the circle of submission. No growling, no aggression, just quiet surrender. Crazy walked toward the two dogs, just a few yards from the first, took careful aim, and fired. His shot was painfully perfect, and the dog failed to make a sound but moved no more. Crazy walked ever so calmly toward the next target and repeated his deed without hesitation. Taking the box of ammunition from his back pocket, he started to reload.

"Why is he killing all the dogs?" shouted my brother.

Mother was screaming unrecognizable words of terror. The

baby was now crying, and my other sister was hiding under the kitchen table, Ginger wrapped tightly in her arms as if knowing she needed to protect her—but who was protecting who? My sisters were too small to have seen out the window or know what was happening. How could they understand? Were they seeing images in their heads like I did? Either way, their screams were needling my ears and hurting my head.

Crazy turned his gaze toward the second-floor windows and stood there glaring, just like he had a short time earlier, watching Duke as he broke free. What was he looking at just above our heads? His eyes must have made contact with someone, or maybe something. He had that look you get when your eyes connect and your mind knows what it is seeing. That look when you complete the process of thought and move to the next stage. A slight squint of heightened focus washed over his face. He knew precisely what was next on his list. The only one who knew the terror that would continue.

Long seconds clicked away in half-frozen time. I could hear feet shuffling about as if gathering items. The footsteps seemed to circle something. Another set of feet traveled back and forth like they were in a panic or maybe collecting items. Crazy pointed at the window with the end of the rifle as he filled its chamber with shining death pills. His action had the intended effect. The steps grew more frantic, more repetitive. Muffled shouts carried below the ceiling, but I couldn't make out the words.

Crazy took that first step toward the side door. Mother

panicked, now at a fevered pitch, her arms flapping like a goose and shouting into an empty direction. There was no one in front of her. She pointed with one hand while looking into the hollow space. She debated, as if she saw the shadows I saw. I didn't see anyone or anything, but maybe she did.

She started to argue with, seemingly, another shadow. She was pointing in all directions like she was directing traffic on a busy city street. Her hands waved wildly, making little if any sense. She seemed to fully understand what she was doing. It looked to me like she was fighting with Crazy only inches in front of her. To her, she was winning the invisible battle. Her face was contorted in both anger and fear as she pointed and wagged her index finger with the authority of a niggling street urchin. It was blindingly painful to witness, and I was lost as to how to help her...or my siblings!

The side door bursting open shattered Mother's victorious, albeit pretend argument. We all snapped our faces toward the entering danger. Was Crazy some kind of protector, or was this just a continuation of the four-legged final chapter? I saw the entire room with a vision so clear, so precise, the colors so vivid—I could almost feel the colors as they popped and changed shape. It was as if another world was waging a war simultaneously with our battle for survival.

Crazy waited just inside the door, scanning the rooms, looking up at the ceiling as the footsteps increased in their nervous venture above our heads. Crazy never said a word, never even took a breath or wiped his face or forehead. Sweat ran down the side of his grizzly face. His old green work shirt was stained with blood and spatter. He looked at the hallway leading to the formerly secured doorway, the renter-occupied rooms. His pause gave us time to prepare for the next step on his path to reclaim his place as the leader of the insanity surrounding our existence. Something was infringing on his corner of the market, and he was coming to take it back. At least that was a thought flashing through my mind.

Without looking in the direction he was choosing, Crazy headed back to the cabinets, where he retrieved the long gun. Stepping on the stool he kicked into place, he reached for the top spot and felt for something until he found his prize. He pulled down a blackened Colt .45 pistol. It was a classic 1911 model with several clips fully ready for use. It was covered by a pinkish-red rag, one of the ones Crazy used to wipe the grease from his hands before picking up a wrench. The same rags he used when he worked on his truck. He unfolded the semiautomatic weapon while gathering the many rounds of lead bullets carefully prepared for the exact moment, as if it had been planned some time ago, waiting for just this very moment.

The Colt brought flashes from the past: Crazy telling us about the Colt Firearm Company and how he worked for them as well as the Underwood Typewriter Company in Hartford, Connecticut, when he was a small boy. His mother and aunt both worked for the Colt Firearm Company. During the Second World War, many young kids worked for manufacturing companies, as he would preach. He'd tell us how he learned all about guns during his days on the run from his father. How he learned to shoot, always stopping just before saying whether he had or hadn't shot someone. He'd end the "lesson" the second the subject got close to that point, yet leaving us with the understanding that he had, in fact, killed someone. Maybe even more than just a "someone."

Watching him make such easy work of those dogs, now former pets, quickly retrieved the thought of his lessons of his youth and his exploits of survival, as he called them. Crazy grabbed another box of shells for the rifle, packing them into his pocket after filling the gun with all it would hold. He never looked at any of us. It was like we were not there. His eyes had a filmlike quality overtaking his normally disturbing dark sockets. He looked so comfortable, so matter-of-fact as he moved through his process. Kicking the stool back, he turned and took that first step toward his next rendezvous. He tucked the Colt into his back pocket after moving his wallet out of the way and put the extra clips into his other back pocket. The right corner of his lips tipped upward in a self-wink and small smile as the pending events waltzed across his mind. His face displayed a field of gratitude, a sign of satisfaction as it clearly motivated him to move one step closer to his final objective. Only he could know the endgame.

For the rest of us, what could we do but stand there or hide under the table and watch? We could spin in circles like Mother, doing a perfect impersonation of Helen Reddy's "Angie Baby," the classic 1970s song about a girl locked in a room filled with her active, aggressive insanity. It was truly like watching a television program with all the players doing their part while the main character keeps the focus of the assembled onlookers, waiting to see how the plot will proceed, how it will end, who will survive, and who will not. To me it was just another day, albeit a very, very bad one.

—⁓—

Crazy marched across the kitchen and past each of us with the ease of an old soldier highlighted in the local Fourth of July parade. His mind was at ease with his mission. His armament locked and loaded. His will unstoppable. The blackness with dark-gray outcroppings completely enveloping his body. An egg-shaped bubble surrounded his body, floating along as he moved toward the opening and up the stairs to fulfill his secret destiny.

Should I follow him, or should I hide too? I wondered. My sister was still clinging to Ginger, tucked under the table. Ginger's head was buried deep under my sister's arm with only one eye visible to see what was or wasn't coming at her. The baby was crying in her playpen, but her heavy fussing was only audible if you listened for it. Mother had the phone in her hand, dialing numbers as quickly as the wall-mounted rotary phone would allow. Her fingers waited for the clear plastic holes to reset so she could insert her digit into the next number and spin the wheel once again. Her hand was shaking so visibly that I was amazed she could dial at all. My brother was lost in the chaos, nowhere in sight.

I decided to follow Crazy to see what was going to happen. I traced his footprints as quietly as I could. As I got to the opening at the bottom of the stairs, I stuck my head around the doorframe until I could see the opening begin to come into view. Then I heard breathing, so I pulled back, thought, and stuck my nose out again just enough to see a bit more. Crazy was still standing at the entrance, gun in both hands, looking into the opening yet clearly afraid to take the next step.

In my mind, I was daring him to go forward, but in my heart, I didn't want the people to get hurt or treated like the dogs. I was sure they had witnessed the carnage from the upper windows.

Their footsteps were still creaking the floorboards, sending echoes into the rooms below. Crazy just needed to cross that doorway threshold and face his fears, assuming that was his plan.

As I kept watch from behind Crazy, egging him into harm's way, I was jolted from behind. A stiff jerk on my shirt collar pulled me out of the doorway and across the bedroom, stopping only when I was at the old couch in the living room.

Mother scolded me about following Crazy and demanded I stay in this room. "Where is your brother?" she exclaimed with a soft sense of bewilderment.

I shrugged, palms facing the sky. "I don't know."

Before Mother could react, the sounds above rattled all of us and left us looking upward at the ceiling...wondering what was next.

—␣␣—

We stopped moving the second we heard the cracking and creaking of the wooden floorboards just inside the forbidden door. Crazy must be heading into the second-floor rooms. The historically old boards from the time the house was first built sprang to life as Crazy ventured closer and closer to those rooms we were never allowed to enter.

The footsteps that had been running back and forth stopped as Crazy approached. Not a sound. I could hear the wind picking up outside the windows, gently moving the curtains as the breeze flowed across the living room. The baby, lying on her back, was still in her safety pen, mysteriously quiet as if someone or maybe something had pushed her off button. It would have been creepy if not for all the other stuff happening around us. My other sister was now at the doorway between the kitchen and living room. Ginger was nestled at her side like a small pony, and they were pressed against each other in a show of support. The wind was all we heard as time seemed to have stopped. Nothing, not a sound, from above.

Mother was looking up toward the ceiling, her mouth slightly open as she pushed her nose higher as if to gain an advantage as we waited for a sound, any sound. The silence kept us in lingering suspense, and I could feel my chest moving up and down with every shortened breath.

Nothing was moving except the breeze and the curtains when, off in the far distance, a siren broke the quiet with its warning, then faded to nothing. Maybe it wasn't coming here. No sooner did my thoughts wonder if the police were going somewhere else than the sound of an approaching cruiser returned with increased volume.

I looked at Mother with my eyes asking if she'd called the troopers. She looked at me approvingly, but I was still not sure if it was her or someone else.

I jumped off the chair to look out the window to the street in anticipation of those flashing lights and well-dressed state troopers. There, on the other side of the road, was an old man staring at the house. He had white hair and was wearing a red checkered shirt and plain pants. He looked like one of the old farmers, but I had never seen him before. He had a slight hunch as if he walked with a cane, yet I could not see one. His face was wrinkled with long rolls of skin folding just below and to the sides of his nose and to the outsides of his mouth. He wasn't very tall. He was thick but not fat, like he'd been a very strong man back in his day. He looked right at me as if he knew I'd be looking for him.

I searched, scanning for his car or truck, but I couldn't see one. He stood just a few feet off the pavement on the far side of the street. He was looking at the second floor. While the neighbors were close enough to hear a gunshot, or several, this old man didn't seem to be with anyone, so why was he watching our house?

I called to Mother, "Hey, there's a man staring at our house from across the street."

Mother dashed over to the window next to mine and pulled back the curtain. "*Where?*" she demanded.

"Right there," I pressed back.

The sirens were getting closer. I could hear them racing in our direction. I pointed back toward the old man. "He's right there; can't you see him?"

Mother looked back toward my sisters and then back outside, and just as she was about to tell me what she saw, *boom!* We all jumped in shock, surprised as the echo of the gun blast ripped down the hallway with a rolling, thunderous sound and stinging vibration. My ears hurt from the sound waves, and I used my fingers to shake the pain inside my eardrums.

There was a second blast, then a third. *Boom! Boom! Boom!* Two more followed in quick succession. *Boom, boom!* Then, from an even louder-sounding gun, came so many shots in a row I couldn't count them. Crazy must have been unloading all the bullets into those rooms. Maybe the people who were creating those footsteps were shooting back? Did someone shoot Crazy? Could I get that lucky?

No one was making walking sounds on the ceiling above. A pause after the last series of shots. Maybe it was over.

—◊—

The cops' warning sights and sounds seemed to be right outside when more gunshots exploded from above. Then silence from above our heads. Outside, the blaring whine from the patrol cars finally stopped as I turned back to see the flashing lights of two, now three cruisers stacking up behind Crazy's truck, almost in the exact same place the two troopers had parked late last year.

"*Shots fired!*" was called out, then repeated. "*Shots fired!*"

I watched as one trooper pulled a large rifle from his trunk and tossed it to his fellow law enforcement agent. Those two looked young compared to the first trooper in the lead cruiser. He had an old face but was still strong looking. They looked at one another and then charged for the door.

My face was plastered to the bottom of the window, my eyes just above the sill. I studied the buildup, and I was amazed at the bravery of these men. Heading into battle to help people they'd never met before. It was a visual that etched itself into my mind.

What I didn't see was Mother. She had wrapped up my two sisters and was making a beeline for the exit. Ginger was right behind her, stopping at the doorway and looking back at me. I watched Mother hustle her two daughters, born to Crazy, out of harm's way and into the security of the state troopers, who surrounded them and escorted them quickly into a cruiser just past the driveway. Two more cruisers pulled up across the street. A senior trooper directed the newly arriving officers to take control of the mother and her babies. The early-evening dusk was now filled with many red and blue flashing, rolling lights.

I looked back at Ginger, still standing at the door watching, eyes connecting to mine as if to say, "They forgot me, too, but I'm grateful I wasn't chained up with the others today." I felt the same—grateful my sisters and Mother were finally safe but per-plexed by how Mother had failed to ensure I was close at hand. I stood there wondering if she even knew I was still here—or where my brother was, for that matter.

Where was he anyway? I started to worry about him, but some-thing told me he would be fine. He always was, as if he had an early warning system that told him to disappear just before events like this took shape. I stood there watching the troopers doing their work, talking among themselves as they tried to figure out what was happening. I saw one standing by the duck pen as he reviewed the carnage and moved to the next scene and then looked over the remains of the chained dogs.

Ginger stood her ground as a trooper entered the door, gun in hand, followed by two more troopers. "Are you hurt?" asked the lead officer.

I simply shook my head as he scooped me up with one arm with the force of a bull—not even a grunt as he effortlessly held me in one arm, still pointing his gun toward the hallway, placing his body between me and his gun. "Where's your father? Who else is in the house?" he asked.

"He's not my father," I responded. "He's upstairs, and there are more people up there."

More perfectly dressed troopers entered the living room, and he passed me off to the much younger and even stronger officer. "Get him to safety," commanded the lead trooper.

"Yes, *sir!*" was the instant response. Without pause I was rushed out of the house, down the driveway, and toward the street.

"I haven't seen my brother. Do you know where he is?" I asked.

"If he has black hair, he's with your mother and sisters up the road with some other troopers. He is safe. Are you hurt in any way?"

I thought for a moment, wondering how to answer. It was a question asked by my teacher, the principal, a janitor. One I never knew how to answer—not truthfully, at least.

"Are you hurt? Bleeding? Cut?" breaks my thoughts.

"I'm fine." It was the only response I had…What else could I say?

The trooper asked more questions, but I stopped talking. Ginger was following just behind me. When the trooper put me down and turned to head back, I reached up for his arm, grabbed his sleeve with my finger, and looked up at him. He bent down to bring his face close to mine. Looking him in his eyes and in a quiet hush, I said, "Thank you, sir. Thank you for getting us out of there, sir."

His smile told me all I needed to know. He quickly returned to his fellow trooper.

After EMS gave us the once-over, we were kept close together with one officer in a suit and tie, asking all the questions. Mother refused to say much.

For the next several hours, we sat in the patrol car until a lady told us we could get our stuff, but "only clothes, and only with a trooper." We were not to touch anything else, just what we needed. We'd stay with the police while Mother went back inside. They said we'd be able to follow in a while, but only after they finished talking to Mother.

Once they had finished, Mother ordered us to gather our things. We filled the boxes she placed on the bed. We could only be in the bedroom or living room. I felt a happiness start to grow inside me. Crazy was not in the house, and the trooper said we wouldn't see him. I asked, "Forever? Is he gone?" But the response was that they'd take care of him. I had no idea what that meant. My hope was that the troopers would treat him like the chained dogs, but that faded away as I rushed to pack my clothes.

Was it over, the life with Crazy? Was Mother finally done with him? Did the troopers kill him, or did the people upstairs kill him? What happened to them? All these thoughts were racing through my mind as I tried to find toys to stuff in between my socks and pants.

Walking outside with a box almost too heavy for me, I saw that man with the plaid shirt. His hunched body was easy to pick up with all the flashing lights. He was staring at me, but not in a bad way. He didn't say anything, made no gestures, and hardly moved a muscle. It was like I knew him, yet I'd never seen him before. Who was he, and why was he watching me?

A trooper offered to help me carry the box.

"I've got it. I can do it," I protested, but with a smile. I looked back to see the old man, but he was gone.

The trooper who had offered to help called back to me. "Oh, the old farmer asked me to tell you he'll see you at your next house. Said you'd understand."

Puzzled, I asked, "Was he wearing a red checkered shirt?"

"He was," responded the trooper.

Who was that man, and how did he know where I was going?

Mother pushed me from behind. "Please hurry up; they're waiting for us."

"Put that in the trunk," said Mother.

Her friend came to take us someplace, maybe back to the city.

There was a commotion back by the house. Troopers were in a bunch just next to the station wagon with the huge red light. There was some yelling as the cluster of uniforms moved in a circled huddle. Mother started to panic once again and shouted for us to "get in the damn car."

We piled into the back seat. The door had barely closed before Mother's friend snapped the column into drive, hit the pedal aggressively, and ripped up the dirt and stone as she steered onto the pavement. As I looked out the back window, I saw the huddle of troopers looking at their feet, but as the car moved quickly away, the scene of flashing lights faded. What were they doing? Where were we going?...At least it wouldn't be with Crazy, thank God!

CHAPTER 4

The morning's distant sun shone on my face once again as I looked out the window at the peaceful calm and gentle winds of a late-summer morning. My eyes remained closed as I soaked in the happiness and joy that flowed into my chest, warming my heart. I was so grateful that I was in a place of such grace and that my brother's feet weren't touching mine. As my mind warmed up, taking in the stillness of a good night's sleep, dreams rebounded around my brain as I tried to remember what those dreams had been saying. What was I watching as they played out their senses and displayed the visions of the past and the future?

I swear, sometimes those dreams would tell me of things to come. Sometimes, when I was awake, standing and watching an otherwise normal day, I swear what I was watching I'd seen before, but when I was sleeping. It was as if someone or something was preparing me, telling me of things to come. A warning at times of what to be careful of, enabling me to see around the corner, so to speak.

I would stand motionless, watching in awe as the play moved forward, knowing I'd been there before, knowing I'd seen this before, yet not understanding how it was possible. My dreams would play out from time to time, just like watching a movie and always slowing down to a crawl as if to make sure I wouldn't miss a single frame. Ensuring I saw the entirety with a wide angle, a scope so big, these visions would allow me to see around the backside of my ears, but not completely behind me.

Many times these dreams would happen just after or just as I fell asleep. Also, at times, just before I woke up. It was magical to me, but no one else understood what I was seeing, so I'd keep it to myself. Sometimes I could see what was going to happen a second or two before it did. Once in a while, I could see things minutes before they happened. It was like knowing what's going to happen next and then watching as it plays out. Sometimes it would make me laugh. These visions would make me feel connected to something I couldn't explain. A feeling that was both distant and so close at the same time. I couldn't touch it or change it from happening or even react in time to prevent events from fully taking shape, although I wished I could. I was almost frozen in time, watching a real-life movie. It always left me amazed and intrigued as to how it worked, and why me? I was never frightened, which also made me wonder why. It was happening more and more, and getting longer and clearer. What was happening to me!

My brother didn't understand, and we'd talk about these things while we waited for the sandman to show up. As I lay there, eyes still closed, I could feel something coming. Far off in that vision that took place in my mind, I saw that rider on his horse with a stick in one hand and a shield covering his other arm. He was charging in slow motion with all the energy of a full-on rush toward the center of my face. A powerful light shone down on him and his horse like sunrays breaking through the clouds with split beams casting light and shadow on his muscular frame. Horns stuck out of the top of his thick dark-brown fur hat. It had the shape of an animal skull. Was the hat protecting his head from harm? Or maybe showing off something, something of value or importance! I could feel a flood of emotions flowing like waves of water breaking on the edge of a lake, gentle and forceful at the same time.

The rider was mostly bare chested, with bands strapped between his biceps and shoulders. Three lines of colored bands signified something important, but I couldn't know what it meant. As he drew closer, you would think it would make me fearful, but it didn't. The opposite happened. I experienced a calming of sorts. Almost an understanding of something in the past telling me to be mindful of what was coming.

Black paint covered his eyes and his cheeks in a curved triangle. His piercing blue eyes had rubicund drops rolling out of his eyes, the red dots pasted like stationary tears dripping down his face. A leather string around his neck held on to what I was guessing was a bear's claw. It gave me the sense he'd taken it from an old king grizzly in a life-and-death battle, one that determined who had the right to continue walking on the earth while knowing the other must perish. The leather chain had some kind of power that radiated like a laser into my chest, as if it was telling me a story, one I already knew but couldn't remember. He was here to remind me of something, to bring it back to the surface of my memories. Maybe to prepare me so I would be ready for something—something unknown but still something that was surely coming.

His slow-motion charge, sitting on a beautifully crafted white horse. A glow that emitted outward as the light shining off the rider danced around the magnificent beast. The horse looking directly into my eyes, telling me something, relaying something I just couldn't quite figure out but telling me just the same. As he moved closer, I saw the stick in his right hand had a sharpened point with feathers floating just a few inches below the mounting of the pointed stone. His shield had a painting on it, the head of a buffalo. The same red dots dropped from the bison's eyes. Thunder from the horse's hooves pounded into my chest so fiercely I felt my entire body vibrating. As the rider approached, he was saying something, pointing with his decorated spear just above my head. Pulling back on the horse's mane, he kept repeating the same thing, but I couldn't make out the words. "Look…life…behind…" Again and again he moved his lips, each time with more and more effort, almost jumping off the horse's back as he pointed with such demanding vigor I decided to look behind me. His shield lifted as if to cover his face, his head, as I started turning myself about.

As my eyes focused behind me, I saw that lady who visited from time to time. The one who brought a comforting feeling. I heard her saying, "Everything will be all right."

I could feel myself focus on them both as they started to fade back in time, retracing their frontal movement in reverse as if to say, "Time's up," until, like the pop of a soap bubble, they vanished.

At that moment, I heard a piercing noise. It was a sound that snapped me back into this world. It happened so quickly there was no time to think. My eyes flung open with shocking authority. I heard Crazy's voice behind me. Dear God, *no*, tell me it's not true!

Instantly, every ounce of my being was bombarded with intense fear, terror, and panic. How was this possible? Turning my neck to its fullest, I realized I was in my bed. Crazy and Mother were standing over me, watching, talking, and looking down at me. I was remembering the walk down the driveway, the car, and no Mother to greet us. No cookies, no milk, nor that warm hug I'd come to love so much. The sun was coming in the window next to Mother's bed, the place Crazy had been hiding. Finding him was my last memory before the horse, the painted man, and the flowing white-dress lady faded in a popping bubble.

"Why are you here?" I demanded. "Mother said you were gone for good. I can't believe you're here. You lied to me, lied to all of us."

Before my words were even finished, Crazy let out, "That's enough! We'll talk about it in the kitchen. Now get out of bed, and get to the table," he commanded in his same old style but with an effort to mask his true feelings.

At the table sat my brother and me, Mother, and one of our sisters. The other sister was in Crazy's arms as he talked to her with sounds that made me want to puke. Mother went into a series of tales, explaining why Crazy was back and what was going to happen, telling us that we'd "be a family again." The last part was a death knell to me. It struck like a knife ripping open a chicken, gutting it after cutting off its head. I had watched the wife next door place a live chicken on a tree stump, hatchet falling without grace or mercy. "This is how we do it in the country," she'd proclaim. I wished Crazy would be the next chicken on the stump.

Mother went on to tell us, "There will be *no* more hitting, *no* more switches, and *no* more belts. Your father promised those days are over."

Looking from Mother's face to Crazy's face, I could see there was no truth in her words, and without a second to think about what was going to pop out of my mouth, I blurted, *"Yeah, right"* as I got up and ran for my bed.

There was no mention of the former house or what had happened, just that Crazy was back, and we were "a family again." I cried myself to sleep only to wake up the following morning wishing it all were a tragic nightmare. The rain was pounding on the bushes and leaves outside my window, where just a morning earlier the sun had woken me with the excitement and glee of a wonderful new day. The air inside the house was as thick and heavy as the rain, pushing its depressing mist through the bug screen.

As I walked past the living room into the kitchen, Crazy looked up from his newly claimed spot at the head of the old shiny metal table with its small checkered green-and-white top. His eyes left his newspaper, his left hand on his coffee mug as he glared in my direction, finally locking his eyes on mine. I kept walking without giving him his due and headed straight into the bathroom. Before I could shut the door, I heard, *"Don't* be long. I need to get in there." And the fun began…all over again.

Throughout the rest of the fall and winter, things settled into a rather quiet routine. Crazy didn't spend much time with his brown bottles or much time at the house. Mother said he was working a lot, but my brother and I thought there was more to it than that. I could hear them talking from time to time about the cops, something about the courts and probation. But we didn't know much more, and when we asked, it was met with a stifling "None of your business."

As spring took hold, Crazy showed up with a box of his brown bottles and a fancy story of winning in court but with "time served." He also lost his car someplace, so his friend kept driving him back and forth. His friend was a big Black man, strong as could be. We called him by his surname, Mr. Means, but he wasn't mean at all. In fact, he was a very nice man, always smiling, laughing, and bringing stuff for us. I really liked him and his son, who was my age. Crazy was extremely "nice" whenever Mr. Means was around us.

As the school year ended and summer was in full swing, life was rather quiet, and it seemed like the past was just that—the past. It was a phrase Crazy would use to shut down any talk of things before the current times.

Mr. Means would pick up Crazy very early in the morning. I remember hearing his car turn the corner before he pulled into the driveway. One day, after a late afternoon of playing in the woods with the other kids, I went inside to use the bathroom. Mr. Means and Crazy were sitting at the kitchen table laughing and carrying on while they emptied many brown bottles and got louder and louder. I was ordered to sit next to Crazy as he told stories to Mr. Means about how I was a troublesome child. At some point I'd had enough. Maybe it was after he'd called me a baby or maybe after he told about the difficulties I had doing schoolwork. Maybe it was the "He's too sensitive to become a man; he's more like a girl."

Either way, I'd had enough and let him know of my displeasure. I cut loose, telling him how happy we all had been without him. How we missed the dogs he'd killed and that if he put a hand on any of us, especially Mother, I'd call the cops. "Where is Ginger?" I asked, "Did you kill her too? Did she die just like

Duke?" It felt *so good* to speak my mind. I felt alive in that moment of challenging bravery. "What happened to your other sons, the ones who only came to the house because they had to? They don't like you either. None of us do."

I could see his face growing angrier and angrier. That old wickedness started to reshape around his neck, the back of his head, close to his shoulders. A floating cloud grew above him like the cigarette smoke spilling out of both men.

The silent pause chilled the room. Crazy slowly turned to look back to Mr. Means. A surprised story of shock caked Mr. Means's face. His eyes left mine and slowly, deliberately walked back to meet Crazy's glare. "Well now, about time I get my boys home to the missus before she starts fussin'," Mr. Means said.

Crazy's left hand moved so quickly I didn't have time to react other than flinching enough to move my nose down just low enough so the force hit me square between the eyebrows. I closed my eyes just as the force shattered my thoughts. My neck slapped backward with a grinding, crunching sound that reflected deep into my ears. Stars instantly filled the entire field of vision inside my closed eyelids. The chair's front legs lifted off the floor before the chair continued its journey past the point of no return.

The momentum of the contact lifted me off the seat and pushed my body firmly against the chair's backrest until the chair and I hit the floor. There was a solid *crack* as the back of my head hammered the floorboard, like a carpenter driving an old iron cut nail with all his might into sturdy old oak floorboards.

My ears rang a piercing tone that only lifted because of the thumping drumbeat inside my skull. Which pain hurt worse was a round robin of misery, one competing with the others for the title of most painful. My shin bones were screaming in agony. They must have hit the underside of the table as I flipped head over heels.

I was moaning in sheer anguish, my lungs weak and unable to draw more than a very short intake. Trying to push air out was even harder than the effort to inhale. Short, choppy breaths were the best I could muster. Fog plagued my mind. I wasn't sure which hurt to focus on, as I still couldn't see past the stars and blackened shades of gray light filtering past my closed eyelids. My head was pounding, and my face was screaming a fiery blaze when a new, more formidable pain entered the arena. My lower legs began to take control as the worst pain ever.

The first attempt to open my eyes sent shock waves across my forehead and jabbing needle points into my eyes. Blinking to clear my vision only caused my eyes further misery, as it felt like glass shards were sprinkled under my eyelids. Please, just let me die right here, right now. That mantra became my focal point. Rolling off the chair and onto the cool floor offered the slightest sense of relief, just enough to know the difference in levels of pain as they competed for attention.

My lower legs revoiced their call for attention. Moving either of them sent wave after wave of brutal pain across my mind with such force I almost blacked out. I must have hit my shins on the underside of the metal table edge as I whirled backward. That second, louder crack, just after Crazy's smashing blow, must have been my legs hitting the table.

"What the hell is wrong with you?" was the first thing I could hear above my moans, grimaces, and grunts coming with the puffs of air escaping my lungs as they worked to regain control and bring much-needed oxygen into my broken body.

"He needs help…" That was Mr. Means's voice, followed by a hand on my arm and my stomach. I could hear Mr. Means talking to me. It felt like he was kneeling next to me, so I managed to open an eye to get a blurry view of his kind face looking down at me.

"Get a wet rag," he instructed Crazy.

I couldn't see him or most of anything, but a few moments later, I felt the cool sensation of a wet towel on my face, my head. Then Mr. Means pulled me off the floor into his arms. "I'm putting him in his bed, and you *better not* touch him again. You hear me, you sick bastard?" It was music to my ears as he followed with "My wife said you was no good, and I didn't listen. Drive all the way out here to help you. I don't want any part of you or what you do." Mr. Means was voicing his position clearly.

He gently laid me on the bed and fixed the pillow to comfort me as best as possible. Blood filled the towel in blotches as I kept moving it around to find the cool spots, a slice of relief to an otherwise battered body.

"I'm out of here, and don't you ever call me or ask me for nothing again. I should have listened," Mr. Means muttered as he marched out the door. I couldn't hear the rest of his words, but his finger wagging told the story, pointing back toward my crumpled shell as he forcefully voiced his displeasure. All the while, I was wishing he'd put a beating on Crazy to settle the score.

As I lay there, my thoughts turned to the horseman and the white-dress lady of comfort, but nothing came forward. I didn't feel abandoned, because they never showed up when I tried to find them, only when they had something to say, something to warn me about.

The rain restarted, pelting away outside, adding to the dismal feelings spiraling in my insides. It felt like the darkness Crazy possessed was trying to invade my entire world. Trying to take over any happiness within me so that nothing was untouched by anger, misery, and a growing hate.

Crazy returned to my bedside, leaned close to my ear, and began to whisper. His nasty steam stuck to my skin like droplets of poison. His vile breath snaked around the side of my head, reaching my blood-soaked nose. Exhausted spent remains of cigarette smoke penetrated my throat, clinging to the back of my tongue as if I'd licked an ashtray. The pasty remains from his brown bottles mixed with the decaying food trapped in his unbrushed teeth made me gag, and I held back my wish to vomit all over him as he launched into his defensive verbal attack. "The cops won't do anything to me, and if you tell them what happened, I'll do worse to your mother, your brother, and then I'll start on your sisters…"

He was planting the seeds of his game of control, fear, and power. Even at a young age, I knew what he was doing, but I also knew he was telling the truth—evil as it was, it was the truth. He'd proven he'd beat any of us except my sisters, who to date he'd never hit or even spanked, as best as I could have seen.

"I got away with it before, and I'll get away with it again." His hurtful intention was very clear, and it quickly became his theme song—his anthem, if you will. "The cops can't help you, and they can't stop me from teaching you any way I see fit." He was filling in his scheme of things to come, his gospel of evil, and a notice of how life would proceed.

"Even if the state takes you, they'll take all of you, and I'll be left here with your mother to do with her what I please, without you brats gettin' in the way and causing problems," he snarled. "You think the state will keep you four in one place? Now look at me when I talk to you!"

He grabbed my shoulders and forcibly rolled me until my face was inches away from his dried lips. Flakes of white foamy spit collected in the corner of one side. I sent my eyes away from his hollow sockets. Looking out the window, I was trying to remember those peaceful mornings before Crazy's return when something caught my eye. I saw an old man across the street looking right at me. It was only a very brief viewing of the old man, but his white hair seemed familiar. Where had I seen him before? His hat fit like a well-worn article and seemed perfectly in place with the rest of his tattered clothing. He was rather short and stocky, but I got the sense he was very strong for an old guy. He was just standing there in the rain, looking at me, yet I'd never seen him next to the fire station before.

It was only the briefest of seconds before Crazy had my face at his, and my feelings flooded back from that momentary respite.

Oh, how I hate him. Oh, how I will get my revenge. Please God, make me big so I can stop him from hitting my mother, my brother, and others—it was a wish that would repeat itself almost daily from this point forward.

The punctuation from Crazy kept coming. "The state will put you all in different places, and you'll never see each other again. Not even your mother." A pause to let that part filter past my rage. "That's what will happen if you tell lies about how you hurt yourself. You shouldn't lean the chair so far back like that, now, should you, boy?" He carried on and on, planting the words, ideas of what had happened and how the story must be told. "It's your fault you got hurt. You brought this on yourself. You did this to yourself."

These were all words he used on Mother time and time again. Always the fault of the one who was bleeding. The one with broken bones, bruises, black eyes, or lumps in places you never thought could swell up, let alone swell up so badly.

I turned my face back to the window when I thought he'd let me be. The old man was still standing there, still looking in the window. I couldn't see his eyes, yet I knew he was looking at me. It felt like I was connecting, and strangely, it felt good, almost peaceful.

Just as the old man's sense of calm was offering relief, Crazy snatched away the lifeline. He jammed my head into the pillow, forcing me to look at him as he spewed his never-ending rant upon my tired, blood-caked ears.

Finally, he left, and I turned back to the window. But the old man was gone. My eyes canvassed the area, but there was no sign of him, or of anyone, for that matter. I folded myself tightly into a fetal position. The pain in my legs claimed the prize for most intense, although its competition wasn't giving in.

I tried to focus on my friends at school and the fun we had enjoyed, but I kept wondering why the state police couldn't stop Crazy. Why hadn't the cops put him in jail for the dogs and the shootings? I was drawing the conclusion the police couldn't do much of anything to protect us. I felt sadness but also anger. What were we to do? No one could help us, and Crazy would just get away with more and more.

The police were useless, and from that moment on, wrongheaded or not, it was fast becoming deeply ingrained into my world. Law enforcement had little power and even less ability to help people. It was a path that would lead to a complete lack of respect for the law and those who were charged with enforcement. Once that thinking took hold, I was hard pressed to change it. Crazy had laid the foundation that would cost me dearly, and I didn't even know it, not yet at least. Something changed within me as I lay there like a wounded wild beast plotting its vengeance.

At that moment, I lost the fear of the law, the rules, the guidelines, and that which governs society. I began to no longer care what would happen. Crazy stole that from me and left a shell of painful tracks that held little value for my own life. When I got angry from that moment forward, I couldn't care less about anything close to law and order. The rules didn't apply to those who beat women and children and killed dogs without remorse! What had happened on the second floor of that farmhouse, and how did Crazy escape the police? It just didn't matter anymore. From this moment forward, I would fight to protect Mother, my brother, and my sisters.

I lay there remembering the story of Paul Bunyan and realizing it was a path I wanted to follow. To stop bullies and bring the hurt back to those who aimed to hurt others. I just needed God to build me a powerful body, one like Mr. Means's, so I could stand in the breach of harm's way. To do what the police clearly could not. If God would build my body, I'd sacrifice myself to protect those who could not.

Making a pact with God and anything else that would listen, I caught a glimpse of that old man again. He was back on the rain-soaked pavement, and this time I was sure he was looking me in the eye. I lifted my head, the pillow in tow, now stuck to my face. The dried blood locked our parts together so securely I had to pull with effort to free its grip. I lost sight of the old man for a moment but picked him up as I pushed the blood-and-tear-soaked linen back in place. The old man didn't move. He just stood there as if to tell me something but without moving a stitch. I squinted and then rubbed my eyes to clear them as I sat up and gained a better view.

He was gone, leaving me alone again. I closed my eyes and returned to the tight circle of self-protection, the pain settling in for the night as I did.

I don't remember anything else until early the next morning, when the sun poked its rays onto my face, offering a bright new day, a happy day. The same as it had been before Crazy returned, but something was different. The sun seemed the same; the breeze seemed the same. The birds, cars, wind, and sounds all seemed the same, but something was missing. After a few pointless thoughts, it became clear: happiness was missing along with my brother's feet.

I let out a sigh and moved to get out of bed. My brother was sleeping on the floor, and I almost stepped on him. My shins screamed out once I put weight on them. The bruises and swelling told the story of broken bones, a story I knew all too well.

The sadness became the new day's calling. No more happy, joy-filled times. Crazy was back, and there was nothing I could do. I knew happiness was gone, most likely never to return. That was the day I knew I'd changed for good. Sadness had won along with Crazy, unless my pact with God was fulfilled!

CHAPTER 5

We were told to move from the Scotland house shortly after Crazy's backhand crushed my face, fractured both my legs as they whipped against the underside of the table, and dented my skull when it hit the floor. Mother and Crazy fought until the homeowner forced the eviction, old Yankee style, at the end of a shotgun and with a lot of help. No one would talk to us after this all blew up. It was as if all the locals were somehow joined in a community-shaming effort or at least "we don't want to get involved in your affairs, so just keep moving along." A swamp Yankee approach to keeping other people's business from becoming their business. The town's folk stuck together like one family unit. I envied those people and wished I'd remain one of them, but it wasn't to be.

Fisher's Market wouldn't let Mother charge anything and asked her to "please shop someplace else. We don't want your kind of trouble here." While it sounded unfriendly, I understood. Scotland was a great place to live—quiet, peaceful, and happy. Until Crazy returned and shattered all that. The community didn't want the problems we created, and while it hurt me to lose the friends I had,

I didn't blame them. At least I didn't have to invent stories about my injuries, the casts, the bruises. Everyone knew what had happened since Crazy and Mother shouted about it so loudly people on the green stopped to watch and listen to the insanity rumbling out of the windows and across the center of town. They had brought big-city "problem-solving" to a historic farming community and tried to shatter the tranquility right in the heart of the village.

Needless to say, they didn't wait for courts or cops. They simply gathered in force, many different guns openly displayed as they "helped" us pack our things and made sure we were on our way. Of course, we didn't have much anyway. All the furnishings had come with the three rooms, so clothes and toys were the baseline of what was being placed into boxes, burlap sacks, and sheets tied at the four corners to keep stuff from falling out. Mother had her friend helping once again, and Crazy rounded up two trucks and someone I'd never seen before.

It became quick work, and as fast as we'd entered, we were gone. This would become the theme of our existence for the next few years. We never stayed in one place for very long. A full school year in the same place with the same teachers was abnormal. We mostly started midstream and rarely lasted a full cycle of the calendar. I stopped trying to make friends, among other reasons because it was hurtful when we left and we knew we'd be leaving either by local force, by court order, or in the middle of the night, slipping away like worms in the dirt, making sure to hide before the morning light exposed our trail.

The banging on the door with "You owe me money" was the forbearance warning, followed by a silky vanishing act we learned to perfect. Packing, stacking, and running to the next place. Then we would wait in the office so the new school could figure out where to put each of us without school records or transcripts of any kind. I was placed in "special education," since I couldn't read or write very well. Spelling was an adventurous word salad, having no base to lean upon. Being labeled "special ed" was as unkind as anything I'd experienced, and to make matters worse, nothing was taught nor learned in that "select environment." We'd sit at a table and play games all day, never taking a second to learn how to read or write. I was trapped in another void and locked into a side room. Isolated from others, pointed at by most.

After Scotland, our next hiding place was Windham Center. We lived in a two-bedroom row apartment with dozens and dozens of identical units, a giant U-shaped collection of overcrowded buildings. The short-lived stay was highlighted by a fight between Mother and some other mother on our front steps. The other woman was on a dead run directed at Mother. A cigarette was clenched in her teeth as she hit her intended target with all her might. The two fought for what seemed like forever. A crowd quickly gathered to watch and cheer them on. They both lost hair, blood, and skin. The scratches and welts grew and swelled with each swing of the determined fists. Mother held her own and fought off the attacker as best as she could, but the other woman had so much anger boiling out of her it would have been hard for her to lose. The attacker kept screaming something about "He was my man" and calling Mother a whore in what seemed like a few different languages. The cops came and hauled the attacker off in handcuffs as she kept screaming, "Whore!" among other awful taunts.

We left that place shortly thereafter, heading into Willimantic and another school system. My aunt was a teacher at Noble School and did her very best to help me. I was so grateful for her attention and her warm hugs when I got to her classroom. She always had something for me to eat, always. I'd eat some of her treats and put the rest into my cloth bag to share with my brother and sisters, but it needed to be kept a secret because if Crazy found out...Well, you understand.

My aunt would let us come to her house as often as we could. She'd cut our hair and feed my brother and me until we were stuffed. It was a strange feeling to have a full belly but one I enjoyed greatly. She never said hurtful things and told me there was a life waiting for me after being a child. I couldn't see it, but it was good to hear. My aunt became a mother figure to me, and when we were removed from the latest house, it was heartbreaking to leave her behind. I built more barriers to protect against the pain in my chest and throat and the hurt that comes with saying goodbye to someone you love to be with. I was learning to shutter myself from within and stop all feelings. "Have you ever done this?" I would ask my brother. "Have you made mental efforts to block off these feelings?" We'd talk about all kinds of stuff, but my brother wouldn't "go there," as he liked to say when he didn't like a topic of discussion.

—⚊⚊—

Lebanon was our next stop. It was another farming town, which was so big it took over an hour on the bus to make the rounds and gather everyone on the bus before dropping them off at school for the day's learning. Again, I was placed in "special education" and isolated from the rest of the kids. Something was wrong with me! What is wrong with me? I kept wondering. Sometimes the wondering was out loud, which didn't help me, as I would quickly learn the hard way. It was as if Crazy's lesson to "keep family a secret" was playing out in school. Learning *not* to voice my thoughts was becoming a hard-learned exercise.

One day I was called to the front of the class to read a story from the book we were reading. I was so terrified I thought I'd wet myself or, at best, pass out. The teacher made everyone wait until I walked to the front of the class and started to read. Of course, I had no idea what the words were, so I just started making stuff up, trying to remember what the story was about and taking it from there. After a few moments, my classmates started saying, "That's not what it says," followed by laughter and taunts like "He can't read. He's a baby and doesn't know the words. Dummy, stupid, idiot…" until the teacher put a stop to the laughter and sent me back to my desk. You would think that was the worst of it, but it wasn't.

After sitting for a bit, the sweat pouring down my face, I had hot flashes followed by cold spells. Tunnel vision came into play, fading back and forth with the laughter echoing side by side with the same words Crazy and Mother used to tell me who I was, what I was. You would think it would have hurt deeply, but anger was now becoming the dominant emotion in my life—a feeling that overtakes all other feelings to protect you against incoming rounds of hurled aggression intended to inflict enough harm to ensure you never get in front of your classmates again.

The teacher told the class to "settle down," but there were two class bullies in the room. One was bigger than me, and the other, his sidekick, loved to pull the hair of girls who didn't unleash a fisted response. He'd taunt them as he was taunting me. I had already concluded a fight was forthcoming, but I never would have guessed it would be caused by my next uncontrollable action. The teacher walked down the aisle toward me, telling the class, once again, to "settle down now."

The bigger bully was just two seats over, still working his tongue like a battering ram. I unleashed the most uncontrollable vomit imaginable. Puke gushed out of me just like those volcano models you build as a kid, except everything in my guts was the lava flow, and the taunting was the gunpowder that caused the explosion.

The chunky liquid sprayed out of my mouth with such force it hit classmates two and three seats away. The teacher was hit with the first round, the biggest burst. I turned my head to avoid her only to cast the putrid stench toward the bully. While I'm sure it didn't hit him in midair, everyone was touched by the spray as it permeated throughout the room like a fog over a pond on an autumn morning. I convulsed, hacked, and jerked until every ounce was released from my guts. Nothing remained. My eyes were blurry with tears, and my nose was filled with the burning aftermath. Stomach acid, a yellowish fluid, oozed out of my nostrils, and with no place to put it, my sleeve became the wiping cloth. The acid burned like the hot-sauce lesson as memories flashed through my mind, adding to the nightmarish scene. Imagine your entire classroom jumping from their seats, running for cover as the new kid fills the air, the floor, and the seats around him with such a smell, too vulgar and disgusting for words, splashing such grossness that it all but causes others to follow suit. One after another, classmates gagged, hands over their mouths, racing to avoid more eruptions.

No one else puked, but honestly, I don't know why not. Classmates were running for safety, with the teacher standing right in the middle, a look of shock smeared on her face. A nightmare her college days never prepared her for, displayed by her growing look of "What the hell do I do now?" The same look must have been covering my face under the chunks and fluid.

"Why couldn't you have gone to the bathroom?" shouted my teacher. A few choice words under her breath were followed by "Get your butt to the nurse's office."

All the kids parted like Moses splitting the Dead Sea as I got up and moved to the door. The exit was blocked by grossed-out girls screaming pleas of "Don't touch me; keep away; you're so *gross!*"

I headed down the hall soaked in my own innards, and just as I got to the door of the nurse's office, I heard, "Janitor to classroom 107, and bring a mop, please. A student threw up all over the classroom."

Now the entire school was briefed on my exploits. If you ever had to change schools as a child, you understand what it was like, especially in the 1970s. Imagine trying to make friends after this event. Imagine going back to the classroom the next day! Imagine the words that would follow you as long as you stay in this school. The fight with the bully was the only bright spot in a sea of swill.

It was the first time I remember wishing Crazy and Mother would do their thing so we could move again. It didn't take long for my wish to come true, although it might have been in motion before my wishful request. We were gone a short time later, but returning to the class was a series of misdeeds that will hurt and haunt me for the rest of my days. A puke bag was placed on my desk. The bully gifted me with an umbrella. The jokes and taunts were endless. No one would sit near me, even in "special ed." While inside I hurt deeply, I was getting better and better at masking and hiding from those feelings. I was falling into a deep abyss and needed someone to offer a lifeline. It appeared from the oddest of directions.

—∾—

Crazy had a brother. He was the nicest man imaginable. I'd only seen him a couple of times, so when he showed up out of the blue, it seemed very odd. He pulled me aside and said he'd heard about my mishap, a polite way of phrasing the puke fest. He told me to laugh about it. To do so in front of the other kids. To poke fun at myself and make a joke of the entire debacle. "Use humor to avoid ridicule," he suggested. "It'll paint you in a different light and help you overcome what you're facing. Give it a try." My uncle left shortly after offering his insight, but he had given me that lifeline I so desperately needed.

The laughter seed planted, I looked to face off with the class bully and his umbrella. The next day, I grabbed the rain shield, popped it open, and started gagging with all my might. Everyone skedaddled, running for cover or heading for the door, the bully out in front of our classmates, now stacked up at the door like cordwood fighting to avoid the flames. I lowered the umbrella, a smile pinned to my ears. The class was relieved at the lack of lava. Laughter and faint disbelief darted across the four walls. The teacher, less jovial but still enthralled by the charade, let out a coy smile before ordering everyone back to their seat. "The fun is over," she proclaimed. And with that, I had found a tool to offset the pain.

Of course, Crazy thought it was funny as hell that I had puked all over the classroom. It wasn't what I expected nor what I needed, but it was something different, so I'd take it. Maybe humor could pierce his evil ways.

—⁓—

Before being tossed out of Lebanon, I became friends with an old man who lived next door. He was a large man with huge hands and fingers like Italian sausages. His shoulders were wide, and his waist was as thick as an old oak tree. He wasn't fat at all, and he had the saddest face I'd ever seen. It wasn't sad like Mother or me. It was a different kind of sad, a distant one that had a mixture of former happiness mingled in with the sad clouds floating around his head and chest. He would always put on a show of being happy and never said a bad word, but the silence that followed him told volumes about his life without speaking a word. At least that was what I saw around him.

He was all alone in that house, a house exactly the same as ours but with very little stuff inside. He worked in his garden every day and seemed to be hiding things in the dirt. When he learned we were to be moving, the sadness grew and spread into a wider circle around his head and chest. When you walked inside that circle, you could feel his loneliness and his hurt. It wasn't a broken-bones kind of hurt, more like heartbreak or the sadness of knowing I'd never see Ginger again. It was a deep sadness I'd never felt, but it made me want to talk to him, to ask him questions. Almost like I had been sent to comfort him in a way I couldn't understand, but that was the feeling I was getting. It was drawing me toward him somehow.

I had no idea why I felt this way, but it was something inside me, pushing me until I walked out the door and over to his house to settle the increasing demand from within. He was happy to see me as he opened the door and invited me inside. "Sit, sit, please sit," he said in broken English. He filled two glasses of water, one for him and one for me, sat down, and asked, "What can I do for you, little boy? I'd offer you a cookie, but I don't have much."

I told him I was fine and that I was there for him.

His eyes lit up as his face and head drew back a bit. The surprise of my statement caught him well off guard.

"My grandmother is from Poland, and my grandfather is a full-blooded Indian. Pawnee, I'm told."

I'm not sure where those words came from or why or how they landed on my tongue, but they had such a profound effect on the old man. I could see his entire grouping of clouds, gray when I walked into the house, turn colors, lift off his shoulders, and fly away as tears filled his eyes. His lips quivered and shook a bit before he pulled a small white pocket towel from his pants and wiped away what had started to flow.

"Let me tell you something," he began. It was the starting point of this old man's life story. I had no idea why it was happening; I just knew it was what I was supposed to be doing at that very moment. A calm had taken hold of me, one that gave me a strong sense of being exactly in the right place at the right time. The only thing off was an odor I couldn't quite place.

The old man talked and talked in a combination of broken English and what I figured were two or three other languages. His hands were telling stories just as fast as his mouth. Emotional energy was cutting loose, free of all restraints, seemingly for the first time in his life. He happily voiced his every thought.

As his life's experiences bounced off the nearly empty rooms of his small ranch-style home, his eyes were aglow. He relived the past with that glazed-over look. The one you get when telling stories so deeply you forget to focus on anything except the visions as they flow across your memories like Kodak negatives racing across a screen on the inside of your forehead. Images so strong you believe and feel as though you are present in the moments once again.

His face leaned slightly toward the dull white ceiling as he questioned and rephrased one part of his tales and adventures, all the while never breaking stride, pausing only to drink from the glass of warm water to recoat his tongue for the next round of pointed memories. When he reached for his water, I caught a glimpse of something in the sliding glass door, a reflection of sorts, a shadow maybe. I got the sense there was someone else there, someone or something that was happy. I saw an image forming in the glass. An outline is a better reference marker. If you've never seen these types of reflections, it was like seeing animals form in the clouds. The ones you see when lying on the beach, staring at the sky and daydreaming about your world.

In the sliding glass door behind the old man, the image took shape. Over his right shoulder as he sat with his right arm on the table, his left arm moving up and down in rhythm with his story, I could see the outline of a woman, older but not as old as him. She had a pretty face sporting a smile and a glow. She was wearing a black lace hat to match the black lace dress with a neckline that revealed an old family jewel strapped to a thin gold chain. Her smile seemed to be for me, almost a nod of approval or a silent thought of appreciation. A feeling of gratefulness filled the air.

I squinted to get a better view just as the old man changed tone with a gruff grunt of "*Halt!*" It caused me to jump a bit in my chair. When I looked back at the glass, the image was gone. Maybe I was just there to listen to his story. That was what felt right, so I decided to keep listening for as long as he was willing to talk. The best I could understand, he was a soldier in the war when the Nazis invaded his homeland. They burned everything! They killed everything! He was a soldier for many years but was a farmer when the Nazis came. He explained how he lost his entire family, his farm, his friends, and his country. He'd been captured, tortured, starved, beaten, and enslaved. Forced to march for weeks from his homeland and into the heart of his enemies' land.

"Skin and bone," he kept repeating. "*Skin and bone!*" Sometimes loudly and sometimes just under his breath, fighting back more tears as the movie replayed in his mind. He snapped his face from time to time to shake off the pictures he hated to revisit, like when he spoke about his children. "*My boys*...gone...all gone! My boys, I miss them...My wife..." Tears flowed each time he mentioned his family, sadness rolling out of him like a tired old steam train huffing and puffing along.

When the Americans came, "I was free." He said he walked back to his homeland only to see the Nazis replaced by the Russians, although he called them by another name that I couldn't understand. "*Nothing,* no more, *nothing!*" he said with a soft pound on the table with his mighty right hand. A red glow rose above his head whenever he said words like "Nazi" or "Russians." "Slobs" was a word he used, but I never understood his meaning. After walking back to his destroyed home—"finding the dead," as he put it—and the "new law," he was a slave again but without the chains. He said it was a "yoke" that enslaved him. I still didn't understand, but my job was to listen, so I kept playing my part.

He said he fled for America after years of "slave work in home-land." Many who tried to flee died, but he made it. Now he was here, but with "nothing," he said. "No friends, no family, and only this small plot the government gives me." The loneliness was clearly heavy on his heart, as were his stories. "My wife...my wife..." The tears no longer held back. His hands held his head just above the water glass. His thinning white hair with yellow-ing streaks showed off his balding crown as his eyes pointed at the table. His sobs softly filled the room. He lifted his head and stared at me as he finished crying out the ending to the story. "I'm alone...no one with me...no one left." Then, just as quickly as it had started, he sat up, looked me directly in my eyes, and said, "You're a good boy, a nice boy. You are going to be okay." He pat-ted my hand before standing up. With a deep, strong voice, he said, "Thank you for visit. You go back to family now." And just like that, it was over.

Listening to his stories made me think about what I was living with and how hard it must have been for him, yet he had survived. It gave me a sense of purpose, maybe, of being there. Maybe I didn't have it so bad, and compared to him I had it easy. At least that was my thought process. He had lost everything and kept fighting, fighting to stay alive. When I thought about him sitting in that house all alone, I felt sadness for him. I felt sorry for him and wondered if maybe he'd take me in, let me live with him. But who would protect the others? At least I could dream.

His story stayed with me, and when I needed to hide from the Nazi who ran my life, I'd think of the old man and his stories. It offered comfort and reminded me that others had it a hell of a lot worse than I did, and it could always get worse, just like it had for the old man, surviving the war only to walk for weeks to get home just to find he was a slave to another master and then trying to escape again. I was glad to be there. To let him get his dark clouds off his shoulders.

The next few days were quiet as we packed up once again for a run to another place. The old war veteran hadn't been around, and I didn't see him in his garden. The day before we were to leave Lebanon, there were blue and red lights flashing in the old man's driveway. Mother was coming back, walking across his front lawn.

"What's going on?" I asked.

"He passed away. Must have been a few days ago, from what the landlord can figure out." Mother put her hand on my head as she continued. "Could have been as long as a week or more, but he's been gone for some time; that's for sure. No one has seen him since last week."

I wanted to tell her about my conversation with him, but something told me not to. I thought about it for a long time, confused as to when I had seen him last and wondering if I was the last person to see him alive. It was only a couple of days ago, wasn't it? Maybe it wasn't me who was there to help him; maybe it was the other way around. Was that possible? I thought about that for a long time, wondering and thinking.

The next day we were gone, once again, on to another place to live, in another town. This house would remain in my memories because of the stories of the old man—the old soldier—and all he lost without giving up hope. It was all he had, and maybe that was the message—hope!

CHAPTER 6

After moving from Lebanon, we experienced a few more midnight escapes from the wonderful world of debt collectors as they tried to beat down the door to get paid with zero chance of that happening. As we vacated the Lebanon ranch, we did so with hunger snapping at our bellies even more than the bill collectors were snapping on the phone, in the mailbox, and in person.

Packing our belongings from the kitchen took only minutes since there was nothing in the food pantry, freezer, refrigerator, or anywhere else, for that matter. We had a pile of potatoes and a tub of old cooking oil as the sole remaining edible items. Thank goodness for salt, as the deep-fried potato slabs held salt much better than traditional french fries, which made you drink more water, in turn filling you up. At least for the time being.

Crazy stopped going to work yet somehow was able to enjoy his brown bottles. That supply never seemed to run empty. My brother and sisters would team up to see who could create a new way to make potatoes. Garlic powder and other spices helped the adventure along, but in the end, deep-fried won top prize. The ketchup packets from McDonald's had run out days ago, but we had so many salt packets we figured the salt would last well past the fast-softening fifty-pound bags of potatoes stacked in the basement. We didn't know where they came from, but Crazy had shown up with them a few months back.

"We can eat like kings," he proclaimed as my brother and I struggled to get them from the car down the bulkhead stairs without damaging a single spud…or else!

When you reach a point of hunger close to starvation, you're so grateful for anything—potatoes, rice, stale bread, even raw vegetables. Even as a child you gain a healthy respect for the very basics in life, like eating. When you've crossed the fields of starvation, it takes you to a place where you feel so grateful it lifts you into a format unknown or understood by anyone who hasn't slept with the hollow drumbeat of a growling, empty stomach or the pain that accompanies hunger.

It changes you at your core and does so for life. You appreciate the simplest of gestures from people, strangers who offer something, anything, even an act of kindness such as a smile, a connection of acknowledgment.

When we were eating potatoes for days on end, my siblings and I worried about one another, and I made sure they got enough to stop the pain and quiet the barking hollows, as we'd jokingly call the never-ending noise emanating from all of our bellies. I swore then and there that I would never go to bed hungry a day in my life once I survived the stepping stones of this life, and I would make sure those around me never suffered this kind of hurt as long as I was alive.

Going without was something I saw as a lack of will, a lack of drive, a lack of determination to work hard enough so you would never run out of food or a place to live. These were my thoughts leading up to the time with the old soldier next door. His story made me more determined to fight, to work hard, and to battle to survive and change the direction my life was heading, to break this cycle of poverty I saw with Crazy, Mother, and her mother.

Each time we moved, I saw people working hard, working together, and fighting to take care of one another. One good thing I gained from Crazy's lessons was what I didn't want to do with life. I had no idea, no guidance, no sense of how to get there, but hard work seemed to be a starting point, so I was going to find work, find a way to make money so we would have food at the very least. The move from Lebanon was a turning point and one I was determined to win. I was grateful for the lessons of that old soldier.

I began my middle school years at the former Windham High School building called Kramer Middle School. It was a classic building constructed when the city of Willimantic was the heart of the universe for silk and all things thread. It came to be called Thread City because of all the cotton turned into thread. If it was made with thread, it most likely came from Willimantic, starting in the late 1800s and continuing until the 1970s. It was the thread capital of the world.

A new high school was built a short distance away in the early seventies. The Kramer building became the center for grades six through eight. The classic building had a swimming pool, old locker rooms, and a huge gym that doubled as the theater with a full-blown stage set up and used for local productions. While I didn't like school, I did enjoy going to school.

Friends were one thing, but getting away from Crazy was the main reason I enjoyed attending most of the time. There was a truancy officer, but we figured out how to dodge him and his early-sixties Remington model eight-barrel tank you could hear coming from a block away. Classes were set up so you had to move around every forty-two minutes, so we'd skip as many classes as we felt we could get away with and hang out around the gym next to Eastern Connecticut State College, a college for future teachers. The college offered many places to explore and hide away, so we could talk about what we were going to do for the day.

The city cops were always on the lookout for us and had taken us back to the school so many times they'd given up and just shook their heads and yelled, "Get back to school!" But they didn't do much more than that.

One of my best friends was Gary Dziekan. He had a bunch of brothers and sisters, who all lived in a quiet housing project a mile or so from my house. He had cool stuff like dirt bikes and off-road motorcycles. He taught me how to ride motorbikes and even how to build them. We'd race around the city and outskirts of town on those bikes like we owned the streets. That, of course, led to more encounters with the local cops as well as the college police. They knew who we were, for the most part, but could never catch us. We'd tear up the ball field with the knobby studded dirt bikes and race around town dodging in and out of traffic causing as much hell as we could get away with.

Cops would come to his house and to mine. We'd deny everything, of course. "Wasn't us" became our mantra. We'd find all the hiding places, from the smallest patch of woods to a forty-eight-inch drainage pipe to the backyards of friends who would know just the right places to stash the dirt bikes until things cooled off. We couldn't go to Gary's house. The cops had someone there, and we never went to my house, so we learned how to avoid the law and have fun at the same time. I had a few other friends but honestly not many, and only a couple like Gary.

For the most part, I was a loner, but one thing I hated was bullies. Crazy was the biggest bully of them all, and his "lessons" turned me into a person who would be a bully fighter. Someone who would stand up and fight back when a bully came calling. I saw boys mistreating girls, and it pissed me off. I would stick my nose into places that got me into trouble just for saying, "*Hey! Leave her alone, or you'll deal with me.*"

It was something that grew inside me, especially as I got older. Gary was the same way. His life wasn't all that different from mine except for the beatings and abuse. He didn't like bullies, especially those who hurt girls, and we really hated the fear a bully created. He'd tell me, "One day you and me are going to cream that guy. We'll make him pay for what he does to you." He was one of the very few who knew what was really going on. At least that was what I thought.

One day an eighth grader was picking on a friend of a friend, a girl who went home in tears and a torn dress. He was older than us, but Gary wanted to right this wrong. He knew the girl's mother. Her father had died some years earlier, so she had no one to help her, as Gary put it. At this stage, I already had a reputation as a fighter, and the size, strength, and powerful build I'd been asking God to provide—well, he was working his magic, because I was growing, and so was my ability to use what I was given to help others.

I never put my hands on anyone unless they started something or they were hurting someone else. That's God's honest truth. I also hung around with kids everyone else called hoodlums, bums, or trash. I didn't fit in elsewhere, and I liked those kids. I understood them, and candidly, they were the ones who would get beatings as well, so it was easy to relate. We didn't have to ask questions; we just knew a black eye was punishment, no explanation needed.

One day, a hoodlum friend got suspended for refusing to sit in his chair. He demanded he be allowed to stand in the back of the class—actually, all his classes. The principal sent him home for a week for not obeying the teacher's orders. No one knew his backside was so battered he could not sit, not for a while at least. I kept him company for most of the week.

Other kids always tried to find out what had happened and asked, "Are you all right? Who did this to you?" If you said what had caused the injuries, then you'd be called to a sit-down where a cop would show up, and the whole thing would unravel. Despite filing a report or taking down names, nothing would come of it. Crazy had taught me that a long time ago, and nothing had changed in all those years, so it was best to just keep quiet.

The only benefit to all the black eyes, bruises, and casts was that kids thought you were a badass. Getting into fights with a high schooler. Heck, you could say anything you wanted. Who'd challenge your story! Making up stories became a pastime, but trying to remember them all was a disaster. At least with Gary and the other guys, we could all just be ourselves, and if you needed to vent, they'd listen. No judgment, no pity parties, and no telling anyone else.

Gary was the best at keeping secrets, and as long as we hung out, he never ratted, not a single word. I trusted him with all I had. Sometimes he'd hide me in his room or sneak me food until his mother would tell him it was time for me to go. His mom was a very nice lady, and I'm sure she knew the score. But she had many mouths to feed, and I was one more she didn't have room for, at least not in long spurts.

One time I was hurt so badly I ran away. I needed a place to hide out for a while to heal, rest, and recover. Gary somehow got his mom to allow me to stay for almost a week before the cops showed up, and she said I needed to "move on." It was enough time to recover, and I was grateful to her, Gary, and his family. I'm not sure I could have taken another beating without that recovery time, and when I got back to the house, not an hour later, the fists were a-pounding. But at least my body was strong enough to withstand the brunt of Crazy's blows.

When Gary saw me the next day, he was furious. But what could he do? He helped me as best as anyone. So it was time to repay his kindness toward me. Someone was hurting a friend of his or his mother's friend. I never really figured it out, but I was going to do whatever Gary needed. Since it was a girl, it made me even more willing.

We found this kid's house. It was a really big house with a huge front lawn. It looked like a million-dollar house to us. It had a big front door, and it was on a dead-end road with a lot of other high-end homes. I had delivered newspapers to this area only the year before, but the *Hartford Times* had shut down. So I lost my route, but I knew the houses.

We also knew the hiding places, so we watched for the kid and spent several days learning how he moved about. He had a really nice bike. In fact, he had a couple of them, a ten-speed and a brand-new off-street bicycle, one we'd never seen. We decided the bike was the starting point, so we planned to steal it and then let him know where it was so he'd come looking for it. The first part worked perfectly, but the son of a bitch called the cops, and somehow Gary's name came up. Long story short, Gary got pinched, and his mother was beyond mad. He couldn't help finish what we started.

A few days later, this kid was teasing the same girl in the hallway along with a couple of his high-end friends. It didn't take long for me to…well, overreact. I double chest thumped this bully so hard he hit the locker a few feet behind him. One of his friends put his hand on me and started a big right hook. I hit him under his chin with an uppercut that wobbled his knees and left him in a pile on the tile floor. The bully charged with little success. Picking him up with a power and strength I never knew I had, I smashed him on his back with such force I wasn't sure he'd ever catch his breath again. Reaching down, I put my right hand around his throat, my knee compressing deep into his ribs, my left hand bending his fingers backward to as close a point of breaking as possible.

Leaning within kissing distance and using a voice I didn't know I had, I said, "If you ever come near this girl again, I will kill you." I let go of his throat and looked around at the crowd gathered in almost a complete circle. As I stepped back, I let everyone know, "*You don't hit girls, or this is what will happen to you!*"

The timing was perfect. Just as I finished my warning, security came along with several administration officials, parted the crowd, and surrounded me and the two boys on the floor. I was suspended, but I didn't care. It was the right thing to do, at least in my mind.

Sometime later, that girl came up to me and thanked me. She had been terrorized by that boy, and even though her mom reported it several times, it was only getting worse. She said he'd never bothered her since, and she was no longer in fear. She could sleep again and was doing better with her grades. She was a smart girl, but the bully had her so stressed, so afraid, that she couldn't function. I knew exactly what she was living through. She put her hand on my forearm, and before turning to leave, she gave me a kiss on the cheek, which warmed my heart before I shut down the happy feeling.

It felt good to help someone and, of course, finish what Gary needed taken care of. Gary also told me his mother and that girl's mother wanted to thank me. They were worried about the trouble I was in, so they reminded the principal of the abuse before the reckoning. Getting suspended wasn't the worst of it, and it wasn't the first time I'd been arrested. It also wasn't the last time.

It was the first time I stood up to a bully for physically hurting a girl and the first time I helped change a girl's life, in this case from terrified to back in control. It wasn't the last time either. Somehow it became my calling card, so to speak. If you were going to hurt a girl, you'd better understand someone was going to make you pay. There would be many more battles—none I looked for, but each of them ended with the girl returning to her life, free from further harm.

It also painted a target on my back. It was a strange way of things but one that seemed to fit with me. Gary and I remained close friends until high school. He went to the technical school, and I went to the other one, the one without an entrance exam. I'll never forget how much he helped, his kindness and understanding. A place to stay from time to time and food to help me survive and to keep moving forward. Gary is the definition of a true friend.

CHAPTER 7

D id you fit in at high school?
High school was an adventure for me. I wasn't a good student, but it was a break from life with Crazy. I learned to use humor as a tool to make people laugh and deflect reality. Fighting was a never-ending battle, and I never lost a fight. When I pulled out the mean person inside me, it carried an energy so intense no one could beat it, not even me. The power within had so much energy it would become overwhelming at times. This led to fits of rage that would return throughout my life, and, to this day, it's not the person anyone wants to see, unless I'm defending someone. It felt like a mild version of the Hulk when someone would push me to the point where I could no longer control the rage, the anger!

Leading up to high school, an event at eighth-grade graduation practice in the gym became a calling card I'd have to face for the next four-plus years. Imagine a couple hundred kids sitting in neatly packed rows of chairs. The energy was very high, with the excitement of the last few days of middle school and anticipation of being freshmen, attending high school. It was electric, and our class was graduating. Everyone's clothing was draped with school colors—well, almost everyone. Memories of the past three years whipped into tales larger than they really were. We all felt so alive and excited, and summer was just a ceremony away.

We were several rows back from the front of the stage. In front of me was one of the class geeks. He wore thick, dark-framed glasses. He had terrible teeth and smelled bad. His clothes were worn, wrinkled, and outdated. His wiry hair stood in some directions and floated in others. It looked like he never used a brush or shampoo. His glasses were always so dirty I used to wonder why he didn't just clean them so he could see better. While he was tall for our age, he was very skinny. He barely had enough muscle to pick up much more than his own skin and bones. You could tell he didn't brush his teeth by the buildup of yellow crud caked where white should be. Watching him eat in the lunchroom wasn't something you wanted to do twice. When he walked down the hallways, everyone cleared the way; the smell always foreshadowed his intent and lingered behind him. Everyone made fun of him, but I don't recall ever doing so. At least I hope I never did.

I remember feeling sorry for this kid and thinking he must have it tough at home too. I felt like we had some kind of kinship or unspoken adjoining force of life. An outsider's position, like being in the crowd but never being part of the crowd. In fact, it was knowing exactly how different you were and that you'd never fit in with the crowd, any crowd. There seemed to be a silent understanding between those who were on the outside looking in and those on the inside.

As graduation rehearsal slowly took shape, we had a lot of wait time, sitting there with not much to do. It was getting hot in that gym, and I started to smell our geek. It was getting the guy sitting next to him rather worked up. Richard Cooper—Dick to those who didn't like him—was a class bully and all-around tough guy. He always had to stick his two cents into anything and was forever causing trouble. He was a fighter. One of those guys who was always looking to pick a fistfight, no real reason needed. I can't even remember how many fights this guy had over the course of my knowing him since grammar school, but everyone was afraid of him. He wasn't a good student either and had a lot of brothers, cousins, and friends he'd tap into for his fighting ways. Cooper voiced how big his "group of friends" was, an effort to strengthen his "bullydom." I'd seen quite a few of his fights and knew he had backup to help him if need be, so it was best to keep this in mind whenever you had to deal with him or his kin.

Me, on the other hand—I was alone, no backup or anyone to step in to help me out if need be. And I knew if I went home on the losing end of a fight, it was going to be a long night with Crazy and his lessons. While I never lost a fight outside of life with Crazy, the consequences of losing were always at the forefront of my mind. Getting a beating—hell, that was easy, normal even. No matter how many times I was hit by anyone, I would never quit. You might "beat" me, but you'll never win!

The first time someone hit me in school, I did nothing except cry. When I got to the house and told Crazy what had happened, it was worse than getting hit by the second grader who felt touching his schoolwork was a punch-worthy offense. Crazy made it clear that I was never to come back to the house after losing a fight or allowing anyone to put their hands on me. (I'm wondering if this is where that famous statement "Crazy is as Crazy does" entered the world). To take it one step further, if anyone put their hands on my sisters or older brother, Crazy would beat me to "within an inch of your life," one of his favorite terms of endearment. He would make sure I was properly beaten so I would have no fear of what anyone else could possibly do to me. The beating I took for getting hit that first time was a lesson that stuck with me. That beating was so severe it released something inside me. It was as if an animal took hold, one so mean, so powerful that when it came out, it felt like pure hate wrapped in unemotional madness with limitless energy and no thought process other than self-preservation by total dominance. By the time I was fourteen, this "lesson" would come back to haunt Crazy to no end.

So there we were, the graduating eighth-grade class, in 1970s vinyl pants, tube socks, and corduroys looking like mini pimp bosses yet feeling like we had the entire world in front of us. As the heat increased and the air stagnated, it became a lot to deal with the smell of the geek. Cooper made it clear that he'd had enough. He started to really dig into him verbally. Some points were funny but truly in a very mean way. After a few laughs egged Cooper on, he went further by hitting the geek in the back of the head. After a few slaps and elbow jabs failed to gain the full weight of his bullying ways, he elevated the force and knocked our geek off his chair and onto his knees. His glasses slipped past his nose and stuck to his chin. As he collected himself without a word, a tear formed as he realigned his spectacles. A kick to his ankle stunned our geek with another agent of pain.

"That's enough, Cooper. Leave him alone" jumped past my lips without any thought.

Cooper quickly began a four-letter attack at me. I could feel his rage start to transfer to me. I could also feel a change in our geek's energy, like a gratefulness or relief of sorts that someone, anyone, would step in to help this poor bastard. I knew if I could keep Cooper's attention away from our geek and directed at me, it should get him through the rehearsal, which had to be ending soon.

Cooper had no intention of stopping his assault. A couple of girls stepped up and told Cooper to leave our geek alone, but it had no effect on the class bully. It was as if the attention served a purpose and fed Cooper's ego. Between his increasing spewing of hate and f-bombs at me and his ongoing physical assault on our geek, I finally reached out and stopped Cooper's next blow.

This really got his attention. He stood up to square off, but his timing wasn't the best. Our beloved principal had just stepped onto the stage and, with mic in hand, took control of the proceedings. While he didn't know what was going on, and I didn't stand up, he told Cooper to sit down and warned everyone to calm down, or he'd ensure anyone misbehaving would not be graduating.

Cooper sat down while pointing his finger at me and telling everyone, "This is not over." At this stage in my life, having a finger pointed at me was a trigger. One that unlocked the safety box where I kept the monster. Crazy would point his finger into my chest, jam it into my nose, tap my forehead until I bled, and poke me to a point of utter madness. I vowed to end it, someday, and *never* let anyone else "point" at me. Cooper had pushed a button without knowing its outcome.

Cooper kept pressing, jabbing, poking, and kicking our geek, doing so in a manner few could see. My anger was growing, but getting suspended, ejected from graduation...What do I do! Part of my mind was saying, "Help him," while another part was warning against it.

Then Cooper hit our geek so hard it made him cry—and I'm talking full-blown, snot-driven, face-contorting sob storm. Cooper went to hit him again. I reached forward, grabbed the bully by his neck with my right hand, squeezed with the power of a hydraulic ram, and jammed him backward in his chair. I grabbed his left arm with my left hand, preventing him from doing more damage to our geek. Cooper winced in pain. A perfectly proportioned dish of cold revenge forced his withdrawal. A teacher in the front had been informed by a classmate of the ongoing troubles and had made his way down the folding-chair aisle just as the two of us were about to take it to the next step in this dance of wills.

By this time, the entire graduating class knew there was something afoot. Something a lot more interesting than practicing our graduation, something juicier. An old-school fight was snatching the headlines—and everyone's attention.

Now what do I do? As I sat contemplating how this was going to play out, when this was going to play out, and where, my thoughts went back to Crazy. I'd surely have to deal with him at some point. Of all the things taking shape, Crazy was the one thing I was worried about. If I lost a fight, I'd get beaten. And if I got in trouble in school, I'd get beaten anyway, so now what would I do? As I sat there deep in thought, our class theme song started to play. The principal keyed the mic. "We're just about done, but we'll all be sitting here until the final bell rings." He signaled to restart our song.

I kept trying to figure out a path forward without success, as all options seemed to have the same outcome. Someone was getting a beating, and I was sure I was going to get at least one regardless of what moves I made. So I just sat there and tried to think about my life and going to high school. I was trying to ignore what was coming until internally, I heard those opening sounds everyone knows from the movie—that song that makes you invincible, that song that opens the power valves inside every kid in America with such adrenaline that you just know you can't lose...the theme from *Rocky...dat da dat da*...started playing, and my insides went full-blown hyper.

Without a second thought, I poked Cooper with two fingers (so much worse than a single finger poke) and told him to be outside right after school and "meet me by the college." Of course, this would keep me from getting into trouble, since it was after school and off school grounds. Hopefully, I had plotted a course that just might keep me from getting that beating from Crazy after all.

Now, the following events would seem to be fiction, and honestly, I still have a hard time understanding how it all played out. This was the 1970s, so no Twitter, no Facebook, no cell phones. A text was a handwritten note passed from one sweaty palm to the next. Somehow, the entire school learned of the pending brawl with the spread of a midwestern wildfire.

The bell rang, and our principal ended the pregrad event with some quick words of encouragement and a final warning. "Don't get into any trouble between now and getting your diploma, or you will be back here next year to do it all over again."

The school day ended at 2:14 p.m., and the prefight planning was only four minutes prior! We exited the gym, shoulder to shoulder, bumping into one another as only early teens can do. There was an air of excitement. The energy of things to come, creating an atmosphere that was hard to imagine, and I was there.

Before I knew it, I was outside the school and walking toward the back of the building and onto the grounds of the college campus just across the parking lot. The school buses lining the streets were half full of sixth and seventh graders, who hurried to get their favorite seats. It looked like a sea of heads roaming around an area the size of a football field. It was packed with kids buzzing around, talking about what had happened, what was about to happen. Betting on who would win, arguing who was right.

Just off to my left was a seventh grader telling his classmate what had happened and why we were all gathering. He said the "hood" had totally beaten the crap out of this "jock," and a riot broke out in the gym, and now there was going to be a rumble between all the jocks and hoods for final control over the right to be cool! Only a couple of people, those who actually witnessed the bully's abuse, those few were the only ones who truly understood what had happened. One endured humiliation, far worse than a beating. In the end, he was the only one who mattered. At least that was my view, and I was willing to fight for a defenseless geek I hardly knew.

It's insane to think that something seemingly so small could build so quickly into something that had the entire school system, including math and science teachers, bus drivers, and the general public, showing up to witness it. I wish I could say it was the only time an event like this happened in my life. Unfortunately, it wasn't the first or the last event like this to take shape.

The noise was incredible. Imagine a few hundred kids between the ages of nine and thirteen, hyped up at the end of the school year, entranced to witness a fight. Dozens of grown-ups, head and shoulders above the masses like trees scattered in a field of wind-blown wheat, were caterwauling as if they were the adolescents.

Before I could think about it any further, a friend slapped me on my shoulder blade and said, "I hear you're in for a fight. Better get on with it before the police show up. I got your back if his friends jump in." Big Red and I knew each other from baseball and football. He was bigger than most and strong as an ox. It was good to hear his offer and know someone was willing to back me up.

As I stepped into the center of the immense circle, Cooper was at the far edge. A half dozen or so of his kin gathered around him, cigarettes fingered by most of them.

I moved to the center, studying Cooper as he sat on a large boulder inhaling his tobacco stick. He glared in my direction, flicked the lit coals toward me, and spit as a warning that he was on his way. Not a single word was exchanged between us as Cooper set a hurried pace, closing the distance with several steps.

He cocked a deep right hook. A fake, and he led with a left jab but missed badly. I'd seen this move from Crazy, and candidly, Cooper's misleading poke to set up his roundhouse was an easy read. I simply moved my head to avoid his first shot and rolled away from his haymaker. His balance lost, I hit him in his right ear with a pounding thud, knocking him to the ground. Pissed, or embarrassed by the crowd's "Ohhh...did you see that...?" he charged from his knees like so many linemen I'd played football against. My thigh and knee top caught him under his chin, sending him back to the spotty grass and packed dirt. Each charge, every attempted punch, even his girly kicks were thwarted with ease. His face was bleeding, and sweat was soaking his shirt and his head as he knelt a few feet away, formulating his next move.

His eyes looked to his kin. A head bob signaled his need for help. "Look out! Duck!" Big Red warned.

I moved in time to avoid a shot to the back of my head and caught the intruder with an uppercut to the bottom of his jaw. He crumbled like an empty plastic garbage bag, lying motionless in the unnatural position with his knee holding his face. The crowd released a synchronized groan followed by shouts of "Did you see that?" Cooper, taking advantage of his helper's attempted double team, caught me from behind, but only for a moment. We wrestled, but it wasn't much of a match. I sat on his chest, hand on his throat, fist cocked for another chin dance…Cooper's hands positioned to protect his face when someone from his corner shouted, "*Enough!* You won; let him go."

Emotionless, I climbed off him. The crowd began to disperse. Cooper's brother helped him off the ground. "You know you're going to get whipped for losing, don't you?" remarked his brother!

And with that, it was over. Couldn't have been more than five minutes. As quickly as it had come together, it had disappeared. However, the remarks by Cooper's brother had me concerned. Was he dealing with the same Crazy I was?

"Hey, you better get. Campus cops are around the corner, and city cops are coming," Big Red told me with a head nod as he started in the other direction.

Cooper was back on his rock, cigarette hanging from his lip, blood scattered about his face and clothes and matting his long light-brown hair. Our eyes met for a brief moment. His look told me our battles were not over. One of his brothers made it clear with a point and then a finger across his throat.

I decided it was time to get distance between me and this campus. In the distance a couple of sirens were calling out the markers, letting everyone know they were en route. So without a grace period to reflect on the events or a single person to share this with, I headed toward the house, quickly but not running.

That day changed things for me, some good, some bad. As I watched everyone fade into their respective lives, moving past the excitement that turned out to be overhyped and ended quickly, I could still feel the energy as it faded away. The kids were getting back on the buses. The grown-ups who had enjoyed the event had a change of outward dogma as the cops and other authority figures started showing up. Acting like they had no idea what was happening.

I tried to fade into the surroundings, but blending in with the others was a little bit tricky. I had blood on my shirt and pants. My knuckles were cut and bleeding, and I had sweat pouring off me, so I just kept walking in the direction of some other kids who walked home each day.

No one wanted to approach me. I guess that was a good thing. I walked a few blocks before turning and heading back toward the house. As time passed and my breath came back, I could feel the cool breeze wicking the body heat away from me, and I began to feel that fear start to creep back into my chest. My shirt was dirty with blood spots in places, and my pants had grass stains at the knees and pockets of blood. I had to figure out how to hide this mess so Crazy wouldn't find out.

I was praying that he was at the bar and not at the house and praying it was one of his days when he wouldn't come back until after closing, around 2:00 a.m. That might give me time to get past this one. I knew Mother was going to be coming from work in a couple of hours—unless she worked a double. Then it would be up to me to cook dinner for everyone and deal with Crazy until he passed out.

I wondered what all the other kids were thinking about right now! Were they worried about getting beaten or what to cook for dinner or how to get bloodstains out of their clothes?

I knew I needed to figure things out quickly, since I had the after-school paper route. One hundred forty-two home deliveries of the local newspaper. I'd hide the clothes for now and deal with them later. I turned the corner to head up my street two blocks away from the house. My heart stopped beating, and I felt my life draining from me. Two cops were on the front porch. I could hear them banging on the door, and I felt it pounding against my chest as if I was standing on the other side of that door. I stopped in my tracks and froze as I drew a complete blank as to what I should do. Without a thought, I turned around and headed back around the block I'd just come from, and I started running as fast as I could. Where to go? Where to hide? What should I do now?

I decided to run into the woods. There was a grouping of trees along one edge of the baseball fields across from the college tennis courts, so I kept running until I was at the edge of those woods. I slipped into the tree line where I'd hidden so many times before, a safe haven of sorts that only a couple of kids knew about, Gary being one of them. I found my favorite sitting rock and claimed my spot hidden from view. From my vantage point, I could still see the two roads in the distance, so I would know if someone was coming.

—⚏—

I put my head in my hands to cry, but nothing happened. The fear turned to anger, followed by hatred for my life and the mess I had once again made of it. Now I was hiding in the woods with no idea of what to do or where to go. As I tried to gather my thoughts, I could hear the birds chirping away and some kind of screaming animal, clearly upset I had invaded his space.

What was that sound, and why was it so loud? While the birds seemed peaceful, that damn screeching was frustrating. To make matters worse, this bastard called in some friends. Behind me I could hear another loudmouth screeching away. I was thinking this one must be huge, as it was a lot louder than his damn counterpart. I turned to look for this churl, and I almost jumped out of my bloody pants. It was an extremely large squirrel clinging to the side of a tree about eight feet up. It was looking at me with its mouth wide open and making a noise you wouldn't believe. I swear he was preparing to do battle with me for some ungodly reason that I couldn't possibly have time to figure out. I wanted to scream back, but it wouldn't help matters.

One fight on the streets was my limit, and this king of the small patch of woods needed to shut up. So I whipped a rock at him, and to my shock I damn near hit him. Then I began to worry he was going to charge me, and I had no experience doing battle with critters of the woodlands. After a few brief moments in a standoff of wills, the nutjob bolted up the tree and went about his business. The other one stopped shrieking as well. It was a nice break, but just like that, my mind was back to thinking about what I should do next. And as I looked past the evergreens and pine needles toward the street, my heart once again skipped a beat.

The cops were stopped on the street and looking in my direction. The same cops who had been in front of the house when I turned the corner. The local do-gooder was pointing right at me. I started to wonder if those squirrels were actually trying to warn me and I had betrayed them by throwing a rock at one. Maybe that was why I thought the king squirrel had shaken his head before shooting up the tree. It was starting to look like I'd be sleeping in a jail cell while the squirrel enjoyed the comforts of his nest, which was sounding great.

As I sat there growing tired and hungry watching the police as they figured out their next move, I got the sense they wouldn't be coming to look for me in these woods. I decided to wait it out. After a while they drove away. I put my head back against the rock I was sitting on and felt the relief only known to those who have hidden from law enforcement or Crazy.

I could hear the birds as my heartbeat slowed down, and the thumping in my ears became a quiet hum. I took a few breaths and allowed myself to feel safe for the moment. The king squirrel would surely send out a warning if anyone else approached, right?

The music of those birds took me to a place of pure calm, and before I knew it, I was fast asleep in my safe spot, on my comfy rock bed with a granite pillow, tucked away in the cradle of nature's protection and warmth, at peace where no one could harm me.

The next thing I knew, my hands and head were hurting, and I wasn't sure why my eyes wouldn't open. All I could see was blackness, utter darkness without a sound. As quickly as I could blink my eyes, it all came back to me, the entire day.

I could see the streetlights in the distance. My stomach was growling, and I was hurting in several places. After a few minutes, I figured I should just go to the house and get this nightmare of a day over with. I ventured out of the woods, back to the street, walked quietly the few blocks to our road, and turned right onto our street. As I got close, the porch light wasn't on, which was interesting. There wasn't a police car in front of the house as before. Then I got one of those senses that seemed to be telling me, "It's going to be okay," and I started to get that calm feeling I'd had earlier in the day, just before the fight.

As I walked up the steps to the front door, things sounded quiet, which was also strange. I didn't see the car, so maybe Crazy wasn't there. I took my usual deep breath before opening the door and walked in. No sounds, no TV, no smells of cooked food, so I guessed Mother wasn't there either. Only a couple of lights were on, so I walked into the kitchen, where my sister was sitting working on something. She looked up as I glanced at the clock. It was just past 9:00 p.m. She asked me where I had been and what had happened to me. I asked where everyone was and found out Mother was at work, Crazy hadn't shown up, and my other two siblings were upstairs. My sister knew about the fight and said the cops stopped by to talk to me, but our parents didn't know anything yet.

Wasn't that an interesting turn of events? I cleaned myself up, hid my clothes, and made some toast. I went to my room, where my brother was reading. We talked briefly, and he said he'd heard about the fight but didn't ask much more. I climbed under the covers and tried to get some sleep. This day was finally over, but I knew it wasn't the end—tomorrow was coming. There was potential trouble with police, and of course there was school and getting out of the eighth grade...or not? Even knowing what might be waiting for me in the morning, I was still grateful to be out of the cold and away from the king squirrel. The uncommon calm of the house seemed to be a reward for stopping a bully. As I drifted off to sleep, I couldn't help but wonder what our geek was doing. Maybe, just maybe, he was sleeping peacefully, without the fear of getting beaten up tomorrow. Maybe he was going to sleep with a newfound hope of things to come...It was a warming thought to close out a very long day.

CHAPTER 8

T he second year of my high school career was a big transition in life, but before that change took place, life with Crazy had to come to a head. That point was fast approaching. Leaving school in the darkness of late winter, following baseball tryouts, was a cold walk. I'd delay the need to start toward the house I lived at for as long as possible. Once I made the decision, my stomach would prepare by churning its mostly empty chamber. Tastes of mild acid would creep up my throat onto the back end of my tongue, leaving that same type of burning feeling the hot sauce did. Those types of lessons, or "training"—Crazy so enjoyed coining a phrase—had graduated into more aggressive torments, but the legacy remained. Slight reminders like black pepper or the smell of spices could bring back the nightmares as quickly as a politician can change their views.

A few deep sighs and some speculating. Would anyone notice if I didn't show up? I made that fateful daily decision to return to the battlegrounds for another round of "stay alive until morning." If there was a place, any place, to go other than back to that house, I would have taken that path without hesitation. But at the moment, nothing but hell house was an option.

A quick message just under my breath, but loud enough to hear my words slip out to whatever or whoever would listen, begging for a pain-free night and a new place to live. A new life free of fear, free of constant survival mode, and free of worry that one day I'd walk into the house and find Mother with her eyes open, soaked in a bloody mess of Crazy's butchery. If only I could sleep fear-free for a night, if only for one night, if only...

As the knots started to collect in my core, my breath shortened to a quick in-and-out rhythm, like half my lungs had been removed and the other half was a clogged mucus brick from the bitter winter air. I turned in the direction of that end-of-days place and forced my feet to take that first step. However, my feet simply didn't want to move, so I mustered another sigh, refocused, and pushed on. "Let's just get on with it"—a mantra to survive the day. That first step, the hardest one, completed, a couple thousand more in front of me.

The freezing wind started to bite through my thin jacket only steps into the count. My feet were getting wet from the frosty slush. My Barkers Discount Store brand Converse All Stars were doing little against winter's collective appearance. The slippery crunch splashed onto my ankles, adding more discomfort to the self-induced protracted walk. Counting each step, I felt the cold sting of prior broken bones. Pain surged in my hands from both old beatings and new bruises that hadn't fully healed. On one hand, pun intended, the cold helped the pain and bruises, but on the other hand, the bones, my shins, the scars, and other mended physique locations reminded me of past ordeals when Crazy had tested the limits of stick and bone.

I paced along under yellowing white streetlights and turned

right from High Street onto Prospect Street. The middle school was across the road; I chuckled as a few memories bounced about my head.

Then something stopped my next step. That old man with his white hair and red checked shirt jacket. He was standing in my pathway, not quite a full block away. His eyes were focused on mine. He looked up, to his left, and above the street. The lady in white. She was floating midtree level, with something in her outstretched hand. "We are with you; you will be okay" entered my mind, as if they were talking without sound. "Remember your past" flashed the next message.

A car horn chirped beside me. "You all right?" came from the rolled-down window. The horn startled me as I waved the driver away. By the time I looked back to the block in front of me, they were gone.

Looking toward my former teaching environment, "remember the past" replayed its silent note. Was I supposed to revisit those not-so-bygone days? Maybe I was needed to help another geek. Was this message about God answering my prayer to make me big enough to stop Crazy? What was the meaning, and why ambush my cold, dank, lonely step count? I tried to think. What memory, middle school?...Maybe!

When I was in eighth grade, before I was sticking up for geeks, I had grown so big I could no longer play in the midget football league. I was asked to play with the high school freshman team. The size limit, 140 pounds, disqualified me. I was well over the cap. I'd been begging the spirit world to make me big and powerful so I could stop the abuse. My prayers were being answered. Not only was I over 150 pounds, the muscles were taking shape, and I was creeping closer to Crazy's eye level. Was this what I was to remember?

Anyway, in eighth grade, John Hope, one of the nicest people on the face of this planet, and I talked the vice principal into allowing us to play at the high school. Eighth graders playing freshman football. How cool was that! I needed to keep it secret so Crazy wouldn't screw it up. Turned out we were the last two guys ever to be allowed to move up to that level, and it came with some positive attention for a change.

Crazy and Mother didn't support anything I enjoyed. There was no way they were going to approve, let alone give permission. Keeping this out of their bonnets was going to be tricky. I needed signed approvals from both Mother and Crazy. Sidestepping Mother was one thing; Crazy was another. So I forged his left-handed mark after expending a couple of ballpoints practicing. The school accepted the fake signatures, and, albeit underhandedly, I was on the team. I was so excited I started dreaming of playing in the pros and even gave college a thought or two.

The night before our first game, Mother found out about her eighth grader playing with the big boys. She told Crazy, who, in turn, presented the school with two options. My equipment was turned over, and my locker was cleaned out the next morning. It was a heartbreaking, painful end to a dream.

That memory helped me recall my freshman year of football. Maybe that was the message I needed to remember. Somehow the steps on this night had to be tied back to those events. What was that old man trying to tell me? Maybe it was about Bethany! He better not venture back there, not again. It had to be tied to sports and trying to make another team. It had to be!

—∿—

My freshmen year was the best ever, starting with football. We had a head coach with a name like Arnold, only more phlegm was needed to pronounce it. This guy took a group of actual misfits and created a sports legacy in three short months. As freshmen, we had the worst gear possible, and the head coach was literally out of the 1940s—a great man, don't get me wrong, but I think he played in college before helmets were required, and some of the gear, for the freshmen, was leftovers from that time period.

The freshman coach from the prior year moved up to handle the JV. This left an opening that was filled by a very young guy. He was built like the Terminator, to match his impossibly unpronounceable name. If someone asked him to pose with the world on his shoulders, he'd be the statue in New York City's Rockefeller Center. His mustache matched his thick black hair, which refused to budge from its perfectly brushed setting. He didn't dress like the other coaches, and he didn't fit in with the other coaches, especially the cantankerous old *Flintstones*-era head coach.

Our first experience with our new coach was in the heat of a mid-August double session, but his introduction was something that would change our lives in ways you'd never imagine. "My name is Swartzenzeplinzeekopinhemmer, and that's my first name. You all need to figure out my last name before the end of the season. You will call me Coach Swartz. *Got it!* We are going to have a *perfect* season. We will not lose a single game, and we will *not* allow our enemy to score a single *point*! I will teach you football, and you will become legends. Do we have a *deal* or what!"

A perfect season...no points given up! This guy was out of his mind, but he had our attention. There were twenty-one freshmen lined up that first day. Short shorts and Gut T-shirts, the latest fashion, strapped around old tennis shoes and Gatorade Gum, the newest thing in sports energy. That coach had a way about him, and the ripples in his arms matched the waves of light that popped with every word he spoke. He called us "men" and treated us like soldiers. I was never so excited to sweat.

While our gear was better suited for history class, our new coach was pumping us up like a modern-day televangelist. He promised, "You do as I ask, and I'll teach you how to win. I'll show you how to *never* lose, *never* give in, and *never* quit"—words that caused my heart to pound without the threat of a stick or a punch. There was something about this guy, and to me, he was a godsend.

We drank from the same water bucket, sharing one another's spit, and had worn-out spikes that attached to shoes with enough rawhide on the bottom to last another fifty years or so. Drinking from the water pail "makes a man out of boys," as he would say. We'd haul all the equipment for the varsity and JV team before and after practice "with pride" because Coach taught us the importance of total team temperament. Our reward at the end was a drill that made us feel like we were unstoppable. He'd set up dummies and make us run over them. We had to do flying leaps from many feet away into the bags while we each had to learn our own special dog-style crawls. And when we tackled the bags, we'd crunch our face masks deep into the leather as we growled like we were possessed. It was awesome!

We were on the field before the varsity and didn't leave until well after everyone else. We trained, we ran, and we learned to battle. Most of all, we learned never to quit. When we thought we couldn't take another step...he'd fire us up and put a charge into that invisible force that lit a fuse inside us and made us do things we never thought imaginable before he came into our lives.

Coach had every single player believing no one could stop us. Excuses were never allowed. When we made mistakes, we had to take responsibility as well as learn from them. Coach always told us that he believed we could do anything and that faith in us turned on our belief in one another. He taught us the meaning of football and how to succeed at anything if we refused to quit.

To focus our toughness, he wouldn't let us complain about anything. He didn't care how hot or cold it was. He didn't care how tired, sore, or banged up you were. "Toughness is a mental game. If you believe you are in pain, then pain will win." He'd tell us, "Lick your wounds tomorrow while you relive the victories of today. The pain will fade, but the win lives forever."

Coach preached, "Hit harder than you got hit. It won't hurt." After a few meaningful drills, I believed him, and from then on, I'd focus all my energy on hitting others harder than they could hit me. He was a godsend, a new revelation, as if someone had opened Pandora's box, one that released a mix of wisdom and worry and gave me tools I could use in real life. It felt like my life was taking on meaning, and he was installing building blocks inside me like a stone mason building a wall capable of withstanding anything! It also touched on the dangers the box was known for, the dangers from within.

—⚍—

I grew to love that man for who he was and how he made me feel. The power within me that he, and he alone, brought to the surface. He could take raw, untamed power and show you how to direct it into something useful, productive, and fun all at the same time. I have never loved running drills before or since. He was magical at worst and godlike at best. He had the strength of Hercules and the voice of Apollo, and when he clapped his hands in your direction, it was as if Thor had unleashed his hammer onto a hurricane—the thunderous sound vibrated your entire being.

Coach could motivate a tuna sandwich into turning itself back into a 327-pound yellowfin and flopping its way back to the ocean a hundred miles away. He was a true coach. He had the heart of a warrior, the roar of a lion, and the mind of a wolf pack leader. He trained us like a Navy SEAL team, and for a group of freshman Whippets entering the start of a high school career, we had the swagger of seasoned pros.

Everything Coach did had meaning, purpose, and direction. He taught us to think ahead, to plan a path, to know where we were going well before we wanted to get there. His lessons on the field held meaning in life, and he made those lessons pointedly clear. He had plans on top of plans, never failing to know the next move even when he paused to ponder a question. Sometimes his answer would be "Give me ten laps" while he'd think out the right approach. Of course, I didn't pick up on the ten-lap delay for some time; he did it so well I just thought it was planned. This guy could command the grass to grow better, faster, and with more pride.

When the weather was nice, he'd break out the water hose and create a mud pit so we wouldn't "get too comfortable or forget how to clean our gear or the importance behind his lessons." He had us running in formation, singing cool songs about an airborne ranger and a girl on a corner in Arizona. I was so happy just in his presence. I wanted to please him, and I wanted his approval and his attention—and he never failed to give it. His smile was always showing his teeth as his grin opened his face like a Saturday-morning cartoon character. His dark-brown eyes were lasers, and when he focused on you, you knew he was proud of you, even when you played poorly or made a mistake. His trademark statement about mistakes was "Don't worry about it. Just hit them harder to make up for it." And it worked.

We'd turn our mistakes into aggression focused on the enemy. We were banding together like a group of West Point grads after four years of military training ready to take on the world. He set up a scrimmage with another local team, and we chewed them up, ground them into the dirt, bit their ankles, and hit them so hard their coach stopped the practice game early because of all their injured players.

Coach had us so pumped up we were thinking we could take on the JV team for our next matchup before our first real game. So we started chirping at the older players, challenging them to play us. But it was quickly silenced by the old head coach, who said he liked what he saw, but we were all on the same team. We didn't agree. We were special, a unit in and of itself, a breed of breed, untouchable as Al Capone until the IRS caught up with him.

As the buzz kept growing and the days got closer and closer to our first game, I couldn't think of anything else but our first real contest. I was an outside linebacker and the tailback. Jonny Bender and I would swap in and out of the tailback position. He had amazing speed, and I lived to hit things—thunder and lightning, long before the New York football giants Ron Dayne and Tiki Barber likened the phrase.

Jonny Bender really was an awesome player. His speed, quick cuts, and ability to move were fun to watch—if not for his one flaw, his only mistake(s). Jonny had a habit of forgetting the ball. He would run like the wind, but somehow he couldn't seem to keep track of that pigskin and keep it with him. He was like Speedy Gonzales running and holding the football like a superhot tamale that burns your hands if you touch it for more than a few seconds.

Victor Agosto was a wideout and had to be the prettiest boy in our entire class. Perfect hair and silky skin most women would kill for. His deep-blue eyes were like the Wyoming sky on a perfect day. A smile that girls giggled over whenever he'd pass them by. Jonny and Victor could handle two things really well, girls and running the football, fumbles aside. I, on the other hand, never fumbled, but I also avoided open-field running since pounding into the defense was so much more fun.

Coach set up a dinner for our team on the eve of our opening game. He called the dinner a "gathering of warriors, to feast and revel before the next day's battle." He said it was a time of bonding. A time to enjoy all the hard work we had put into becoming "men," as he would call us. It was so much fun I almost didn't believe it was real.

Before the pizzas hit the tables, Coach Perfect rolled out the game plan for the next day. He gave a speech letting us know how proud he was of all of us. He went on to call out each player with his special brand of recognition for the growth and accomplishment earned over the past month plus. One player reminded Coach of his statements from the very first day, and Coach never missed a beat. "You've done what I've asked. You've put the blood and sweat into learning to battle. If we don't have that perfect season, it will be my fault, not yours. If you execute, if you never lose faith and never quit, you will be legions. That I promise you!"

After a moment of quiet pause, our team captain piped in. "You coached us perfectly. We won't let you down."

Before the captain's words could be placed in their proper folder, deep in our memories, someone added, "Coach Perfect." A few others followed before the entire team said, "Thank you, Coach Perfect."

And with that, the name stuck, as did our intentions. We were not going to let him down. We'd fight, battle for the man who had trained us to be warriors—Coach Perfect.

When I got to the house after the team dinner, Crazy was waiting for me. He started making demands about my working after school. My paper route had to be given up because football was after school, and Crazy said I needed to get a "real" job. A new requirement came into play as well: getting on the honor roll if I wanted to play football. Of course, I still needed to have a job. Getting a B average was not in the works. Hell, just getting a B was an adventure for a single class, but a B average to make the honor roll was never going to happen, and he knew it. I would have to leave the team, and there was nothing I could do to stop it. My heart ached all night as the dream season slipped away along with the slice of happiness holding me together.

The next morning, I was turning in my gear. Coach Perfect came to talk to me and asked if he could try to do something. I wanted to play so badly that I sidestepped my fears that Crazy would take it out on Coach Perfect (I could only hope, right?)— or more to the point, retaliate against me or Mother, my brother, and the poor dogs, kicking them out of the blue with no warning. It was never fun to witness, but here it was, the life in front of me. I should have known better than to get my hopes up. "Coach, if you can keep me on the team, I would be forever grateful. But be careful." My words slipped past my tongue without thinking.

Coach Perfect never let his smile fade, never hinted about his plan. He just said that if it was all right with me, he'd like to give it a shot. When he asked, "What do you have to lose?" I wanted to answer, but he cut me off, saying, "You don't have to answer that."

Then his face changed to something I'd never seen before. It had a look of fortitude, of resolve. Not mean but, rather, a surefire determination in his eyes that made me feel like there was a chance.

I wished him luck and told him that if he could get me back on the team, I'd never let him down.

His response was "Are you kidding me? You're a great kid with a huge future in front of you. Let me down? That could never happen. You have a special way about you, and I want to help where I can. I see greatness in you, with football as a learning field. You have a great life ahead of you."

—◆—

He made me feel like I mattered, like I meant something to someone, and that place in my chest normally reserved for that foul, hurtful pain and anguish melted into a powerful happiness that felt as if it would explode through my chest bone and pop right out onto the locker room tile. This was such a better feeling than what I was used to; Coach Perfect had done it again, given me hope and a glance at life aside from that which made up my daily existence. Before I could say another word, he wrapped his bodybuilder arms around my neck and with a pat on the head told me he'd go to battle for me.

"Go to battle" for me. He loved to say those words. "Men, let's get ready to go to battle." He used "battle" to describe our practices, to signal we were warriors preparing for battle. Our helmets and pads were our gladiator tools, the armor we donned before entering the ring. Now he was using it directly for me—someone willing to defend me, at least to get me back on the team. My hope to remain part of the best thing I'd ever been involved in was in his hands, and I quietly asked for help from any other sources. I wanted this so badly I couldn't stand it, but for now, it was in Coach Perfect's hands. As he marched off, he turned his head back to me. "Keep the faith, and I'll be back soon."

Crazy was a huge thing, and compared to Coach Perfect, he was outright tiny. He had long, pointed fingers with the strongest nails known outside of hell's creation. When he poked you with a finger, it hurt, and he knew it. He had a method of jabbing your chest or your forehead in rhythm with his rants. His black hair was slicked back from his forehead with the sides greased over his ears, something right out of fifties films. He wore white T-shirts with his cigarettes rolled into the sleeves until he was ready for the next smoke.

Crazy had a beard sometimes and was clean-shaven other times. One look wasn't worse than the other, as both gave off the same appearance of wicked delight. His arms were muscular, enough to impress a child, but by high school, their threatening size was waning. He was not tall but not short, maybe around five foot nine inches when he wore his hardened boots with lifted heels. He didn't shower much or brush his teeth very often. The yellow plaque would build up so much he would scrape it with those devil claws from time to time. The smell coming from his mouth of decay, cigarettes, and alcohol created a scent that has never been replaced—nor will it ever, I hope. That smell just under his breath carried a body odor he tried to cover up with Right Guard out of a can, which he'd use like a woman spraying her beehive hairdo, hoping it would hold for eighteen hours without reapplication. It only worked for a short while to mask his unpleasant if not offensive aroma, which showed up several feet before he did. If he passed you on the street, you'd think a garbage truck was parked at your next step.

He was a machinist by trade, and grease and oil were always part of his perfume combination. His hands were stained with oil, and when he hit you after his workday, that smell would dig deeper than the cuts and bruises, remaining and reminding you as it tickled your nose for hours on end like a torturer's vise clamping around your emotional grip on reality, swinging back and forth from current to past memories. You never could get away from those smells, and to this day, I get sick to my stomach when the right combination of odors connects with my nose and attacks my senses, triggering a violent reaction.

Crazy was about 175 pounds at his height of monstrous affairs, but that wasn't his weapon. It was his temper. His temper had a wild life of its own, and when it got loose, it had a strength that can only be described as demonic or maybe possessed. It had to be witnessed to truly be understood. While I don't encourage anyone to truly witness this level of insanity, I'll do my best to walk you through it.

Crazy had some strength to him, but when the other animal came out to play, you could watch it overtake his physical body. It would transform him into a powerful being not of this world, yet when you looked into his eyes, it was him, all of him, staring back at you with death in full view. Even on his best days, little did real life stir from his darkened sockets, as if a temporary mask was in place over true evil.

When Crazy called for a dog, Mother, or a child to come and they didn't, he'd transform like the Hulk focused on pure harm, absolute pain, and how best to administer the joyful delight with the wooden stick, a backhand, his fist, or the seasoned leather strap he cherished so much. Crazy had a coil-like hair poking out of each nostril. You could see he'd use clippers to shorten them, but only just past the openings. The buildup of hair poking down those two holes made for a ghastly sight. Looking someplace other than his eyes, nose, or yellowed teeth only angered him more, so it was best to blur your vision so you weren't focused on any part of his outer being. Of course, that opened another quatrain that led to seeing what floated around him!

When I was young and looking up into those hair caves and the hollowed, rotting mouth, it was terrifying, and when I got older, it was just gross. He'd spit when he got in your face, and it would stick like glue until you could scrub it off. When the darkness inside Crazy made its appearance, it would give him a strength several times his normal handiwork. I don't believe Crazy could control the animal. It lived within him and came out to play once his buttons were pushed or he was triggered like a switch. There was never a real way to know when it would appear. But you could see it wind up or start to take shape, and when it started, there was no backing down until the animal had been fed. It was like an energy field started to build around him, a bubble that grew, much like a child playing with soap and a plastic circle—just add a puff of air, and watch the bubble grow. Except this bubble was a ball of evil with the power to cause damage, hurt living beings, or worse. I was hoping Coach Perfect wouldn't have to deal with either Crazy or his animal partner.

Dealing with teammates over leaving football was as tough as it could get. Telling Beth was even worse. She was my heartthrob and the best friend a guy like me could have. The rest of the players sported their game jerseys while mine, number 42, sat in the coach's office with the rest of my gear. It was a long morning until just before lunch. The speaker cracked to life ordering me to the coach's office. It wasn't the main office, so it couldn't be that bad, I hoped.

I was surprised to see Coach Perfect talking to the old head coach, who had my helmet in his hand. It seemed Coach Perfect had some news and wanted the old coach to be a part of it, or maybe a witness. They informed me my parents had changed their minds, and I was back on the team. My heart raced with excitement and disbelief. I could hardly believe it was true. Coach Perfect had somehow pulled off the impossible but didn't want to say much about how he had done it, and I didn't really care. I just wanted to play football, and now I was back in the game.

I gathered my gear and found a small pile of twenty-dollar bills in the helmet. No note, just a small pack of money. When I asked Coach Perfect about it, he just said it was part of the deal. I should buy lunch or something, and if I needed anything else, just let him know. Once again, Coach Perfect had given me hope and let me know someone cared. He had gone to battle for me…"keep the faith" flashed across my mind.

On the bus before each game, Coach Perfect would command us to keep quiet on the ride to the battlefield. Think of all the plays we worked on, visualize how we'd perform each play and how we'd tackle the ball and keep our enemy from our land, our end zone. "Nothing can stop you," he would say, "except yourself, and you've been trained. You've worked harder than any other team, so together you are unstoppable."

If he heard a sound coming from within that bus he didn't like or felt we were not preparing for battle, he'd lecture us on mental toughness, mental discipline, and preparation as keys to success in any of life's endeavors. He had us ready to fight before the opening bell. When we got to the field, he'd tell us to put on our helmets and *"prepare for battle!"* Coach Perfect would do this in a way that shattered any fear that entered your existence. He had our energy at its peak power setting, ready to redline and chew through our opponents at the sound of the first whistle.

We'd get off the bus in perfect formation, lining up like the best World War II vets at a November 11 parade, pumping out the same pride and eagerness presented only by those who had earned the title of warriors. We were Coach Perfect's warriors, ready to face the enemy and eat them alive—or at least pound them into the muddy ground of a middle-class auxiliary playing field used by the varsity squad for practice. But to us it was the parade grounds of Utah Beach, and we were landing like my grandfather nearly four decades earlier. We were walking on air while our historical footwear was clinking on the pavement in drumming unison, each step in harmony with the rhythm of our determination. As we marched from the bus to the field, eyes looked upon us as if to say, "Holy crap! Who are these guys?" and "How come our team doesn't look that good?" It was another masterpiece of discipline by Coach Perfect.

You could feel the fear growing from the opposing team and their fans as we quickly and efficiently moved in perfect concert across the parking lot, double-time marching once we hit the edge of the playing field and its few remaining blades of grass, locked inside the old gated fields of glory—and I mean past glory, as some of the fields still had potatoes on the ground from last planting season's harvest. But it was the Notre Dame stadium to us, and we loved it so.

We won our first few games but made a number of mistakes. If not for our training, we might have surrendered to frustration, but Coach Perfect kept us focused. Our defense had done a masterful job by shutting out our opponents, keeping them out of the end zone, and we had a perfect 3–0 record without giving up a point. The buzz was moving around the freshman class. Even some older players were encouraging us during school and at practice. We worked harder and harder without failure. We would hit the dummies like Superman flying through the air, our cloaks and capes as protection. We kept ourselves laser focused, still first on the practice field and last off.

We pounded away game after game, hammering team after team. Day in and day out, Coach Perfect taught us lessons of football and how to win. He set goals for every aspect of our training. The harder our bodies became, the harder he'd press us on mental toughness. Being mentally prepared was "second to nothing," Coach Perfect would preach. He was always teaching us, and we soaked it in.

After each game, Coach Perfect would huddle us away from the waiting crowds, parents for the most part, giving us final notes on the overall effort and our performance throughout the sixty minutes of playtime. Coach Perfect never talked down to us, never blamed anyone for mistakes except himself. Everything in my life to this point had been my fault. It was my fault Crazy lost his job or the rent didn't get paid. I was the reason Mother lived in such poverty. It was me who ate all the food, which was why my sisters didn't have anything to eat, no milk to drink, or any breakfast. It was my fault the lights got turned off—I didn't run fast enough to get to the power company before they closed at 5:00 p.m. to give them one month's payment on the three months owed. It was my fault. I was the reason Crazy was beating Mother and me. I caused him to whip the dog or blacken eyes with his fists. It was my fault he had to rip out chunks of Mother's hair and smash her to the floor. I was the reason Crazy kicked her broken body. Even as Coach Perfect mouthed his words of praise, the hurt was so deep my soul would feel it for lifetimes to come. This was what played out in my mind when I listened to Coach Perfect take full responsibility, full blame for all mistakes. He'd take all the responsibility for our mistakes, the team's error, a single bad play, or even when Jonny fumbled the ball. It was his fault and his alone. Coach Perfect would go on to tell us that leadership starts and ends at the top—the failures were caused by a lack of coaching, a lack of the people in charge to fully train us so we wouldn't make mistakes. Lessons without blame!

This concept triggered great havoc in my mind, at the same time opening a new manner of thinking. Maybe I wasn't to blame for all the troubles in Crazy's life or in mine. Was that possible? The building blocks Coach Perfect placed inside me cast a concrete foundation that started a change in my fundamental way of thinking. A new approach to my life, the past, the present, and where I was going. Was it possible that life and a football coach's words could be interchangeable? As he spoke, I entered into a subterranean thought process, playing out how this concept would work in real life. How to use football verbiage in day-to-day matters as they came along. Would I be able to translate his words to real-life battles, or did I dare not open myself to hope, as it surely would be smashed under Crazy and Mother's boot print of disapproval?

While Coach Perfect was continuing to speak about the game,

I looked over at the sidelines in the vain hope of seeing someone who was there to watch me play. I searched the crowd of teammates' parents and family as they talked with such big smiles. Bouncing happiness surrounded them as they tried to keep warm in the biting cold of late fall in New England. I searched the crowd hoping to see a face, any face that knew me, knew who I was, or knew something about me or how I played that day—how I played any day. But once again, nothing. No one was there for me. No one had watched me run the ball, pound the pigskin into the defenders, and fight for yardage with a resolve to never fumble and always keep moving forward. There was no one to see me tackle the other team's running backs or intercept a pass meant for the sideline with the hope that the outside backer wasn't paying attention—but I was always on my toes, never asleep no matter where I was or what time of day it became. I'd never let Coach Perfect down by failing to do my job, to cover the receiver in my zone or let that ball get out of my hands.

As the team broke from the coaching debrief, everyone was allowed to head over to the sidelines to share their joy with parents, friends, and so many family members attending a late-afternoon freshman football game on a weekday. I was amazed to see just how many people had shown up for some of the guys. We all dispersed and moved along toward the cheering fans with smiling faces: grandmas bundled up with curly gray hair poking out of their hand-knitted yarn head coverings; grandfathers with their hands and arms over their heads like today's version of "raise the roof." There were cheers to greet their pride and joy, pats on the shoulder pads of a son for playing so very well, proudness beaming from their faces.

It became overwhelming, so I turned away as sadness gripped my chest. I looked at the ground as the only place of comfort. I started toward the bus with my head facing the broken shards of grass as the excitement of the game began fading into a memory. The thought of an hour or two from then, having to make that daily decision to put one foot in front of the other and head back to that house. My stomach started to growl with the early-evening hunger calls of a slim promise of filling its requests, just one more worry to build on during the short couple of hours until I was back at Crazyville.

As I cleared the muddy field, I was joined by another teammate who didn't have anyone there. We ended up meeting just past the fan section and together finished the lonely walk to the empty bus. Of the eighteen or so freshmen on the team, my Ukrainian friend Myron, perfectly named like the fifth-century BC Greek sculptor, also didn't have many guests show up to games, but he did have some of the best sisters a brother could ask for—five of them. They'd come to the games when they could, which always made him smile. As we met just off the muddy field, we'd bump shoulder pads and kick around stories from the game like how I needed to stop running up his ass and pushing him into the guy he was going to block.

Myron was a hell of a blocking back, and between him and John Hope, they could help open a hole for the ball carrier like no others. Of course, I wouldn't agree with his review of the event and told him to run faster, or I'd keep pushing him face-first into the oncoming tackler's traffic. Myron and I would meet for that slow walk after half the games. The other times, I was all alone.

On the bus, Myron and I talked about the game, girls, and

other things young men discuss, but we never talked about family. We both had a life outside of normal, and we never really let it come into play. We just knew it was what it was, but at the same time, we could relate without sharing a word. We had a kind of kinship known only to those who have suffered through lives like ours, so to us, there was nothing really to talk about. It was just known and understood. It sucked, and that was that!

As the other players and Coach Perfect filled the seats and the driver revved up the motor, we got our postgame report and preparation for the final game. We quickly settled in and let the day's victory fade once Coach Perfect raised his commanding tone with a call of *"Listen up!* You played a great game, but we have a lot more to learn if you want to keep your perfect, undefeated streak alive. You're going up against the very best team in the state next week, and on their home field."

It was New London High School, which had a huge team, with more than fifty players on the freshman team alone, compared to our now seventeen players. For us, it was impossible to field fully staffed offensive and defense teams at practice, and we'd have to play both sides of the ball, which I really enjoyed. We were going up against the Whalers. They, too, had a perfect record, and like us, not only were they undefeated, but they were also unscored upon. It was as if Coach Perfect had predicted the future and warned us of things to come. His words from that first meeting echoed throughout the bus.

That's right: neither team had given up a single point in the entire season, not one single point. We'd be heading into the final game of the season going to battle with perfect records. You can't make this stuff up, and believe it or not, it's God's honest truth.

Two Connecticut freshman teams with literally perfect records, undefeated and unscored upon, going head-to-head for the bragging rights to be called the very best—perfect, in fact. The battle line was drawn on the gridiron as the local press jumped into action promoting the upcoming showdown. It was the most exciting time of my life!

Now, I have to tell you, New London is one of the largest cities in eastern Connecticut. It was a rough place and not a backwoods farm country community. They took football as seriously as a Texan does a longhorn brisket on a spit, man-size trucks, hunting, the Second Amendment, and oil rigs. New London had a fan following like no other. They traveled extremely well, and home games were a must-attend no matter what level of football, from peewee to midget, junior high through each level of high school, and when they put players on the field, they were trained and battle-tested combatants.

Losing was not the Whalers' motto; nor was it acceptable. Winning at all costs was their all-or-nothing summation. We'd played against them growing up, and never—I mean never— could we beat those guys. They had heart, iron in their muscles, and speed from the fattest offensive guard to the free safety, who'd claim Barry Sanders couldn't catch him in his bare feet. They had quarterbacks who could throw the pointed circle like a fastball from a triple-A Pawtucket Red Sox pitcher ready for a debut at Fenway Park. They had a ton of coaches, from line to secondary, running back coaches to middle linebacker, and one guy just to teach the quarterback how to move, how to place his feet, how to dance in the pocket, and how to read a defense.

We all knew what we were going into, and it was hard to believe we would come out with a victory, let alone an unscored-upon legacy. Hell, there was no way we could win. No sooner did those thoughts enter my mind than Coach Perfect, who was still giving his prep talk for the coming week, must have read my mind, for just like that he put it out there: "So you guys don't think you can win against such a team, do ya?" How did he do that—read our thoughts like he was in our minds, always one step ahead with a plan for our next mindful wonderment even before we knew we were having the thought? It was almost like he could look into our eyes and see what was behind them, see what was in our hearts, see the fear floating around within us like a Nostradamus predicting trials to come. Those thoughts were locked inside our personal space, where no one was supposed to be able to get a glimmer. Yet somehow Coach Perfect was able to see inside our minds, and I wanted to know how!

It was startling how Coach Perfect could perform this magical mystery, but he could, and when you lost focus, he'd snap out a deep bellow to get you back to where he wanted you. On this day, he was looking at me and caught my focus elsewhere. His words came alive as he said, "You can do this, but it starts with today's mental planning. If you work harder than you have, the hardest in your lives, you can slay this dragon and claim victory over the best football program in the state." The confidence in his voice was contagious, but we all had that nagging history poking at our sensibilities.

New London had become so powerful that a new rule had to

be written just to keep things from getting completely out of control. The league passed a "fifty-point rule," which was directed at New London, who would beat teams so badly, with scores at or near a hundred points. Teams refused to play them, and if a team won by more than fifty points, the coach would be forced to miss all or half of the next game.

New London also had the oldest and longest-running high school football rivalry in the nation with its annual Thanksgiving Day game against Norwich Free Academy. The matchup dates back to the latter half of the 1800s. So when I say they had a following, it means they literally set the bar, along with the historical charts. This was the mighty empire we'd need to strike back at in order to reach our dreams.

Coach Perfect laid out the framework and gave us an attack plan, but would we have the nerve to play it out? That was the question each one of us would work through over the next seven long days. For now, we had the victory bus ride in front of us and a bucketload of youthful, unadulterated singing and backslapping. Coach Perfect gave us the hour-long ride to enjoy the feeling, and then we were to get back to our next game plan, start thinking ahead, and be ready for the next day's practice. Coach Perfect even got us film room time, weight room passes, and special permission to practice the day of the varsity game so we could work on our plan to take down the mighty Whalers.

—⚋⚋—

New London is an old-town whaling and seaport village dating back to just after the *Mayflower* gang struck their rock in Plymouth,

Massachusetts. It's also home to Benedict Arnold's historical and treasonous attempt to steal the American Revolution from those patriots who fought so hard for freedom from taxation without representation. Ironically, the New London versus Norwich Free Academy rivalry, the campus of our nation's longest competition, is just a few minutes' walk to the place where the General Turncoat family home had been, back before someone decided it wasn't worth saving as a national landmark. There is a small plaque along the edge of the current homestead so locals can remember the West Point–selling egghead who, quite candidly, would have become a national treasure if not for the little mix-up in the color coordination of his final wardrobe. Coach Perfect used the traitor's namesake to fuel our team harmony and paste the Whalers as yellow-and-green cousins to Arnold. "If you stick to the plan, they'll turn on themselves. That's your edge," he'd hammer from that ride onward. I didn't understand his intention, but I believed him all the same.

As the week wore on, the school days were as enjoyable as I can ever remember, with happy times and feelings of being involved in something bigger than ourselves. It seemed everyone was getting in on the festival, the buildup to the pending fight of the century. Even teachers were excited for us. It felt so wonderful, and I wished I could live in those moments for the rest of my life. Of course, I dared not mention a word to Crazy, nor bring the happy excitement to that house. I locked it away steps before I reached the side door on my paced nightly journey.

At the same time, teachers were trying to get me to work on my grades, but I had little interest. Many teachers tried to help, and honestly, without their constant pushing, pulling, and heartfelt efforts, I never would have made it past my second year. And if not for football and a coach who had my attention, things would have ended so much differently. The reality of my life outside of school was only a part of the difficulties I was facing, and again, few knew the factors handicapping my abilities.

At one point when a teacher challenged me to read the questions before filling in the circles, I frustrated her so badly I had to deal with the principal. The teacher wanted to get Crazy and Mother involved, but somehow it was agreed that it might be best to see if he and I could figure out a path to advancement and better grades without Crazy getting a call. If my grades slipped further, the school would suspend me from the team. I had to find a path forward.

I agreed to be in school an hour early to meet with this teacher each day. Halfway into the first hour session and with the teacher's growing frustration, I finally let the cat out of the bag. "*I can't read*" roared past my lips.

With a quiet sigh and a thoughtful pause, this teacher said, "Well then, we know where we stand. That's our starting point."

This revelation opened doors for the teaching staff to work with me in a fashion that could get me learning while not publicly exposing my limitation. It also kept the embarrassing secret securely placed in professional hands. More importantly, at least to me, it kept me on the team.

The day before the big game, Crazy asked me about the pending matchup. I'm not sure where he learned about it, so I had to ask.

Turned out the local paper had run a story about the successful young football team and the gridiron matchup the following day. Crazy always wanted his hand on the wheel so he could "educate" me on the ways of life. We spent the entire night splitting time between his brown bottles and his wisdom. He enlightened me with his expertise on New London, its people, and his vast knowledge of how professional football was to be played.

I made a conscious decision to keep as tight lipped as possible, not getting into it with him, as I was sure his plan was to prevent me from going to the game or somehow make something happen so I'd end up having to sit out the game. He made it clear we had no chance to beat the souped-up Whalers. He let me know I was too small for football. I was too fat and too slow to "ever be any good," and I should just give it up and go to work. I'd never be smart enough to learn the complex plays, which required a machinist's knowledge to advance in that field, and of course my lack of skills would have me on the bench pouring water for the players as my best contribution. Mother did her best to keep things calm and push back against the onslaught of negative assessments, including the team's chances of winning.

There was something in Crazy's tone, though, something that had my mind wondering why he didn't go down the alley to make sure I would miss out on the big game, and after his dark bottle of rum or scotch was almost gone and the 1:00 a.m. clock hands met, Crazy let something slip that made me think Coach Perfect may have paid him a visit. Crazy mentioned the size of the coach and his accent—while he didn't have a strong one, his voice did have a sound that stood out. When Crazy commented on the sound of Coach Perfect's voice, and I knew he'd never been to a game—or anything else at the school, for that matter—I wondered if it was possible that Coach Perfect had had a one-on-one with Crazy.

Was that the reason Crazy had left me alone since I had been allowed back on the team? I liked to think Coach Perfect flexed his Hercules-like arms around Crazy's stranglehold on others and let him know he'd be back if need be. Thoughts like that made me smile, but at the same time, it was troubling because as soon as the season was over and Coach Perfect had no leverage over Crazy, things would be back to normal, and I was sure Crazy would take revenge, claiming I'd sicced the gorilla-sized coach on him. That was something I'd deal with later. For now, Crazy was off to his nest with a freshly opened bottle and one hazy eye closed.

As I started up the stairs on my way to bed, I swear I heard Mother yell out, "We'll try to make your game tomorrow!" It was a strange thing to hear from her, but a hope all the same! Crazy and Mother had never been to a game, so why would this one be different? On one hand, I wanted anyone to be there for me, but on the other, I would just have to worry about what they would do. It was best if they just didn't show up. A new worry for my tired plate.

I went to my room, barricaded the door, and tried to sleep. My brother, awakened by my shuffling, offered a heartfelt "Good luck tomorrow, brother" seconds before his snoring filled the small box of a room.

My stomach growling, calling for a meal to fill that void, I pressed my eyes closed and focused on my assignments, now only sixteen hours away. The hunger waned as I basked in the dreams of scoring a touchdown and sacking the QB. Crushing tackles of the ball carriers. Making hits that would create fumbles and playing a perfect game. Fantasizing a final score of Whippets 75, Whalers 0.

With that smile locked across my teeth and my pillow snug under my ear, I started to drift into a deep, calming sleep.

As I felt peace taking hold, I saw a burly, furry, four-legged beast standing in the distance, a golden sun-draped sky behind his magnificent, statuesque figure. Dark shades of brown curly fur transitioned to lighter-brown textures toward his tail and under-belly. Two powerful horns atop his mighty head. Huge round eyes, black in color but a lightened black, one that felt inviting. A snort sprayed a mist from his nose, as if he were offering a gesture of greeting. A head bob just as his left hoof pumped the dirt below his hardened shoe. His eyes provided a knowing that rang deep within my bowels—an understanding of things to come without a single word passing the mind. A feeling that would cling to your viscera, as if someone were giving you a hug from the inside out. Such a warm embrace—I felt my cheeks touching the corners of my eyes just before I slipped into the most peaceful night's sleep I could remember. The mighty beast stood tall as if a protector against un-seeable forces that would not get past the four-legged guard.

What was that sound snapping me out of a restful sleep? A crack from the bottom landing where the stairs turned toward the second landing just seven steps from the hallway, and then only feet from my bedroom door. That brief relief just before the sounding alarm felt so good, but it was dangerous to get comfortable in this house. Crazy could sneak up on you like a snake in water on a moon-less night with your dreams dangling like toes above the water on a dock before fire rips through your body with pain and venom surely intended to kill you. If not today, it was coming, so never let your guard down, and always keep one eye open in the house of Crazy.

The next sound I heard was at the top of the stairs. A little creaking, but which way was he heading? There was a long pause of heart beating and breath holding as I waited for the next sign, the next signal of where this thing would be heading.

And then it happened. I heard a slight jiggle of a metal knob. The turn-of-the-century door hardware let me know Crazy was at the door and headed into the room, but this time it was Crazy's bedroom and not mine.

I heard the sound of his door closing and the rustling of bedsprings followed by the headboard hitting the wall as he flopped down to pass out for the short remainder of the night—or at least I could hope. I looked at the clock by my door, and like every other time I saw that replacement clock, its predecessor having bitten me so hard in my face only a few years back, it reminded me of the terrifying night, waking soaked in blood and lost in conscious understanding of what had happened. The peaceful sleep I was enjoying reminded me of that fateful night, the one that changed my face, my nose, forever.

It was 1:27 a.m., and I was in middle school, a sixth grader. I had managed to get a little over an hour's sleep before this latest round of terror never sleeps. Knowing Crazy couldn't make it until morning without having to empty the liver-soaked remains of the brown bottle and its bubbly friends, I knew better than to close both eyes. On this night, I broke that sacred rule, and I never heard him coming.

My brother and I had a digital clock radio. We'd let the music play as we shut down for the night. We'd been warned before not to "waste electricity" playing music while we slept. The clock radio was a rather good-sized one, made from hardened plastic in a stocky, flat, boxlike configuration. It was solid and heavy with its mechanical numbers flipping and clicking as each minute passed.

I don't remember being in a deep sleep, but I do remember what I was dreaming and thinking I was in a pool of water. A beautiful red-tailed hawk was flying against the amber-blue sky as if night and day were mixed into the twilight. As I looked up at the sweeping wings gliding amid the winds, the hawk screeched its mighty call. A warning maybe! At that moment I simply enjoyed the beauty of its phantom brown feathers with cloud-white lines painted in a pattern of shining streaks, watching its peaceful grace floating effortlessly as it searched the land below.

Without warning, the mighty hawk started to dive-bomb straight at me. As it closed the distance, it changed into a monstrous-looking turkey vulture. Its coal-black wings spread to enormous size. Its face changed into a nasty beak with a blood-red attachment flopping from side to side. Its menacing eyes glared, squinting into mine as if it was trying to get me to cover my face, my head. But I couldn't take my eyes off the creature as it plummeted toward my head until *bam!* It crashed its mighty curved flesh carver square into my nose.

Blackness followed. Stunned confusion as to why the mighty hawk would do such a thing. Warm water flooded my face in a blanket of moist heat. The feeling washed into my ear and down my neck. A starry sky replaced the amber blue with total black. Spots twinkled off the shiny, coal-dark backdrop. Just before the crash, I thought the vulture was trying to wrap its wings around me as it changed back into a hawk, its wings trying to gently lower me to the ground under her fluffy, soft protection just before sharp, painful spikes drove across my nose, into my eyes and teeth, piercing deep into my forehead. A crisp flash of light flushed away all the images in a burning sting against my eyes.

—◊—

"I told you *never* to play that damn thing when you sleep."

The shuddering shrill slammed my senses back from the silvery screen and wrapped feathers. My eyes strained under the bright light Crazy had flipped on. His voice rang along with the buzzing in my ears, in my head. My face was soaked and dripping as I tried to make sense of what was happening. Pounding pain peppered my mind as I fought to regain a foothold within. My mind was caught in limbo as it tried to reboot from the jarring of what I had thought was a bird landing on my face.

Reality quickly changed my understanding as the crimson-red blood covered my hands. Shock replaced confusion. The digital plastic box rested beside my pillow. Blood dripped onto its clear screen, covering the numbers. My face was shattered by its weighty bulk.

"If you hadn't left it on, wasting my money, you wouldn't be bleeding, now, would you?" Crazy's next montage of reasoning. "Get yourself cleaned up before your mother gets home, and *don't* get blood on my towels."

My shirt was the closest cloth I could reach to try to smother the gushing bloodstream outside and inside my nose. I made my way to the bathroom. It was a ghastly scene looking back at me in the mirror. Skin was ripped open along one side of my nose. Layers were cut from the bone housing the bridge, folded away from its normal position. Blood poured from the exposed flesh until I rolled the skin flap back into position. My nose crunched with the slightest pressure. Blood was running out of both nostrils, splashing in all directions as it hit the old cast-iron white baked-enamel sink. I knew stitches would be required, at the least, but Crazy was never going to take me to the emergency room. Mother would be at work for several hours.

I cleaned up my room as best as possible. The black-and-white numbers were visible behind the dried-blood-coated clock, its digits stuck at 1:27 a.m. The mattress held another souvenir trademark from Crazy's teachings. Sheets, pillow case, and clothes put into the washing machine. Tape holding a chunk of my shirt over my nose to steady the bleeding. I decided to wait on the front porch for Mother. Crazy was tucked into his private hole, his snoring vibrating the house. As long as that noise was heard, I'd know where he was. How did I allow myself to close both eyes? Had I been alert, I could have protected myself.

Mother's friend pulled up to the curb an hour or so after dawn. She closed the passenger door with a polite "Thank you, and I'll see you this afternoon" before turning to see my bandaged face. "What did you do?" was her greeting as she climbed the steps before we started that long walk to the hospital.

I peeled back the tape, blood sliding from underneath.

She gasped before almost puking. "We need to get you stitches." Three hundred ninety-seven steps to the emergency room double doors.

—◈—

That was a warning in the furry four-legged's eyes, and maybe it was reminding me not to sleep that night. The memory of that night the clock flew snapped me out of the dangerous double-closed-eye sleep. It was just before 1:00 a.m., and I'd better wake up, get dressed, and get out of here. But where? If I brought some blankets, the woods I'd hidden in before, the ones on the college campus. That was my plan, at least for now. I needed to move quickly but ever so quietly.

I danced around the creaky floorboards, balancing along the outer edges, toes tight against the baseboards, a blanket wrapped around my clothes and gear for the game later today. I carefully placed each step, avoiding the stairs known to creak under a foot-step. Squeaks of a bedspring, Crazy moving in his room. I used his noise to quickly yet softly jump the few remaining steps and reached the first floor. Ever so slowly I opened the side door and slipped through the framed gap and into the stiff, cold breeze of the night air. Safety reached, I exhausted my locked lungs, not real-izing I'd stopped short of breathing as I exited hell's grip.

As I went down the side of the house heading toward the street, a slight smile cracked my cold cheeks. Then, suddenly, a flash of light froze my planned steps. Above my head, the light from the bathroom bounced off the white semigloss siding of the neighbors' house. My shadow hit the wall next to my rigid posture. The light shuffled my shadow as the curtain moved in the window above. The pounding in my ears drowned out all sounds as I fought to train my hearing for anything, everything. I stood motionless like a frightened deer poised to run but not sure which direction pointed to safety.

The flush of the toilet sounded exactly like the one in Archie

Bunker's house at 704 Hauser Street, Queens, New York. Water rattled as the flushing gurgle vibrated the wall holding my shadow. The bathroom light went dark, but the hallway light shone through the front window and onto the street. My planned route now illuminated, I held my position. That wasn't normal if Crazy was going back to his room! Behind me another light passed its glare across the small backyard. He was in my room. Noise, voices…shouting! Without thought, I ran toward the street, down the three steps, and onto the sidewalk. I didn't stop running until I was blocks away from that house. The blanket wrapped around my clothes and gear popped open from bouncing on my shoulder. As I tucked the package back together, it felt like something was missing, but I didn't have time or the light to figure it out…"Keep moving. You need to keep moving" flashed across my mind.

The quarter moon and scattered clouds cast darkness over the fields leading to the small wood patch, my intended resting spot. It was too hard to see where I was going, so I decided to keep moving and find another place to get a few hours' sleep. A college cop's cruiser drove along the edge of the field slowly, as if searching. I moved toward his rear, knowing he would turn the corner and be out of sight. This path was the shortest number of steps back to the school. I could tuck myself into an alcove by the gym doors.

The cold air was starting to bite as sweat soaked my underclothes. A film was clinging to my skin, wicking the warmth from my body. I worried that a passing city cop would see me, see the blanket sack hanging over my shoulder, and stop to question what

I was doing on the street in the middle of the night. I watched and listened as if I were still in my room. My ears searched in all directions as I paced the steps toward a cubbyhole and some much-needed sleep. My stomach groaned and tussled with a mighty call for something, anything, to fill its empty space. I knew how to ignore its calls, and I had nothing to offer.

I jumped the locked gate protecting the side entrance and shuffled down the frost-covered grass hill and across the student parking lot. Just behind the varsity locker room door was an emergency exit from the large pool room. That door was never used and had a three-sided brick and cinder block covering—a perfect place to snuggle into a corner and get some rest. I spread out the blanket and assembled the contents into a makeshift pillow. I put on tomorrow's clothes to fight off the cold, crisp air and wrapped the blanket under and around me. I pulled my ball cap over my eyes, rested my head on the frigid steel door, and closed my eyes. My stomach gave one last call before quieting down.

As I drifted off, a snort-filled picture of that four-legged fur ball popped into my mind. A smirk seemed to light up his face as he moved toward me in an ever-so-slow march. The mighty beast settled down right beside me and tucked its legs under its chest. His head and shoulders pressed against the weathered side of my concrete box shelter. It was as if the animal was trying to provide his warmth and keep the wind from penetrating the thin blanket. It was so comforting. Sleep quickly followed with a feeling of protection hulked next to me...I was safe!

—◈◈◈—

"Hey, you can't sleep here. You need to get moving. Students will be coming soon."

The warning jarred me awake. Lifting my eyes, lifting the bill of my ball cap, I saw the old janitor, Mr. Spencer. He was a kind man, always had a smile on his face and a cheerful tone in his voice. This awakening was not as friendly until he realized who I was. "Boy, why you sleeping out here? What's going on?" he asked. Without waiting for a response, he said, "Get up, and I'll let you in the locker room. But you better not tell anyone I did this, you hear?"

The morning's light was just breaking over the hillside parking lot as I gathered myself and headed inside the musky-smelling sports center. The warmth felt like a godsend as my body tried to stop shivering from the cold bricks lining my bed.

"You should take a hot shower and warm up."

A great idea. I shoved my blanket into my locker and stripped down to my birthday suit before heading into the steaming warmth of a hot shower. Mr. Spencer left the room, but not before telling me to find him if I needed a place to sleep again. The gesture sent waves of emotion through my cheeks, my head. I give him a nod of appreciation and respect.

Cleaned, steamed, and warmed to the bone, I wrapped the musky towel, which smelled of locker room and jockstrap, around my waist. Sitting in front of my locker, I saw an envelope sticking out from under my blanket. It was a note from Coach Perfect. Inside, a meal pass for the cafeteria. Breakfast and lunch passes along with a twenty-dollar bill. The note said, "I need a star player to be fully charged for the game—get plenty to eat and get ready for BATTLE!"

I almost started to cry, but if I did, it wouldn't look good, since the locker room was filling up. So I sucked it up, put my head down, and simply whispered, "Thank you." Who I was talking to was both Coach Perfect and whoever was helping me without showing me who they were or how they managed to hear my whispered pleas for help. Somehow I had what I needed, as if someone was watching over me! I wiped the mist from my face and quickly made my way from the gym to the dining hall.

I filled a tray with everything the ticket would allow—and I mean everything. My stomach reached for items faster than my hands, piling more on my tray than John Belushi in *Animal House* just before the "guess what I am" scene. The lunch lady started to question my choices but decided against asking questions.

As I was handing over my meal pass, it hit me: "star player"? Where did that come from, and how could it possibly have been in the note? I looked over the note again, thinking I was not a star. It made me smile, but the checkout lady wasn't as pleased, as she questioned how much the pass would allow on a tray. Maybe it was my brown eyes or my smile. Maybe the growling from my stomach. But she didn't debate long before sending me on my way with my pyramid of treats, eggs, and pancakes.

Now, this might sound strange, but I so enjoyed school cafeteria food. Maybe it was that much better than what I was used to, or maybe those lunch ladies knew exactly how to feed kids from the wrong side of the tracks. I would listen to my classmates bitch about how bland and gross the cafeteria food was, but to me it was heaven. Every bite was a flavor fiesta of happiness crossing my hot-sauce-fearing taste buds, which were jumping with delight at the variety of swirling goodness dancing on my tongue.

I picked a table away from everyone else. That is, until Victor, a favorite friend, strutted through the doors. He made a beeline for me, and as he sat down, he told me, "Your brother is looking for you." He followed with "They called my house looking for you really early this morning. Said I'd hadn't seen you." Victor was at odds with his Puerto Rican father, and they seemed to be waging war, at least since his sister was killed in a car wreck two years back. I was going to offer him my tray, but he was already picking at it, so I pushed it toward him.

My brother walked into the open area and picked me out without much effort. "He came looking for you. Where were you?" he asked.

Victor pushed the tray in his direction, and they both dug into the variety of treats. I never would have finished it all anyway, and I knew others would be hungry, maybe part of the reason I overloaded the ticket.

"He's pissed and ripped up the place looking for you. Cops were still there when I left. Not sure who called, but might have been the neighbors. He was pretty loud. Good thing you weren't there; would have been a long one. Anyway, good luck at the game, and I hope he doesn't find you before the game."

I didn't respond to either of them, but that was normal, so they didn't press the matter. It was just short of eight hours before the big game, and I was hoping—praying, really—that nothing else would get in the way. At least for now it seemed to be working out.

Belly full and with a bag of goodies for after the game, I headed off to homeroom, trying not to worry about anyone coming to find me. Who'd think about looking at school for a missing kid, which would be the last place you'd run away to, right?

Wrong. I wasn't in my seat more than a minute before the vice principal, along with a cop in full uniform, was standing in the classroom doorway. He pointed to me and motioned with his finger, a polite head pull, and a silent mouthing of "We need to see you."

You would think a cop pulling a kid out of class would have the school abuzz with rumors. Yet when it happened to me, it didn't seem to generate much attention, at least as I saw it. The cop questioned my "whereabouts," and I simply told him I had left early. He laughed a bit, and to my delight, that appeared to be the end of it. Of course, I'd need to go back there at some point, but for now it was over.

I sat in English class as the teacher rambled on about pronouns, how to write a sentence, and "adjunct professors" of some kind, and I frustratedly thought, I'll never need this crap, and who cares about the use of punctuation? It's a complete waste of my time, right? I was bored to sleep and thinking there were only two classes until we headed to the big showdown.

The loudspeaker in the English room crackled to life with the principal calling attention to everyone in the school. He authorized all freshman football players and those who were taking the bus to the game to be excused from class and report to the gym immediately in preparation to leave before the end of the day. *Woo-hoo!* I was breaking free just like Willy, and before the teacher could get a single word out of her mouth, I was out the door, down the hall, and past Orca, our "fake-pass-killing" hall monitor, who approached her job as if she were undercover for the CIA. She was demanding I prove I had permission to be in the halls. "I'll write you up, young man. Get back here," she shouted.

I showed her my signaling finger as I turned the corner and

went down the stairs to the gym. My feet barely touched the ground, as my level of excitement was so great I felt I could fly the rest of the way. All my worries disappeared, and nothing mattered except a single football game—perfect versus perfect!

—m—

Fifteen excited young football players piled into the yellow chariot. Gear was packed into adjacent seats. The air crackled with a hum and buzz like high-tension electrical wires. There were hand slaps and high fives as we fired one another up. I could feel the scent of nervousness drifting through the winds of hyped manhood. The feelings of fear were masked by the bravado of raised chants and fist pumps. Coach Perfect squeezed past the door and up the rubber-coated steps. "Settle down, get those game faces on, and start thinking about the battle plan."

Coach Perfect's command, as if he had snapped his fingers, brought each of us to attention, then into alignment. We took our seats and settled down for the hour-plus ride. The soft moan of the wheels and the engine vibration and lack of sleep put me into a very relaxed state. Without realizing my eyes had closed, I drifted off into a peaceful, calm sleep.

The rumble of the bus and the bumps in the road kept me fast asleep. Knowing I was someplace other than the house of Crazy, I felt a deep sense of REM take hold. The sounds drifted into the background, and the lush green turf of a well-groomed football field materialized, like the view through a kaleidoscope. It shifted in and out of focus until it rested in a perfect vision of lines, numbers, and sideline markers.

High above the field, a hawk glided on invisible currents. A light-blue sky highlighted her outstretched wings. She looked down with her yellow-streaked brown eyes as if she were looking directly into my soul. She was telling me something, but I couldn't understand it, and words were not her medium. A sense of knowing transferred from her to me, yet I couldn't know what the message was. It felt right, as if everything was going to be okay. Still, a bit of doom was mixed into the missing words.

The hawk nose-dived toward the field. A flash of chaos shone across the grassy surface. Hundreds of images packed into one. A feeling of hate and fear lashed out as the shifting mass thrashed like prey caught in Charlotte's web. The focus shifted once again as the kaleidoscope repositioned. The hawk flapped its wings before being lost in the distant tree line.

As I looked back at the field, off to the side, close to the stands, an image took shape. My heart smiled as I sensed her face, her short, slender build with her perfectly dressed appearance. A fan at the game for me? It couldn't be. Was it real? Bethany shone through the haze of the dream. Her smile lit my heart as she'd done so many times since the first day I saw her in seventh grade.

The beauty of seeing Bethany disappeared as the kaleidoscope shuffled the image, and a feeling of evil gripped my overstuffed stomach. Gray shadows crept over the field like storm clouds in front of a hurricane, its leading edge giving warning of tidal surges and deathly winds. Cold snapped against my face as if I were just waking up that morning in the frigid, biting brick Bilco door opening.

The scene showed the parking lot as my fellow players charged toward their destiny. A sense of fear tightened its grip, as a cop was waiting as I stepped off the bus. Next to him, Crazy stood with his infamous look of triumphant glory gleaming its martyrdom glow. He pointed and nudged the cop toward me. *"Arrest him,"* demanded the vision. My stomach clenched into a fist of knotty pine sap, threatening to expel my best meal in months. The sound you make as you hover over the flushing throne became so loud it slashed me out of the kaleidoscope's tube and back to my seat.

My mind had barely reset when a teammate three seats in front and to the left fought to open the double-latched window. His cheeks filled; his head pumped back and forth; his neck bulged. A couple of inches of air blew inside as he heaved a mighty burst, mostly hitting the glass and ricocheting in every direction. The opening served only to whip the puked remains into a swirling mist. Several more pumps of gut juices caused the entire team to revolt in disgust and shock, the stink forcing others to hold tightly so as not to follow.

The bus pulled off the highway and shed the sick player, leaving him to a following parent. Our water bucket cleared most of the mess. Shirts, towels, and rags did the rest. "Anyone else eat too much before getting on board?" Coach Perfect asked. "Get your heads back where they belong," he said as the bus tussled out of the emergency lane. The team having only fourteen players left didn't seem to faze our leader. The rest of us were as concerned as we could get.

Coach Perfect didn't let the chatter go unnoticed. "Listen up," he said, collecting our attention, and then he walked through the first series of plays he planned to call. No time to think or focus on our lost mate or my trending visions. Coach Perfect kept our heads exactly where he wanted them, focused on his words and the game plan. He didn't stop until the bus was parked in our enemy's lot. "Put your helmets on, and *get ready for battle*."

As we filed off the bus, the sound of a marching band beat in the background. Assuming the band was at practice, we used the thumping sounds to energize our internal beats. I strained to see past the players, hoping not to see police or Crazy. My heart stopped, as two policemen were on either side of the disembarking teammates. I stepped to the asphalt expecting to be grabbed, but the cops were looking away from me as if searching for something else. Crazy was nowhere in sight. I followed the formation of friends, and we marched in step toward the gridiron. I was relieved that a visionary precept was not fulfilled.

The drumbeat grew louder and more in line with a varsity game day than with practice. We steadily double-timed across the parking lot, down the hill, and through the gate opening. As we entered the field, the stands were filled with hundreds of people. Many more lined the chest-high fences separating the game field from the other parts of the sprawling campus. In the seats to our backs, a few dozen faithful followers had collected in the dropping temperatures, bundled like ski season at Mount Hope in February. Two or three buses of students were yet to arrive, but still, it would be only a fraction of our opponents' community support.

The practicing marching band, a lockstepped horn section followed by a dozen banging drummers, rolled down the hill and onto the sidelines. They were *not* practicing. They were there to perform, and there had to be sixty or seventy members. The sounds were both intimidating and rousing, shocking the senses and mind that a freshman game would generate such a showing. New London was once again showing its colors as the green and gold flashed in every direction, with the exception being the limited attendance behind our bench.

The game clock read two minutes to kickoff. The referees were at midfield. The band was banging away, and the crowd turned to face the oncoming freshman players. Running at almost full speed, the line seemed to stretch the entire hundred yards from end zone to end zone. Their freshman team had more players than our entire high school football team, coaches and fans included. It was a sight to behold and one that took the wind from our unbeaten sails.

National anthem complete and coin toss settled, fourteen shabby friends huddled at midfield. The hammering beat of the band's drums, along with the thunderous chants from the Whalers' fans, reverberated so loudly it was hard to hear the team captain call out the play inside our eleven-man circle. We were spreading our line for kickoff when a sight caught my eye—that hawk, swirling above the far-end goalpost. She wasn't very high. In fact, the bird seemed to be planning to perch on the goalpost, as her circles were growing tighter and tighter before she pointed her beak skyward and shot toward the heavens. Watching the hawk cleared away my pregame jitter as if it was all part of some grand plan.

The whistle collected my focus. The kick drove the ball downfield, and we raced to tackle the opening play. I was moving as fast as I'd ever run, ready to put a hurting on the kickoff returner when my head snapped back and I was plastered to the ground, sliding to a stop, crushed from behind by a blinding illegal backside hit. My breath gone, I gathered my senses and popped back up and joined my fellow teammates in downing the runner. No flag in sight!

We battled with all we had, but the Whalers were running over us. We were intimidated, and it showed. Worse still was the manner of play the Whalers engaged in. We'd learned to be disciplined and focused and to believe fairness would prevail. Between intimidation and unkind play, we were being manhandled. The Whalers drove the ball from their own nineteen-yard line all the way to our ten-yard line. Our scoreless record was about to be blown apart.

"*Time-out!*" shouted Coach Perfect. It was first and goal for the Whalers. The foot stomping from the bleachers matched rhythm with the drumming band. A slow-walking Coach Perfect pointed to huddle up. "So you're gonna let these blowholes outclass ya? Never thought I'd see this group scared, let alone terrified. How come you're letting 'em run all over you?"

Before Coach Perfect could get his next word out, Waz, our captain, piped up. "Coach, they're bigger, stronger, and faster than us, and they're taking cheap shots, holding, punching, kicking... Hell, Jonny's got teeth marks on his leg."

"So, you guys done being pushed around? The cheap shots tell you they can't beat you fair and square! Flags will come; trust me. Now, they've given you everything they have. You've seen how they play and who's who. They are not better than you. In fact, they are worried, *very* worried. They can't understand why they haven't scored yet. If you stop them, keep them from scoring, you will win this game! Now shake off the pity party, get into the fight, and *don't give up another yard*!

"Oh, one more thing: they're getting tired, so when we go on offense, we are going to pick up the pace. *Go get 'em, men!*" Those were Coach Perfect's final words, and he calmly walked away from the huddle.

A new hyped-up ball of energy filled our oval. With a few fighting words tossed among ourselves, we broke the huddle and lined up to stop the surge.

The defensive line broke into the backfield and tackled the running back for a loss of four yards. There was stunned silence from the Whaler fans, but the Whippets assembled let out a roaring cheer of approval. The Whalers' running back pointedly showed discontent with his blockers. "You guys need to do your job..." The rest trailed off under his breath.

The next two plays, we managed to lock them down for a short gain and a loss of one yard. Fourth down and thirteen yards to goal. The Whalers came out in a shotgun. The quarterback took the hike and rolled right. Two receivers broke loose in the end zone. The ball passed the scrimmage line on a frozen rope for their six-foot speedster. Our cornerback, a five-foot-five-inch Italian we called Geo, had great speed and fought to keep up. The Whalers' receiver was putting his hand up, ready to catch the first score against us, when the racing Whippet jumped in front of the pass and intercepted the ball in the end zone.

Without hesitation, Geo bolted forward. All the former defenders picked men and started to move a path of blocks past the ten, the twenty, before a speedster with green and gold ran Geo down from behind. Our fans, our coaches, and the three players on the sideline were screaming with excitement, jumping up and down, yelling as the enthusiasm lifted our spirits as well as our confidence.

Coach Perfect, after settling down from his own jumping jacks, roared for us to line up on the ball. "It's our turn to drive the field." The air was crisp with renewed confidence and a huge dose of relief from holding our scoreless year intact. Three fresh helmets charged from our sidelines as eleven new faces walked toward the opposition's huddle.

We fought and battled our way across midfield, and the first quarter closed out. Coach Perfect stood in the center and gave a vociferous set of "attaboys" and "great jobs," tied to compliments on what we were doing right.

Then he hit us with what we needed to work on. It was as if he wanted the other team to hear what he was saying. It seemed strange, but I caught him looking across the field, wanting a reaction, begging even for the enemy to know that he was rewarding our efforts.

The Whalers' sideline was less positive. Some coaches were belittling players. One coach screamed so loudly I was sure our fans could hear the sneering tirade. It reminded me of Crazy's hurtful words. A sense of sadness washed over me for the players on the receiving end.

Coach Perfect must have noticed that my attention was pointed at the other side. A sharp *"Hey!"* redeployed my focus. "We need to pound the ball until they break. They will get tired, and your training will win the day. This is going to be a *long* battle, so buckle up, get your heads in the fight, and *no* mistakes!" he declared in his softer, determined tone meant for our ears only.

We battled and fought but only moved the ball to just inside their twenty-yard line before turning it over on downs. The Whalers' offense pushed back, but we stopped them at midfield. A squib kick on fourth down netted only eight yards, giving us the ball on our forty-four-yard line. We hammered and hit with all we had without gaining much ground. Our punt pushed them inside their ten as the first half drew to a close.

—∞—

Halftime sent us away from everyone, down a short hill to the backside of an old metal shed sixty yards outside the fence line. Our fans cheered and shouted sentiments of helpfulness: "You can do this. You'll get 'em next half. We believe in you." Family members screamed, "*Proud* of you" toward their offspring from atop the stands. I took a short glance at the excited crowd, not wanting to scan too closely, as it would only get my hopes up, yet I still wishfully held my eyes on the scene until I picked up a familiar face. My aunt, the grammar school teacher, was waving her scarf fringed in school colors. A smile grabbed my face as my heart skipped a beat—someone was there for me, and it felt awesome!

Coach Perfect remained on the sideline for a bit. He was watching the enemy intently. Watching like a lion in the brush, studying its prey before deciding its best next move. He turned and jogged to our gathering place. The other coaches were discussing the pros and cons of our first-half performance, extremely upbeat at our chances for victory.

All eyes followed Coach Perfect as he darted toward us, his white teeth showing off his happy smile. As he came to a stop, his smile grew even bigger before he opened his halftime speech. All eyes were directed at him. His black mustache held firm atop his mighty smile. His eyes pierced ours with his look of sheer excitement.

The air was broken when he launched, "*Mental toughness.*" A pause as he looked across each player. "*Mental toughness!*" This time with much more bravado and a bit of spittle from the force backing the *t* in *toughness*. "Maintain your mental toughness, and you will win this game."

He paused again but this time added a trademark finger pointing to his eye contract, making sure each player knew he meant each and every one of us and not just key members. "For months you have been put through physical rigors to ready you so no other team can outlast you in strength or stamina. We pushed you in sprints and conditioning to harden you so your bodies can outlast anything, everything an enemy brings to bear. Look around. You're not even winded. You're not tired in the least. You could go on for eight more quarters without so much as a water break. Your enemy is already sucking wind. Their hands are on their knees. Their lungs are searching for oxygen while you *men* are standing tall, ready to charge."

Coach Perfect's smile raised his upper lip even more as he held his next words, letting the full weight of his speech settle into our minds.

"Mental toughness is the key to victory. If you maintain your focus, don't get baited into doing something stupid, your opponent will dismantle from within. They do *not* have the training, nor the physical or mental toughness to beat you. Only you can lose this game. It's yours for the taking, but only if you don't let them get in your heads or fail to keep disciplined. It all comes down to thirty minutes of mental toughness and discipline. They will come at you with the dirtiest of play. Expect cheap shots, hits after the play is over, and trash talk to get you out of your game."

Coach Perfect kept talking to us in tones that seemed to stick to our innards like superglue on our fingers—it wasn't coming off anytime soon.

As his words kept penetrating our minds, that hawk returned to glide above the field, casting its shadow from end zone to end zone before turning, sending its outline along the sidelines as if tiptoeing along the edge just inches from going out of bounds. A high-pitched screech cast its sound over Coach Perfect's final words before he ordered our hands into the center for a quick "Whippets!" team chant, and we broke for our kickoff return team formation.

We opened the second half with the ball on our seventeen-yard line. The running game, handing the ball off to me, Jonny, and Waz repeatedly, hammered up the middle and then swung to the outside. Play after play, gaining three to five yards. Losing yards some plays and getting a few big gains on others. We moved across the Whalers' forty after I pounded the ball over center and gave a crushing hit to their powerful middle linebacker. As I walked back to the huddle, proud of the hard run, my head cracked with a star-filled darkness as if Crazy had caught me sleeping.

Lying with my face in the dirt, groaning in agony, I heard my teammates yelling profanities as whistles blew nonstop. A yellow flag inches from my nose, I rolled to my back as my lungs fought to regain control and intake. Victor and Geo lifted me from the ground. "You all right?" came from different directions. I shook off the cheap shot and saw yellow flags scattered throughout the area. Surely we'd gain fifteen yards from the postplay illegal blindsiding.

The pinstripes' discussion took on a different tone, one of home field advantage. We'd faced several calls going against us thus far, but nothing so blatant. "Personal foul—unsportsmanlike conduct against Windham. The player is ejected from the game" came the verdict from the New London resident and his fake "equal justice" commitment to sports refereeing.

Waz pulled our players into a huddle while reminding everyone "mental toughness" was key and what we were doing was not helping. Coach Perfect was going bananas from the sideline, using every nonswear word known in two or three languages. His jumping and arm flailing made such a spectacle we almost started laughing, which broke the wrongful tension and helped us regain our poise.

Huddle reformed, Victor chimed in with "Coach is right. We can beat these bastards, but not if we lose our heads. That was a chickenshit call, but look at them. Their heads are down, sucking wind, and they're getting bitched at from their sidelines. *We can do this!*"

His encouraging words took a bit of a hit as Geo was told, "You need to get off the field. You've been ejected" by the head referee.

With Geo gone and the loss of a player to a broken hand, we were left with only one extra player. If we lost any more, we'd have to forfeit the game. We knew we needed to pay heed to Coach Perfect's halftime speech and refocus our mental toughness.

We punted two plays later and held the Whalers to their side of the field, forcing them to punt as the third quarter drew to a close. Coach Perfect gathered us on the field and said, "Listen to their sidelines."

We could hear the unhappy sounds of fighting, bickering, and blaming one another for the score being tied at zero with one quarter left in the game. Then, like a shot of cold steel, their head coach screamed, *"You're going to lose this fucking game. You're an embarrassment to our fans and what we've built."* He threw his clipboard to the ground and walked away from his players.

Quietly Coach Perfect laid out the plan for the final fifteen minutes. He had a surprise pass play that was sure to "open the field," and we'd be using it on our next play.

Sure enough, a fake handoff to me, a quarterback rollout, and a pass to Victor down the sideline for a gain of sixty-four yards before he was run down by a speedy defender. We pounded the middle and swung to the outside until we were on their seven-yard line with a first and goal. Coach Perfect had a "time management" plan to eat up the clock by using all of the forty seconds allotted between plays. We worked his plan flawlessly. The scoreboard clock showed just four remaining as Coach Perfect slowly walked to our huddle during the stoppage of play. Four-minute warning.

"We are going to run the ball over center until we score. Quarterback, you call out everything you can think of so they think we have changed plays, but keep giving the ball to forty-two until we score. Switch formations with ends and wideouts. Waz, you switch from left to right each play, but lead the blocking. They'll be forced to call time-out, and I won't be coming out here again. You men have this under control, and I trust you to complete your legacy."

As he walked out of the huddle, he looked back and gave me a wink and a nod while mouthing, "You got this." I wasn't going to let him down.

The ball was handed off to me three times in a row as we hammered away, down to the one-yard line. The Whalers' players at their sideline were screaming to hold us. Our side was cheering as loudly as a Yale versus Harvard game from the 1950s.

Fourth and goal. Our last play, with just over two minutes left and the Whalers expending their last time-out. Waz look at me. "You can do this, so don't stop until you're in." He looked around at the rest of the heavy-breathing gang and grunted, "*Score on three—break!*" We grumbled to the line and set our formation. The quarterback rattled off a series of nonsensical numbers and pointed to the outside as if a signal of our intent.

"*Hut-hut-hut!*"

Plowing ahead, I got the ball and slammed into the pile of blockers and defenders, but nothing moved forward. A momentary stop, a shift to one side, then the other. An arm grabbed my leg, and I jumped to loosen his grip, jumping just above the heads of all the players. In that split second, I saw that four-legged beast off to my right, just past the end zone. The noise of the crashing titans drifted away like the calm of an ocean breeze carries a seagull into the distance. "Spin and roll right; head for the outside corner" flashed across my mind. It was like both words and an image displayed at the same moment—a movie-screen-like series of pictures showing the path to success. A thud shook me backward before I followed my mind's image.

I spun from my left to right in a full 360-degree circle that propelled me toward the outside of the mayhem. Two steps backward put me at the three-yard line before I headed sideways, toward the outside corner. The mighty middle linebacker followed my every step. The picture of the four-legged hulk gazed at me with his beastly size, commanding me to break through and reach for its warm coating. Free of the tangled mass mingling back and forth, I planted my right foot, and with shoulder and head down, I pointed forward and charged toward the end zone. The defending shadow met me in a crashing crunch feet from pay dirt. There was a moment when it seemed like nothing was moving, a stalemated force of wills and power halted, as if two atoms had met and split but not yet decided which direction the more powerful force would project. One destiny to yield while the other blasted into the heat of glory.

My tenacity focused as I ground my teeth, and with all my being and a push from an unseen gust, I willed my way forward. With the crack of a thousand claps of thunder, my ears cleared as the middle linebacker crumpled to the turf, my knee driving over his falling body. With his arms wrapped around my left foot, I pumped with all I had and lunged forward until the ball crossed that chalky-white line and into the end zone. *Touchdown!*

I lay on the ground looking to my right. The ref had his hands straight up with all his fingers toward the sky, signaling the successful effort of my exhausting endeavor. I lifted myself from the grass and to my feet, expecting a team celebration but witnessing a fighting mass of fists and punches. The thrill of the score vanished as Victor was leveled and stomped by a heel spike between his helmet and shoulder pad. The placement struck him on the round bone where his neck met his shoulders. I rushed to his aid as the assailants bounced away like schoolgirls playing hopscotch. He rolled to his side, eyes wide open, his arms limp.

Flags flew through the air. Whistles blew at top speed, their siren-like screech having little effect on the players pushing and shoving one another. Coaches from both sides were ordering players to part ways. I hovered over Victor, asking him to speak, to say something, anything. Please, God, don't let him be hurt, I begged in a softly worded commanding prayer.

He moaned and rolled a bit, but he wasn't making any sense. I waved to Coach Perfect for help. A shout and hand gestures got the needed attention. As he took control, he signaled for the EMTs. "Bring your bags," he yelled.

"They jumped on his neck," I told the coach.

"I saw it," he responded.

Victor was put on a stretcher and wheeled off the field. The refs called offsetting penalties but determined the waylay happened after the touchdown. They ejected three Whalers and warned us, "One more incident, and both sides will forfeit the game."

Great. We were winning, so if they wanted to beat us, just create another incident, and the win would be erased.

The fans on the Whalers' side were fit to be tied. They were mad as hornets after their hive had been ransacked.

Lining up for the extra point, the Whalers jumped offside, landing blows to half the guys up front. Even with the shortened distance, we missed the point after. I think it had more to do with nerves and anger than ability.

The kickoff had four more penalties, all against the Whalers. It was getting ugly. And with just under two minutes to play, we had eleven players left, so if anyone else got hurt or tossed out, we'd have to forfeit, and they knew it. With no time-outs left and the ball seventy-four yards from scoring, they needed some big plays. We fought hard and gave up little as the clock ticked under thirty seconds with a fourth down facing our nemesis. A Hail Mary pass deep down the middle hit the ground with a thump.

We raised our fists in a show of power and victory. Coach Perfect screamed at us to "knock it off, and get in the huddle." One snap later with a taken knee, the clock ticked down to zero. The score: Whippets 6, Whalers 0.

We did it! Yet we were being forced to keep our emotions bottled up. No celebration, no dancing or man hugs. "Line up, shake their hands, and get on the bus…*Get moving*," commanded Coach Perfect in a voice, a tone never heard from him. He had a look that caused me serious concern. It almost looked like one of those faces Crazy had before something really awful was about to happen.

That stinging knot, that special dark pain began to take hold in the center of my chest. A feeling of dread and a sense of hate was taking hold, but not so much toward me. It was as if it was descending around the field, around our team like an evil spell had been cast. One destined to rip victory from the jaws of defeat, to steal our legacy and shatter our earned rights of a perfect season.

Most of the Whalers' team was milling about and refusing to line up for the postgame "nice job" hand slaps meant to show respect to fellow combatants. We gathered at midfield, eleven dirty, smelly, sweat-soaked victorious warriors. Three coaches secured the tail end of the short parade line. We waited, standing in our pent-up excitement until a few Whalers made headway toward our meeting point. Some green-and-gold players were shouting, sweating, and blaming coaches and everything else for the loss. Gear was being thrown; fans were shouting vile insults at the gathered eleven. Our team was a mix of nationalities, but not until that day did it sink in how we looked to others, even though our team held the same colors and spoke the same variety of foreign languages as those shouting slurs. Confused, I waited and watched as more Whalers trickled into formation, and the precession began to slowly drift past our short line of eleven.

From the middle of the pack, I could see guys in front of me exchanging words, and it appeared to change from a semicheerful exchange into bitter words and sharp retorts. A wind passed over me like a warning; something was about to change, something terrible and nasty. I pressed my head around the player in front of me with an urging from within. That old man with white hair and red checkered shirt jacket was coming into view, just between the Whalers as they muddled along the sidelines. An overpowering sense followed: "Put your helmet on!"

Before I could reason out the thought, guys in front of me started pushing and shoving. In the blink of an eye, the scene transformed into an all-out brawl. My hand held strong to my face mask hanging beside my thigh. I started to look to my left as a *thump* bounced off my shoulder pads and stabbed my ear. The force crushed my upper ear into my head and burst into bloody shooting streaks of red like a cartoon fireworks display.

My head was ringing in pain as I launched out at my attacker. Without a thought, I charged like a bull in heat, striking him midchest and pinning him to the ground with perfect precision and tackling form. My shoulder firmly lodged in his cheek as we hit the dirt. His back landed solidly as my weight and force drove deep into his flexing, straining rib cage. A torrid crackling penetrated past the blood flowing into my ear drum. I could feel his pain explode as his body went limp after the recoil from the powerful landing. I gasped for air as I reached for his ribs and lifted myself off his crumpled remains. Rage was coursing through my veins. Power pumped my arms as I turned to look for the next victim.

Our team formed into a half circle of protection against the vastly outnumbering and extremely pissed-off Whalers. Helmets swung in all directions. Punching, kicking, and headlong rushing attacks pulsed left and right in a small wave of desperate defenders. Coach Perfect pulled combatants apart like toy soldiers, tossing each one a few feet in the opposite direction. Fans from both sides raced onto the gridiron, some to rescue, others leading with wild swings and sweeping hooks, clutching steel-like knuckles and handbags. Watching the flow of parents crossing the fence line was like witnessing the marines landing on a beach with overwhelming superior force. We were in a fight for our lives.

"Form a huddle behind me," commanded Coach Perfect. He grabbed one player at a time, peeled them out of their fight, and shoved them to his rear. *"Keep your helmets on,"* he barked. With his mighty bulk, he reached player after player and flipped them behind him. It was like witnessing Hercules wading in a waist-deep surf and plucking fish from the waters with the ease of a trident-wielding Aquaman. Coach Perfect held point at the crest of the *V*-shaped reverse huddle, slowly walking us backward and away from the battle grounds. A green-and-gold swarm washed against his girth but without penetrating the shield set five wide in the descending curved V.

Parents clashed, fathers on fathers, mothers fighting mothers. Coach Perfect kept forcing us backward until the sea of families swept around us, forming further protection. Several cops struggled to contain the swirling crowds with little success. Sirens wailed in the background. Blue and red lights with screeching tires raced into the parking lot, then descended across open grass. Dozens of cruisers littered the grounds just as the pulsing wave rifled through the bitterness.

A gunshot reset the entire playing field. People ducked and scattered. A second shot rang out, and the families formerly fighting now looked to one another for a safe direction. The gunfire changed the course of action from a disgusting dysfunctional display into a common community cluster searching for safety and helping those who, moments ago, were striking blows and hurling hate.

Coach Perfect corralled the team onto the bus, and parents stuck close at hand. Students and fans rushed to join loved ones gathered in the buses and parked cars closely packed into one visiting section. Several cops surrounded the area, ensuring no further fisticuffs.

As quickly as it all had started, it was over. The crowds vacated the stands and left the campus. The coaches gathered our gear with some help from a few parents, escorted by a couple of policemen.

"Keep your helmets on and windows closed until I say otherwise," directed Coach Perfect. "Keep the chatter quiet and eyes, heads forward," he added.

The cops escorted the bus caravan and trailing parents past the city limits. Two state troopers picked up the pack with a cruiser in front and one at the rear.

The ride back was intentionally silent. Coach Perfect made it clear: "We are not going to discuss anything until we get everyone safely back with their families. We can talk about the game and the season another time."

We had accomplished such a great feat, and here we sat, unable to savor the victory. No one to share the feeling with. Not even a pat on the back for scoring the only points of the game. It was like I was around Crazy but at another house of horrors. At a time when

I should be living in pure joy and explosive happiness, the feeling of sadness and despair started its climb into my stomach and my head. It was as if nothing good was ever going to come my way.

Fathers, mothers, grandparents, and friends were gathering, packing the area where the buses stopped to let us out. The cheering and callings from their proud family members tricked my heart into thinking I was part of the celebration, but it only lasted for a moment. Oh, how I enjoyed that moment, but no one was calling my name or shouting at me with bubbling excitement. I simply wasn't part of the freshman football heroes of the gridiron but more like the ball boy, noticed but never part of the community. Even Myron had his sisters to hug him and tell him how proud they were. I turned my face away from the happiness bursting everywhere around me. The loneliness climbed back into its proper home.

I waited and got off last, knowing no one would be cheering for me. I was hoping my aunt would be there, but it wasn't in the cards. I helped the coaches with the gear while my teammates crystallized their legacy. Afterward I headed for the shower and, before sitting quietly, ate a few of the treats I'd stuffed into my locker, leftovers from my breakfast tray.

"Great game"—the final remark directed in my direction as I sat staring at metal folds. With a familiar sigh and face pointing at the floor tile, my thoughts turned to that fateful end-of-day decision. Half the lights were turned off before I heard the voice of the varsity head coach.

"Let's get moving, kid. You're the last one, and I've got dinner waiting for me. So finish up. Three minutes. Lights out."

I finished dressing, putting on the musky-smelling pants and shirt. My old socks damp with the moldy scent of the never-washed towel. The lace on my right shoe broke as I tried to tighten the rabbit ears. It was the third time this week they'd broken.

"Come on, kid. I got to lock this place up," softly barked the growingly impatient coach.

I headed for the double steel doors leading to the cold darkness waiting for me once again.

Standing twenty feet from my sleeping spot half a day ago, I considered reclaiming it for the night. The debate raged in my head: Sleep with the cement blocks and bricks, or take the first step toward Crazy? That was the never-ending decision I'd come to deliberate nightly. I felt the dark, frosty air chase the blood from my face, the cold sting quickly changing to a hot burn, the kind you get when you wait too long before covering the icy patch. It was fast becoming a bitterly cold night. My feet began to feel it taking hold through my tattered sneakers. Holes in the bottoms wouldn't be helpful against the fast-freezing sidewalks.

What do I do?...Where could I go? I wondered, gripped by that lonely process of deciding when to put one foot out and point it toward that house and whatever awaited me on this night. I wondered again if anyone would miss me if I didn't show up or if there was a plate of food or anything at all to eat. I wondered if I could just sleep in the locker room and start the day tomorrow without having to worry about closing my eyes in fear of what Crazy would do to me next.

Coach pushed open the door, breaking my thoughts, and asked if I needed a ride home. I said, "No, thanks, Coach. I got it."

And he followed with "Well, you can't stay here, so get it moving," as if he'd read my thoughts or knew what I was considering.

He hustled to his car and sped off as I wondered what he was having for dinner.

I gave that sigh and decided to put that foot toward that house, the toughest of all steps, the first one. Decision made, I started down that well-worn path toward a life with Crazy, but tonight something felt different. Not a huge difference but a bit different. Normally I didn't think about tomorrow until I got closer to that house, but tonight seemed different. Maybe things had changed. Maybe tomorrow would be a better day; hell, maybe tonight would be a better night.

Off I went. The cold started to freeze my hair, and my toes were already feeling the Arctic bite. With the school lost in the background, I stopped for a moment. I'd forgotten what number step I was on. Should I go back and start over? I'd never forgotten to count the steps before, but it needed to be done, so back I raced, back to that varsity locker room door. My goofy excitement and the short run warmed me up a bit. Now, let's get back on track... Step one, two, three!

CHAPTER 9

The starting point, once again, was 2,442 steps from the school to that side door. Two thousand, four hundred forty-two was the number I never forgot. My pace varied from less than twenty minutes in the pouring rain to over an hour or two on those afternoons or nights when my mind wandered to different places. Places I dreamed of, places I'd rather be than on that hated pace-by-pace trek back into the despised fighting cage with little hope of escape or quiet. I kept walking off those steps, hoping not to reach ground zero.

What would be waiting behind door number three today? Was it a cold dinner plate to fill the howls of an empty tummy or the crack of a whip to greet me as I turned to close the cold off before Crazy started bitching about opening his door and costing him so much money to keep himself warm? Maybe door number two was the order of the day, with Crazy sitting at his favorite watering hole telling the world how wonderful he was and how much his kids should get out on their own or pay for their upbringing.

Just a few dozen steps left. I decided to stop and sit on the rock wall several houses from Crazy. That feeling of horror was starting to clamp down tighter and tighter on my insides, like a vise squeezing my guts into a milkshake of frozen chunks of vomit that wouldn't dislodge and melt until I reversed my step count and headed in the opposite direction once the sun returned. Of course, that assumed I would make it through another night of indefinite doors of terror and if I got to experience door number one. Those were my thoughts as I sat in the dark under the moonless sky on this crisp late-autumn evening. Please, God, not door number one. Not tonight, please…not tonight.

My body was killing me from the hard-fought battle to preserve our perfect season. My bloody ear was tucked under my hair and ball cap. My ribs were bruised, and pains were stinging across my battered frame. These hurts were enjoyable, for the most part, as they were earned in a worthwhile battle. A battle that meant something other than survival. Each mark told a different story—a tackle, a great hit, running the football. I felt a smile cross my lips thinking of the war badges.

I was struggling to muster the strength, the will to take those final steps, so I decided to sit there a bit longer. My mind was exhausted, and sleep was what I wanted as much as something to eat. The thought of which door I'd be walking through held me content on the cold stone of the neighbor's rock wall. If only door number one and no Crazy. Not tonight. Please, God, not tonight! Give me this one, please!

My thoughts fell back to the game and those words Coach Perfect preached about destiny. If we'd fight, work hard, and stick together, we'd find that, for the rest of our lives, we'd get to walk with heads held high. A legacy to play back any time we thought about giving up. We'd just need to recall our perfect season. We would have something no one could take from us, not even Crazy. Although he would try somehow. He hadn't done anything to earn the right to claim the title of "perfect season." And no one could get a single point against the best freshman defense in school history—heck, maybe even state history!

Somehow, Crazy would take credit or diminish our accomplishments. I needed to find a way to get out of that house, this life—but how?

—∿—

My prayer requests and memories of the game canceled out the final steps to that house as I decided to finish the long walk. I made a hard turn up the old, crumbling concrete stairs that connected the sidewalk to the small front yard two feet above it. I went down the broken overgrown pathway and up the rotting wood stairs to the side door. I paused, taking as deep a breath as my battered rips and clenched stomach muscles would allow, thinking of the feeling that would return the next morning as I walked out this door and away from this house. I knew that would be the only way for the knots to loosen and the air to fill my lungs once again, sore ribs aside.

But for now, I gauged another sigh and begged God to watch over us, protect us from Crazy. And while you're at it, please send him back to hell or that place he slipped out of when your guards weren't watching. Maybe the devil let him loose. Either way, see if you can round him up before he kills more innocents. Before he kills me or Mother or, worse, my brother.

Crazy never did hit my sisters, at least not that I recall. It must have been a biology thing, since my sisters were his offspring, and my brother and I came as a package deal. I could feel the difference when he looked at his daughters and then at me. The hatred coming off Crazy's face when he looked at me was as thick as pea soup. I could feel the bitterness piggybacked on that leather belt as it whipped across my lower spine and snapped my ticklish fleshy sides. Crazy raised those welts all over my body and in places where it hurt just to be mildly slapped, let alone hammered by a two-and-a-half-inch-wide heavy rawhide mule mover. It took days, sometimes weeks, for those welts to retreat. Sometimes the branding failed to disappear, leaving its mark like a skin-tone tattoo twisted within its fleshy meat.

With those thoughts replaying like a flashing traffic light, images of past lessons I needed to learn, I paused at the door for those last-minute requests, hopeful prayers really, when it hit me: there were no sounds coming from inside. Maybe Crazy wasn't home. Maybe Mother had the car, or maybe the car had run away without me. Maybe the car was hiding for the night as well, or maybe it had stopped working again, just to "teach" Crazy a lesson. I held my breath, peaking my good ear's volume, searching for sounds of Crazy but hearing nothing, not a sound. Was it possible that it was going to be a calm night?

I twisted the cold, rusted doorknob and gently jiggled it in and out to get the latch to let free and release its sticky grip. The latch was like a warning not to enter, resisting my efforts to gain entry before letting go. You had to know the secret password, the correct sequence of wiggles and shakes, as if guarded by an ogre of dark magic. The old door stuck to the jamb, and you had to put a bump into it with your shoulder to get it unstuck and open.

I softly hit it with my right side. I felt the pain shooting down my arm and neck from the aftereffects of the day's earlier encounters.

Those discomforts should be part of dramatic discussions of post-battle banter, served alongside a hot supper. A celebration of the hard-fought victory, sharing the achievement with family members. The stories cast into verbal bronze like your first baby shoes.

No such greeting awaited my arrival. Not even the smell of warm oatmeal.

I had long dreamed of living in a family sharing happy times. I imagined creating hallowed grounds within the confines of a house where love and joy were the heartbeat of the family tree. A home where the replaying of warrior tales was the light that sparked the excitement after the dinner dishes were put away. Tales of shining knights rescuing damsels as you get tucked into clean, fresh-smelling sheets. A gentle kiss on the forehead from your mother as she securely crimps the blankets under your backside and offers you "sweet dreams." Then you quietly drift away into a peaceful night of fairies and friends. All the while you feel safe, secure, and protected as you replay the scenes of glory again and again until sleep takes hold and your body recovers and rebuilds, ready for the next day's adventures. It was just a fantasy, but one that would pop into my mind from time to time. Seemingly at the oddest of times, like this one!

What was behind the door this night? With a painful shoulder push, I entered Crazy's habitat once again and walked straight into the deathly silence of Mother and Crazy sitting at the table as if lying in wait for this exact moment. The taste in the air stuck to the back of my throat like flypaper glued to the webs between my fingers. It wasn't the prayerful door I'd requested, and it didn't take much to see it wasn't going to be a quiet night!

—⧗—

Have you ever walked into a room or someplace where you could literally feel the tension in the air? Like a thick soup of bad perfume that clings to you no matter which way you move, which way you look, or no matter how you try to clear the invisible fragrance from sticking to you? You have a feeling of "Ugh, this can't be good," and in short order you get confirmation of just how right you really are. That's the feeling I got when I walked into a room filled with Crazy and his unique brand of insanity. The only question remaining was to what level would this Burt Reynolds–like deliverance contain tonight. A soft landing of verbal fungus that would grow on me for decades to come or a battering of fists and objects close at hand, denting my bones or crushing already bruised muscles?

There was never any telling until things played out, and this night appeared to be stalled, waiting for the accelerant—or maybe the detonator. A fully charged bomb waiting to be let loose. It felt like death was coming, I didn't know what form it would take or how soon, but death was coming. The air was certain of it. Was death coming to me first, or Mother? That was the question. My brother had a way about him that didn't lead me to believe he'd be killed at Crazy's hand, but the mental cruelty—now, that was a totally different story. The damage in that field was complete.

So put yourself in that room, in that kitchen with its washing machine along the interior center wall. The table for three was pressed against the wall between two windows that were partially open if it wasn't humid. The drafty old windows gave a clear line of sight from the neighbors'. Easy access to watch the nightly fights. The other side of the small kitchen held the antique gas-fired stove. Crazy had set up a bypass to ensure he wouldn't have to pay a gas bill until he got caught again. There was the constant fear of a house fire or blowing up from the leaky regulator he had jerry-rigged in the basement. He had just stolen it, telling us it was because the power companies had all the money they needed and won't miss sulfur-smelling gas. Sometimes I wondered if it was the gas smell that visited the house or something more dangerous.

His thieving lasted for years before the cops showed up with the real gasmen from the city. Crazy refused to pay his water bill, so they shut the valve outside and came to take the water meter. The city official noticed the illegal rigging, which wasn't a surprise to the police or public gas services. It was the start of a long week and fuel for Crazy as he sat in his chair watching me climb over the threshold and into his domain.

Mother got up from the table without saying a word and walked to the sink pantry area. The butler's kitchen, as Mother called it, was a squared-off nook built in between the old mudroom and the formal dining room. The dining room was an open space connected to the living room. The living room was Crazy's territory. An old couch and two chairs. The new one was his spot, and God help you if you sat in his spot. He'd unfold the recliner and put his stinky feet high into the air. He'd bitch at the world as it presented itself in black and white with a late 1960s antenna fixed to the roof. The remote of the day was me. I would stand there for what seemed like hours flipping back and forth, station to station. Of course, there were only four or five channels that came in. Sometimes he'd fall asleep with me standing there. Hours would pass, but I had learned my lesson: never move without permission.

If he'd been sitting in front of his TV, it might not be as bad. But tonight, he was perched on his throne at the head of the table. Brown bottles were lined up like old soldiers waiting to be released from duty. His scowl told me all I needed to know. He was pissed and had planned his punishment well before I pushed open the old pine door. My second glance, after leaning into the door with a bump to close it, told me the level of darkness surrounding his mood. The anger coiled about like dozens of venomous snakes thirsty to latch their fangs into the softened flesh bruises walking into their viper's pit.

"Sit down!" was the order bellowed in that smoke-choked, gravelly voice. Crazy pointed to the chair just within arm's length of his backhand. I was looking toward the seat opposite his swing. "Here. Sit here," he commanded.

I don't move right away. I just looked at him as I debated internally and presented a show of defiance. He started to open his mouth to repeat as I moved forward, pulling the seat away from the table. I sat down with one eye trained on his hands, his arms, so I wouldn't miss a muscle movement meant to mash my face. I knew this game and his tricks.

"Your mother and I need to talk to you. Maybe you can explain to us what is going on," he said in a half–"you're dead" voice and half-curious tone.

The curious tone made me think it might not be so bad. Kind of like sleeping with one eye open and being hungry most of the time. Of course, there was no telling what Crazy had up his sleeve or what direction he was planning, so it was best to avoid answering at all costs because, as the commander said in *Star Wars* as the fleet decelerated from hyperspeed into Darth Vader's domain, "It's a trap!"

—⁓—

I was wishing I was at my auntie's house with a belly filled with warm homemade brownies and a cold glass of milk, but as that thought crossed paths with my hunger pain, my stomach let out a vociferous call to action; Crazy replayed his statement as if I hadn't heard it the first time. Sometimes, if I paused long enough, he'd forget his question. On the backside of the table, behind three empty brown bottles, was his square clear glass filled with extra-strength liquid. This was going to be a long night.

I looked over my left shoulder at Mother, who was working on a dinner plate for Crazy. "I have a plate for you."

Mixed signals were flapping in the room. Confused at what path this was going down, I gave Mother a short head bob and a "Thank you. Yes, I'm starving."

Chances were Crazy had just gotten home and was, most likely, hours away from exhausting his rage. It was going to be a long night indeed. With his mood seemingly tame for the moment, I responded with "I'm not sure what you mean" and waited to see what he'd offer next.

Mother reheated dinner plates the old-fashioned way, before microwaves and cooktops were an everyday thing. She put the plates inside the gas-fired oven and let everything warm up and, of course, dry out. Crazy was still trying to figure an answer to his baited question. His next move was to try to trick you into thinking he actually cared about something in your life. On this night I let my guard down precisely at the wrong moment. I made the mistake of thinking I was going to get a compliment, or at least an "attaboy" or even a "good job." Crazy said, "So, I hear your team did well today. Your brother said the team won the game."

It seemed like Crazy was setting the table for a nice talk and some positive support. Dare I think it would lead to pride or happiness coming out of his fire-spitting, gray-toothed, vile piehole? Feeling rather proud of the day's accomplishments, I responded with a smile. "Yup. We played very well and earned a victory to become the only freshman team in history to be undefeated and unscored upon."

Crazy leaned back in the creaking wooden chair. "So, you think you're something, don't you, smart-ass?"

His response told me the jig was up and he had no time to play around with the happy times. He was heading quickly into one of his fits. There was nothing better to light Crazy's spark than fresh success. To trample all over and squash out dreams before they could fully bloom. If he were a rose bush, he would be only the thorns. He was going to make sure I didn't spread my wings and flap a beat of happiness as long as he was in control.

Mother placed the plates down on the table just in front of Crazy using a towel as a potholder. The semi-dried-out shepherd's pie stuck to the plate like duct tape to a rug. Normally, shepherd's pie has 50 percent ground beef and 35 percent mashed potatoes and is topped with canned corn. A rather easy meal to make, one I'd learned to prepare almost a decade earlier. It's so hard to mess up shepherd's pie; like ramen noodles, it's a no-brainer. Of course, you must factor in one ingredient not included in a recipe—love. Shake love out of a package or sprinkle it onto leftovers, and you have a meal from heaven. Cook without love, and you have dehydrated, repurposed smashed beef under white paste and covered with unpopped Orville Redenbacher. This was not going to help the atmosphere!

She placed Crazy's fork next to his left hand. Not his right. It had to be his left hand because that was his dominant side, and he demanded his fork be placed on that side or else. One time when his fork was placed by his right hand, it found its way into my right shoulder blade. Crazy had lost it and stabbed me from behind, right through my shirt, and left the fork sticking up in the air as if it were a modern-day body piercing, a bolt placed perfectly by a tattoo artist with four tines meeting at one intersection to form a metal stick handle that freely swayed forward and back in rhythm with my body as I fought to reach behind me to pull it out. After enough tries and with the help of the doorframe, I pushed my left arm at the elbow over the top of my right shoulder, just enough to finger pull the eating utensil out of its lodging. I kept the shirt but threw the fork out the door. I never forgot which side the fork was placed on with Crazy ever again. Mother had her own lessons.

The shepherd's pie was on superhot plates, resting on a plastic table covering in front of Crazy and now me. The table was set for what was surely going to be an adventurous supper. Crazy never looked at the food but rather made his face twitch as he reached for his bottle of strength on the far side of the small three-quarter circle. "You didn't tell us the rest of the story, did you? Well, did you?" he asked with a knowing question mark.

I figured he was heading into the postgame fights, but I hadn't done anything wrong, so how bad could this get? I let him know how we lined up after the game and how one of the other guys hit our player in the head with his helmet before everyone got into the huge fight, and gunshots happened, and we got a police escort out of town. I said I wasn't really involved in the fight, and I wasn't in any trouble.

Well, that wasn't what he wanted to hear, and he lit into his facts of life by saying I must have been a coward if I let a team-mate get hit like that and didn't do anything to the other guy. So I started to claim that I did have a bigger role in the punch fest, but Crazy quickly flipped his "you're a coward" attack into a show of faint shock that I wasn't the aggressor and how he had been told I was one of the troublemakers. "You may not have thrown the first punch, but you dishonored this family and disrespected your father," he said. Boy, if there was ever a word he could use for fighting purposes, claiming to be a "father," let alone my father, was on the top of the list of fabricated statements. Crazy continued. "By allowing yourself to be involved in a rumble on school grounds."

"You're not my father," I quietly whispered and masked within an exhale.

You could see he was winding himself up, winding up the faint energy of his life, and using this day's events to justify his pending attacks. I knew it was coming, and I should have let it go, let it just take its course like my brother was so good at, changing the subject or just agreeing with Crazy no matter what came out of his mouth. My brother was the master at this. Crazy would tell you it was going to be a warm day, so put shorts on. Then he'd start bitching we weren't properly dressed for the cold weather and we needed to go change. My brother would just go back upstairs after a brisk "yes, sir" and come back with pants and a winter hat if he thought it would appease the crazy bastard.

I, on the other hand, hated him and his insanity, so I'd push back, let him know he had told us to put the shorts on and it was getting hot out. While my brother was already re-dressed and ready to go, I'd demand I get to go out in shorts, which would lead to Crazy sticking to his guns, and a search for the leather strap would commence before I'd relent and put on pants, normally over my shorts so I could take off the pants later.

Of course, my brother was the smartest. He'd simply put his other clothes in a paper bag—this was long before backpacks were commonly used, unless you were a Boy Scout. My brother would just bring the paper bag with him as if it had been going with us all along, and he would do whatever Crazy said, no matter how crazy it was. My brother would simply play along like it was normal to go outside and find a branch just the right size so you could get whipped with it or turn over the garden when the ground was still frozen and you had to use picks to break up the frozen surface so we could plant whenever Crazy said it was the time. My brother did whatever he was told, and I...Well, you get where I stand with bullies!

After flip-flopping from me being a coward to being all but the cause of the postgame riots, Crazy walked me through his theory of events. Nothing at all how it played out. He said he was told by the "school" I was going to be suspended and removed from the football team for fighting on the field and hitting coaches with my helmet. If Crazy didn't get involved, I might be expelled or, worse, turned over to the police for attempted murder. *Attempted murder?* What the fuck was this crazy bastard talking about? He let me know he could save me, but it wasn't going to be easy for him. He'd have to "call in favors" to get me out of the mess I was in.

He rambled on for so long the hot in the supper plates was long past gone, and a crust started to build on top of the mixed-together layers of mashed potatoes and corn, as there wasn't much ground beef to see, mostly lumpy potatoes and really small, wrinkled corn kernels. But I didn't care; I was hungry. If only Crazy would stop ranting so I could eat.

Tonight I was determined not to take the bait. I was going to keep thinking about our victory and how Victor was doing. Keep it cool here and see if I could manage this like my brother, the pro. Crazy wouldn't stop his jaw fest, and you had better not pick up your fork before he did, or you'd be sitting in front of that plate all night without touching an ounce just because you started eating before the master did—a sin of the worst kind and a guaranteed way to find the floor with your face.

Crazy kept talking and talking without touching his fork, drinking his bottles and ignoring the shepherd's pie until Mother spoke up with her oh-so-endearing and gentle soft tone. "Come on, can't we let the kid eat while you keep talking? The food is getting cold."

It was as if you had just told the Chinese Communist Party leader you wanted to open up the World Wide Web without limitations or restrictions and forgotten to bow afterward. Explosive charge loaded. Fuse lit. The countdown began.

Crazy just lost it. He sat up straight in his chair and started screaming at Mother about how she had disrespected him demanding the "useless bastard" be allowed to eat, that he didn't pay for the food; he was "good for nothing," one of the most common lines in his inventory, and "a waste of life." Crazy went on, raving about how he never should have married her or taken in her "ratty, sniffling, shithead" kids. He said he worked his ass off to pay for her brats, who never appreciated him. "And this one, this one here, is the worst of all. Now you want me to let him eat? This punk will never amount to anything. He'll be in prison before he's eighteen. And you, you fat pig…" His nastiness held no bar save the one he just left. A thick black ball of swirling goo started to take shape in the center of his chest as if coming from some faraway place and forming where a heart should be.

I knew this was building into something more than just yelling and mental vindictiveness. This was preplanned, and I was getting the sense it was heading down a ruthless road of raw rage and resentment. There was real fire coming out of his pores. The energy that surrounded him was gaining strength, as if all the buildup was drawing evil from a black hole, from some distant place only known to Crazy and his partners. That switch flipped by Mother's ask. It seemed to open the gates and funnel some kind of power into a bubble around him. A bubble that he didn't fully control. It was as if a godlike strength was offered but only to cause hate-filled damage. All his work-up was needed to prime the pump. To call upon a secret source that resided within him. He always had a full well of hate at the ready, but for him to fully execute his vengefulness, he needed something else to come alive. Or was it calling on the dead? Either way, I'd seen this many times before, and I was confident I was going to be getting a pounding very soon.

Mentally I started to prepare myself for the punches and the kicks. I wondered what he'd hit me with tonight; I needed to protect my sore spots. I was sure he'd keep me in the ring until all the rounds were played out. So as long as he vented all his hate, all his anger on me, Mother and my brother and even my sisters weren't in real danger. At least that was my hope. It had worked so many times over the years. If he turned to head toward my brother, I'd push myself into his path until he exhausted his fight and quieted his demons.

I could hear my siblings rustling around on the floor above me, running from their room to the top of the stairs to get a better hearing spot. My sister most likely was considering a shout as she'd done in the past. "Stop it! Please stop it!" Those crying screams would echo so loudly, bouncing off the walls around the staircase. The stomping of their small bare feet as they paced up and down the short hallway. I was sure both my little sisters were in full terror mode. Their poor hearts beating in fear. Frightened and shaking with no one to comfort them until Mother let loose a shrill *"Get in bed and shut your mouths!"* ending the pacing...for now.

If my sister had a phone on the second floor, she would have already called the police. The only phone hung on the wall next to the pantry door. My sister had called the police so many times before, memorizing the seven-digit number well before Willimantic was part of a 911 system. She could dial that number on the rotary phone like a modern-day call on speed dial. She would get the cops to send someone, everyone, "before he kills my brother." I have no idea how many times I heard my sister screaming those words as Crazy hammered away. She was so determined to save her brother, and I'm confident she did, many times. Tonight was looking like another one of those nights in need of a savior.

—◆—

Crazy was focused on ending my life one way or another. At least we believed that was his plan, and tonight might just be that night. While all these different signals jockeyed for position in my head, Crazy was still working his devil mouth at Mother and me without taking a break. He was succeeding at building that bubble of power, that ball of energy to launch himself into whatever sphere of destruction was heading our way. He was getting closer and closer, building with every hate-filled tongue waggle.

My sister must have known this, too, as the stomping feet above my head were getting louder and more forceful, as if trying to send a demand through the floorboards and past the smoke-stained ceilings. She wanted it to stop, but it wasn't going to work. Crazy seemed to thrive on the labors to stop the lunacy, almost as if it added fuel to his bubble of growing power. Cries to make it stop backfired, and Crazy knew if he kept raising the insanity level, nothing could beat him, nothing could calm him down or stop him. It simply had to take its course. It was like a demon was controlling the entire play, and we were its puppets. Crazy would alternate levels of anger, rage, and hate as he built his bubble of power. You could feel it growing, shaping itself in waves of flowing invisible clouds like a heat mirage rising off the road surface on a hot summer day. You could see the rolling thunderclouds billow to life, its worst form taking hold, mounting, planning out what was next, like a supervillain taking his drug of choice at just the right time to attack the side of goodness and put down any hope of safety, peace, or happiness.

Crazy looked down at the dinner plate with that look I'd seen so many times before, and with that, I knew what was next. His mind would pause to help the angry pockets of power collect into one force of violent, fixed, targeted mass of naked rage. His eyes would almost turn a full black from eyelids to pupils. All humanity would be erased from his consciousness. Whatever soul remained was being coated in that black mass of malevolence that enveloped his being. It was like a cold front moving in from the north with such speed that by the time you realize it's coming, you're encased in a frozen tundra of bitterness, and you know it's too late to avoid the storm. You know what's coming, so you try to figure out how to protect yourself. You mentally fight to become ready but with little hope as the hurricane winds spread farther and faster than your mind can track.

I was bracing for impact without knowing what form Crazy's storm would take—a blow to the head or a full-body lunge taking me to the floor with Crazy mounted on top with all his devilish might ravaging my body. Punches hitting flesh or bone. Biting my ear, my shoulder, or that muscle that connected my arm to my neck. Perhaps it would be a head butt to the nose. Or would he grab both ears with his toughened, cracked, callused fingers, pressing his palms so hard into my eardrums I would lose all hearing except my pounding heartbeat as it raced blood to newly forming bruises and pumped to get adrenaline into places so I could fight back and protect what was left?

I knew if he got my ears into his bear claws, my head would be smashed repeatedly into the floorboards until darkness and stars revisited and I drifted to the peaceful place I'd known so many times before. Was this going to be his game plan, or would that plate of shepherd's pie get a flying lesson along with the entire table, which was already glued and taped back together from prior incidents? Would Crazy's opening salvo be the flying table, the flinging plate, or the flying fists?

I glanced at Mother, who was transforming in her own right. Not in a retreating way, but more like when a killer bee emerges from its honeycomb lodge for its first day in the new world, knowing its job is to be a soldier whose only purpose in life is to fight and die for its queen. Mother's transformation was like watching a Broadway play open with the first act being of little interest to those who filled the seats. They had been advised it was a slow start but to wait for the *bang!* that would happen when they least expected it. It might be the same play time after time, but the fight scenes were never really the same. Would you get a piece of ear bitten off, à la Mike Tyson, or a head butt to the bridge of your nose, which would lead to massive blood loss and a sticky mess as it covered your face and dried quicker than you could imagine?

Mother's face was turning white as her blood supply started pooling its reserves in a storage area to help prepare for survival. I could see her reposition her body. Her left foot pushed just forward of her right, and she leaned her upper body slightly forward and pushed her neck as far out front as possible to allow her face to get as close to Crazy as it could be without her stepping closer. She was daring Crazy with her chin to "come on, you fucking bastard, I dare you" as she helped ramp up the power play, adding moisture to the storm clouds. I'd seen this move my entire life, and it never ended well when she baited hell's fury.

Fire was starting to form on her face as she all but cheered Crazy on to his next level. Pushing him, daring him to do something with that plate of shepherd's pie that was no longer anything but room temperature and drier than a dehydrated bag of MREs left over from the Korean War. Mother pressed her position, knowing where this was going and still shoveling fuel into Crazy's furnace, as if he needed help getting to that place he craved so much. His powerful, unstoppable force of lava was ready to blow and maim everything in its path. It was like watching two knights of darkness stoking the fires of hell to see who could force open the other's nasty deeds. It would have made a good miniseries if it had not been so tragically ruthless.

Mother never raised herself to the same levels of hate and anger as Crazy, but she did try to compete. Watching her create such a bubble—small waves, really—to push back against his power was a magical thing. The magic plumes of rolling counterhatred bounced up against one another like drumbeats competing in your ears for dominance. She would try to generate the same levels but never succeeded, never came close, really. Her rage was always overpowered by Crazy's majestic gifts and abilities to muster more evil than anyone present. Both had a way of parting from reality and digging into a place where anyone can figure hell exists. That place they threaten you with if you don't behave or do as commanded. That place called hell with its fire and brimstone. That place with no hope for mercy. The place the Bible tells us exists under the earth. I was walking through it every day. It was something I had witnessed so many times it would surely give the biblical writers pause for reconsideration. Now, I know the Bible doesn't say all evil is locked in hell, but unless you really witness someone walking around just like the rest of us and you can see that transformation firsthand, the theories your mind creates when reading or hearing parts from a biblical story just won't do justice to what your eyes witness when watching pure evil materialize in storm clouds of rolling energy. If you can see, feel, sense, and know they exist, the Bible isn't just a book of stories!

—⚶—

Mother would try to compete; however, she was more like an injured bobcat with its tail pressed against the end of the underground burrow it called its safe haven. As Mother dared and pushed Crazy with hurtful words and her body posture, she took a quick look to her right to see where she had room to maneuver, to run, once the physical war broke out.

The froth of revulsion from both sides met just above the table. My ears popped from the sound waves of yelling and screaming. A piercing ring followed as a warning of unearthly "incoming" presences broke through a veil protecting our world from the likes of Satan. Little feet stomped on the flooring above. The panes of glass in the window beside Crazy vibrated from all the noise like plastic wrap placed tightly over a bowl. The glass appeared to transform into a liquid flowing in waves like a pebble tossed into a perfectly settled pond and casting its circling ripples in all directions.

I didn't think it could get worse, but here we were. Broiling, steaming close to the point of explosion. It didn't seem much different from the days of the liver rebellion to the current shepherd's pie crisis as my mind walked me back to the present. The sounds of Mother screaming her share of vile, hate-filled viciousness into the air added to the bubbles of rolling anger collecting at the midpoint of that kitchen table. Competing insanity surged and commingled while tethered to each host like the cord of a newborn. Its lifeline was the mouths of Crazy and Mother, supplying its source of fuel until it reached a point where it could breathe on its own. Spinning counterclockwise, it grew external rings while darkness thickened among the internal spirals. Pieces broke off to form new pulsating circles, offspring of a diseased parasite with its tail connected to its originator. The more they fired off hate-filled rhetoric, the stronger the dark balls became. It was a mesmerizing display that left me lost in both thought and wonder. One thing was certain: it now had a life of its own, but my senses told me it was still not quite where it needed to be.

I looked away from the swirling balls and connected my eyes on Mother and then to Crazy. There was still one stage left to go before that point of no return. It was a lifting of sorts, a clearing of anything good that might remain within the sphere of his domain. As if anything of kindness, anything of love or remorse would gather into one final glow, wrapped in a protective shield against the onslaught of negative waves. It was the last bastion of anything good as it slipped away from the ever-growing hate and took over all that was. This I learned to watch for, as it was the true gauge of things to come, the tell that poker players say is the key to knowing the other players. The tell that gives them the advantage, the ability to sniff out a bluff or a hand that can be beaten if you can read the signs. I was learning to read the signs, but that was all I could do—except prepare for a beating.

The final feeling of hope was swept from the supper table in a flash of white light that seemed to momentarily blind me like a Kodak picture being snapped from a 1940s camera. It was as if any remaining goodness was scooped up and saved from that room. I watched as the darkness thrived at the same instant, jumping in size and strength. Crazy's eyes lost all but the black of anger as that thing coiled over his head and down his body. Fear and nastiness filled the few droplets of kindness.

Mother must have sensed it as well. She pulled her face back from the baiting chin wiggle, withdrew her leaning presence, and took a half step backward. She had gone from fight to fear in the blink of an eye. Her mouth shuddered and halted its death march as she took a quick glance at the direction she'd run once Crazy made his intentions known.

The voices became deathly quiet, the telltale warning that the storm had arrived. Crazy was now standing with his hands on his hips. Somehow I missed him standing up and readying with hands on hips. That was his well-known striking pose. Once those hands rested on the hips, the die was cast. Survival was the only option for anyone in the looking glass of his beady glint.

The pounding bare feet from above silenced. A deafening numbness reverberated in a silhouette of black shadows and thickening dank smells. An eerie calm gripped the tense moments, broken once Crazy lifted his hands from their starting gate and reached for that dish of shepherd's pie.

—ɯ—

The plate was Crazy's focus. The armatures were ripped, locked, and loaded, and so it began. Crazy moved his dominant hand down toward the plate. My mind raced to track his next moves. I began to stand up at the exact second Crazy's fingers reached the outer rim of the blue-and-white cheaply decorated ceramic dinner plate heaped with what was, at the least, a filling supper.

Crazy picked up the dinner plate with one swift motion and tossed it across the table like a pro throwing a rising fastball right down the middle. Amazingly, the shepherd's pie stuck to the plate as it passed just inches from my face like a cream pie thrown in an episode of *I Love Lucy*, without the staged laughter to follow. It was heading directly to its intended target and right at the perfect height to strike his fastball into the center of his second-favorite target, Mother's nose. My nose had been broken several times by Crazy, and I'm guessing Mother had lost count herself as the pitch moved ever closer to the catcher's mitt.

Mother was never a limber woman. Top-heavy with an average build. "Fleet of foot" was not a phrase promulgated to feature her flexibility or her agility. I sometimes wondered if she led with her face on purpose, or maybe she was just so used to getting hit in the mug. Maybe for her it was somehow rewarding after pushing and pushing until the plate was airborne and making a slight whistle as it closed the final few inches before making contact.

Mother's effort to dodge the ball of food and ceramic was pointless, but at least she tried, even if it was more like trying to dodge a punch from Iron Mike Tyson. It was just not going to miss. Even her effort to raise her arms was a fruitless endeavor. By the time her hand led her forearm into the strike zone, the plate was well past being deflected, and like a Tyson blow, it landed perfectly centered on the right side of her nose. With a splat and a thump, the rim lifted and caught her just above her eyebrow.

I reached out with my hand to intercept the pitch, but I was far too late. My mind was caught up in the mystical endeavors floating above the table, my concentration lost in that maze of spinning evil, setting its game plan and growing in strength. I should have been studying Crazy's moves, his plans. Had I kept my focus on him, I could have stopped his dinner bullet. It wasn't the first time my focus had been taken over by invisible abnormalities, and as they buzzed about, it wasn't going to be the last.

Mashed potatoes clung to her face, with speckles of yellow and brown bumps completing the dinner mask. If it hadn't been so tragically sickening and the follow-through so devastating, it might have ended in a laugh—laughter of stupidity over the pointless argument leading up to the dinner plate flying saucer. Looking as briefly as I could, knowing I needed to be ready for Crazy's next assault, I watched as Mother's eyes widened in shock. Indignant disbelief replaced her chin wiggle and former righteous stance. A look of pain started to caress her fast-changing temperament as the plate drifted toward a crash on the floor, seemingly in superslow motion.

The plate clanked, shattered, and sent shards of razor-sharp death nails in every direction. Mashed potatoes refused to move from Mother's face, and her raccoon eyes opened wider for a brief moment before the slice just above her eyebrow produced a deep, dark, reddish-brown river that spilled onto the potatoes like ketchup oozing out of the bottom of a Heinz packet. As insane as it sounds, a picture of steaming-hot salty french fries popped into my mind as the blood squirted from the opening just like squeezing the packet after ripping it out, only without the feeling of happiness. Maybe it was the hunger tapping at my ribs, or maybe it was my brain trying to protect me, trying to keep my anger in check as I watched Mother bleeding once again at the hands of the bastard Crazy. We both knew this was only the beginning.

Mother's knees wobbled, and her body dropped a couple of inches before she regained her balance and grasped what was happening. The blood now pumping all over her face was creating a horror scene worse than any Halloween creation out of Hollywood. The crimson creases created a blood cavity as they wove their path through the smashed potatoes, dislodging bits of corn from their hold, sending them down her cheek before coming to rest just below her collarbone. The off-white mashed ravines, now awash in a gravy-like river of running red plasma, broke loose and fell from Mother's face and splashed at her neckline. With a moment of hesitation, she scooped a chunk from her chest and flung it back in the direction it had come from, flicking bits of blood and spud in a cascading carousel, catching Crazy right in his open mouth.

Crazy didn't waste a second as he flipped the table in the same direction as the plate but with much less accuracy. It was a good thing I was standing up, or that table would have hit me square under my chin. The contents of the table shot in every direction. The four legs were now facing upward.

The sounds of shuffling baby feet slipped back and forth but only traveled in short walks. A scream from above was masked by the tumbling of so many objects bouncing, breaking, and banging across the kitchen walls and floor. A knife whirled past my arm before clanking off the oven door. That knife was Crazy's mandatory eating cutlery, even when serving soup. Its placement, just to the left of his fork and on the left side of his setting, made it readily handy for the left-handed ogre.

Crazy charged toward the flicking fingers that had dared to push back against his pitched authority, full of fury and out-stretched arms, fingers, and thumbs pointing as his upper body led his feet in the race for what was looking like Mother's jugular. The table was still settling down from the flipping as he stepped onto its underside. The sounds of crunching broken glass filled the room but did nothing to slow down Crazy. Racing feet above broke past the short path and crossed the hallway. Screams came from the top of the stair, begging Crazy to stop without even seeing what was happening yet knowing from past lessons, beatings, and bloodshed.

Crazy had flipped the table with such power that two of the legs were now standing upright while two broke free from their mounts. As Crazy charged forward, one table leg caught him in the left thigh, blocking his attack momentarily and tossing him off balance. As he looked down to avoid the obstruction, without a thought, I pushed him with open palms. Both of my hands jolted his dominant shoulder, shoving him off balance even more and redirecting his attack away from Mother. The table leg snapped back in a counterbalance kind of way. The round knob caught Crazy square in his privates. The shock wave curdled his face and crumpled him into a hunched-over holding pattern. It wasn't a hard hit, but it got his attention. It wasn't entirely my doing, and I swear I heard a slight giggle a second or two after the table's toe tapped his tallywhacker.

It wasn't the first time I had stood between Crazy and Mother. The blood on Mother's face left me determined to stop any further beatings. You'd think I was full of fear, but honestly, the fear left me, replaced by a sense of purpose, a sense of protection. I'd get the same feeling every time the buildup transformed into actual fighting. But somehow, this time was different. Maybe it was the lessons from Coach Perfect and the success of slaying the mighty Whalers. Whatever the case, something had changed with me, and I was ready for the next level in Crazy's world of evil.

The fear vanished, and anger became the prevailing force, with a matching sidekick of calm resolve and determination. It felt like I could never lose—not in a short-term kind of way, but more in a long-game sort of thing. I knew I'd get beaten by him, but he'd never succeed in killing me. I didn't care if I lived or died, as the pain of living this life was unbearably difficult. Dying was easy; it was living that was hard. If not for that feeling, that sense of purpose, that sense of knowing that resonated deep within, I might have given in and taken the easy road.

But that sense of knowing was so profound I just knew that "there is something I'm here to do," but I just couldn't figure it out. So I trusted my instincts and learned to believe in something greater, something I couldn't pinpoint but knew to be true with all my being.

As this battle ramped up, those thoughts flooded my mind. It was as if I had to go through all this insanity in order to understand the future. As nuts as that sounds, that became ingrained in me, even as the shepherd's pie dinner war unfolded.

One of the most difficult things to reconcile deep within was striking Crazy. When I was alone and dreaming of ways to fight back, I could see me punching, hitting, and ripping skin from his flesh. I'd visualize smashing his face into the table. Bashing his head against a wall and whipping him with that lethal leather lasher. My steel fists knocked his smoke-stained brown teeth free from their decaying mounts, wiping the smug smirk clear out of existence.

The reality of striking back was, somehow, an entirely different matter. For some reason, when it came time to implement my planned assault, my arms did little more than raise a defensive posture, like the chicken flapping its feathers as Duke snapped its neck.

I used to dream of all the ways I'd fight back and protect Mother against his poundings. I used to dream I'd become big enough to stop him, to hurt him worse than he'd hurt Mother.

But to date, it was only a dream. It was only thoughts and wishful thinking. Was the shepherd's pie war a new beginning? A starting point after all those nights crying myself to sleep, begging God to make me strong enough to fight back? Had I just palm shoved my death certificate and unleashed more harm than ever before? Was the calm taking hold within me a signal of the raging storm about to make landfall?

One thing was certain: it was an entirely different set of feelings as a power started to circulate in my chest, my lungs. The rhythm of my breath began to shorten, as if setting a pace to supply both calm resolve and fiery rage in perfect harmony of a power yet to be unleashed. It was like letting go of all thought and letting fate decide the outcome. A release of control, a surrendering without quitting. A freeing of the force within me that I knew was there but had never fully trusted. At this moment and without realizing I had done it, I decided to trust the power within. It felt like the calm and the power were one and I was simply along for the ride. As long as I didn't try to reclaim control, I would be just fine. That was the feeling whispering in my ears.

The calm was a warm sensation that seemed to flow all around me, almost as if it was the opposite of the bubble of hate engulfing Crazy. As I looked down at him working to right himself, that calm expanded its reach. It was like I was outside my own mind, my brain watching, looking around as if floating outside myself, watching what was unfolding. No thoughts or plans came or went, just calm, quiet, slow motion without thinking. An observing of sorts. It had a feel like a third party witnessing the event to make sure they could fully write the report without emotion, just the facts and no more. I was sure I knew the outcome, but I still couldn't explain it. It was like knowing something without knowing why or how or even thinking about it. You just know what's coming next and that it's going to be all right.

As the scene unfolded, a scream filled the room from another direction, just behind me and to my right. My sister, who had been stomping her feet, racing back and forth down the second floor, had finally come downstairs and walked into what must have looked like a true nightmare. She and my other sister, five years younger than me and two years younger than her sister, were both staring at the mess, screaming for it to stop.

Taking my eyes off Crazy was a big mistake, a big mistake. He hit me at the beltline and drove us both into the gas stove, still hot from warming up the dinner plates and still kicking out heat into what had been a rather cold space before all the objects were tossed about. Now it was as hot as all get-out and getting hotter. My last look at Mother had her moving into the small kitchenette, trying to avoid her daughters witnessing her blood-smeared face.

Crazy controlled my midsection and started to pick me up. I lost contact with the floor and part of my leverage. Off the side of the stove and onto the floor we went, just inches from my sisters, who kept screaming for it to stop. Crazy was now fully on top of me, my back and head hurting from the body slam onto the hardwood flooring with him on top, knocking the wind out of me. Crazy turned to his daughters like a wolf to its pack and, in a hideous guttural-sounding voice, ordered them to "get in your room, or I'll kill him and then your mother."

Through half-open eyes, reeling in pain, I could see both sisters running up the stairs, screaming, crying, and frightened beyond belief. A white shadow stood against the wall as if to shuttle them onward while looking at Crazy.

Crazy turned back to me and readjusted his hip so he could pin me down and control my movements below the waist. Straddling me, he positioned a bit higher, sitting directly on my stomach high enough to put pressure on my lungs. I was gasping for air the way you do when someone sucker punches you in the diaphragm and you can't catch your breath, nothing in and nothing out. I was lost in the feeling of helplessness, struggling for air and thinking it wasn't coming back. Crazy didn't waste time fine-tuning his position and reached to my throat for a short squeeze. But after several long seconds, he decided on a better course of pain.

Grabbing my ears, one in each hand, he forced my face to look directly into his lifeless dark eyes. The back of my head ground into the wood floor. My eyes pulled toward his face as he lifted my head off the hardwood flooring, then brought it back down with a deadening thud. My face raised again...*thud*. His viselike grip on my ears, forcing my head up and down, beating my skull like a jackhammer trying to break concrete. Crazy was panting like a sick dog that has run much too far, much too long, and needs time to regain its facilities. He had exactly what he wanted—complete control and domination over my crumpled body. I couldn't remember my last breath. His weight compressed my lungs like a snake's bowing grip, constricting my ability to inhale even the slightest bit. My eyes rose toward his again and again, the thuds muffled by a crunch. "Dying is easy" flashed across my mind. My eyes were starting to tunnel down a keyhole of light and darkness.

Visions of white flowing garments dangling off an older woman took my focus off his face and eyes and the helpless feeling that was gaining control over me. I could hear Crazy's rapid breathing, see his spit and drool dripping amid the foam forming from his mouth and nose. That feeling of rage was so intense it felt hot in the air around every inch of my body. The older woman was dancing in a slow circle around Crazy. Her dress was flowing several inches above her ankles. A blouse with a pretty pattern of pink and rose-colored flowers, and a white see-through lace scarf that caught the wind as she circled around on her toes.

It felt like she was at the beach, but I could only see her. Nothing more; just her with a clear background with no time or space to judge where she was or who she was. I just had a sense, or maybe a knowing, that she was at the beach. A light-blue sky opened above and behind her. Colors started to form under her feet in differing light-sand tones. Sounds no longer came from any place except the beautiful old lady with shoulder-length gray-and-silver hair as straight as straight could be but with a little curl inward as it touched her back just below her shoulders. Her wispy hair and gown blew in a soft breeze with such elegance I could feel a smile come over my face. The grip on my ears let me know Crazy could see my smile as well.

I started to hear a thumping I'd never heard before—or wait, I had heard this before, but as I started to think of when, the old lady stopped dancing and faced me with the kindest smile I'd ever seen. Her teeth were perfect, white without gaps. Her lips were thin with a touch of bright-pink shading to highlight her welcoming smile. Her eyes were radiant and inviting, caring and comforting. The kind that make you forget all of life's worries and fill your insides with complete warmth and happiness. The scent of chocolate chip cookies caught my nose, and I could feel my eyes smile back at hers as if to say thank you. I don't know why I wanted to say thank you, but I did. My pain was fading away, and a feeling of pure love started to penetrate my chest, replacing the remaining torment, the leftovers of a lack of breath taken away, like the flap of a bird's wing as my lungs completely stopped hurting.

Peace was taking hold. A feeling like I'd never had before took over my entire body as that calm I was feeling resonated across my existence, growing so strong I felt a smile locking across my face. It was the happiest I can ever remember feeling. It was pure joy wrapped in the most serene feeling I'd ever experienced. It was the answer to my prayers.

Then, without warning, without a sound, without notice or explanation, the old lady seemed to whisper in my ear, "It will be all right." And with that, everything went dark. Was this death? That was the last thought I would remember. The light faded into complete darkness and the ultimate sense of silence.

Without a concept of how much time has passed, I started to hear voices; sounds in the distance; faded, faint, broken speech; and background noise. But where was I? What had happened to me, and why did I feel like I was moving even though it felt as if I was in my bed? That gruff, smoke-strained sound I knew so well was right in my ear, but what was it saying? It was garbled and not making any sense.

God, my head hurt. Victor jumped into my mind, an image of

him as he was carted off the field. Was this a replay of that scene, a rerun of today's events? Was I dreaming? And if so, turn down the lights; they hurt my eyes, and I didn't even think they were open. Maybe I was in my room, and the sun was bursting through the dirty window glass and hitting my face. It didn't feel like the warmth of the sun, but my face did feel hot.

I tried to move my head, but it felt like it was stuck to something. It felt like pillows were on both sides of my cheeks. The cool pillowcases felt good, but why were they so hard? My pillows were supersoft, old with most of the feathers lost to time, as I'd had the same pillows since I could remember. My pillows were only about half their original size, and only one pillowcase remained. The other one was torn apart the last time it got washed, trying to get the bloodstains out of a formerly white casing. I tried to sew it back together, but Mother decided it was too far gone and promised to replace both pillow and case. As usual, it was an empty promise that disappeared the second Crazy found out.

This wasn't my pillow, and who was making that noise? Another grizzly whisper crept into my ear, shaking my senses and awareness.

The sounds of people and the pain in my head caused a throbbing, but from a distance. The pain felt far away, but I knew it was going to come ever closer. It was like looking down a tunnel to a point far away and seeing the scope of light widening as your focus opens and you can feel more and more of your surroundings. Another sharp whisper of that voice started to reemerge as the dominant sound, pushing its way into my head past the other sounds to take priority, but I still couldn't make out what it was saying. "…don't…better not…kill…else…"

What was this message, and where was it coming from? The

pain was becoming very sharp in the back of my head, shooting across my skull and blinding my eyes until I faded back into the darkness and silence behind my eyelids until there was nothing more.

If you've ever awoken midstream during your dreams, kind of a sleep-wake combination where you know you're dreaming and you know you can feel your surroundings but you try to stay in both worlds while you mentally dance in both places, that's what was happening. It was kind of cool until the pain returned and traded in the dream-wake combo for a shot of brutal agony so sharp it forced complete blindness inside my eyes. One so dark that even the stars that would normally accompany the thumping darkness didn't seem to want to come out and shine.

What happened to that old woman with the scarf and the white blouse with the flowers, and who was she? As my thoughts started to reform and my mind felt like it was trying to reclaim a hold on what was happening, the light started to peek through my closed eyes, telling me it was daytime. Or maybe I was in a room with big lights above? I had no idea how much time had passed or even what day it was when I first started to regain a footing on my surroundings. It was as if the lighting in the room had entered my vision well before the actual light became real. At the same time, I felt lethargic, slow minded, hungover even. Nothing was moving. It was a pace that wasn't slow motion—rather, a time line different from what I was used to.

Beep…beep…beep to a pulse in the background as it started

to pull me forward like a vacuum sucking my thoughts back to a place away from where I'd been. The quiet and silent peace kept my head pain at a distance. *Beep...beep...beep*, chirping chatter, bringing me closer and closer as it got louder and louder, but more as a distant sense of noise and not so much as an approaching sound. I knew it was a fixed sound, but I couldn't put my finger on it. Voices in the distance started to enter, different-sounding chatter, a woman's voice, a woman of authority just in front of another voice that was softer, gentler, and more soothing as it became the voice to focus on. I liked the sound of her soft voice, and it helped me bring myself back to the present, where the beeping was more in the background and the sounds of activity became more prominent.

I opened my eyes to see a white ceiling with boxes, squares, and tiny holes with black specks around the white patterns. Some had bright lights filling the boxes. I still heard the beeping off to my left, and there was something around my head. I strained to focus my view. It took a bit, but once it cleared up, I could see light blue on the walls below the boxes above me. I started to lick my dry, cracked lips.

A woman came into view. She was standing next to me with a smile, and when she spoke, it was that soft voice I had heard a moment ago. She was a pretty lady with bright-greenish eyes, a wonderful smile, and a feeling about her of pure comfort. A feeling almost like a mother's safety net when you're swaddled in her arms of warmth and protection. It made me smile and feel good as I tried to figure out where I was, what was happening—hell, who was I?

As a round of thumping dull pain radiated across my entire head, starting at the lower backside of my skull just above my neck, the soft voice of the pretty lady standing beside me said, "I know it hurts. We're working on something for the pain. It will come and go, so try to relax, and it will stop; I promise." She never stopped smiling as she gently fluffed the pillow next to my ear and adjusted my blankets with a tender hand. "You've had a tough few days, so take it easy, and don't try to move around too much until the doctor gets here. He's on his way."

—m—

A tough few days? The doctor? What was this pretty lady talking about? She said she'd be back shortly to check on me, so just sit tight, I was going to be all right. My mind wandered, and as I looked around the room, I saw there were three other beds but no one in them. The beeping was a machine connected to wires, tubes, and cords running in all directions. I reached up to my head and felt some kind of wrap covering my entire head above my forehead and just above my ears. I searched around the rest of my body to see what else was hurting, and all seemed to be fine except my head. The throbbing came and went, sometimes with authority but more times just to let me know there was pain coming from that area. I was starting to get used to the pain, and it seemed to dull a bit as long as I didn't try to pick up and move my face again.

I reached for my ear, and a grimacing cringe was my reward for touching that part of my body. It felt like a giant turkey vulture had tried to scratch it off. I gently touched the other one, with the same results. My heart raced, and the beeps got shorter, quicker, and louder. I put my arms back to the bedside and took a deep breath. My chest hurt when I inhaled. What had happened, and how had I gotten there?

As I closed my eyes and tried to remember what had happened, I saw a flash of Victor. Was I carted off too? I had flashes of other images—a face, a sound, the lineup after the game. The bus ride and a crunching inside my ears from something I couldn't dig out of my memory. Mother blinked past my closed eyes, and then the image of Crazy sitting on my chest with his hands securely clamped onto my ears.

I saw my face rising toward his evil glare, and then the heart-pounding vision was broken by the sound of "I'm Doctor Petrel. How are you feeling, young man? You had us very, very concerned about you."

My eyes opened to see the warm face of a dark-skinned man with a heavy accent, somewhere between a British army officer in a Monty Python film and an Australian outback commercial. I didn't say anything, and he followed with "You have a concussion, a bad one, and you took quite a hit to the back of your head. Do you remember what happened to you? Do you remember falling down the stairs?"

I had fallen down the stairs? That couldn't be right. It hurt my mind to try to replay, to recall what had happened, so I tried to re-member falling down the stairs. Was Crazy trying to help me after I fell down the stairs? Was that why he was on top of me with his hands on the sides of my head? As I kept trying to replay what had happened, to try to remember, the doctor broke in, saying, "Don't try too hard. It will come back to you; just give it some time. Your mother is doing fine. She said she tried to stop you from falling and hurt herself when she hit the railing. Do you remember any of that?"

I didn't, but I also didn't say anything. My throat was dry, and I signaled I needed water.

The doctor handed me the ice chips with a warning. "Not too much. Your system hasn't had anything in three days, so be careful not to eat or drink too quickly."

Three days? What the heck! Three days—that was how long it had been.

"Your coach has been in to check on you. He didn't think you had a concussion, but I understand there was a lot of activity after the game. Did you get hit with something in the head, or did you get hit and lose consciousness during the game?"

None of this made sense. I didn't remember anything he was saying. What was *wrong* with me!

I just looked at him with a puzzled stare and no other response. He took the hint and did some checking on my head and my body, asked some other questions about the injuries, repeated that I was lucky I didn't get hurt any worse taking such a tumble down the stairs, and it was a good thing my mother was there to stop me from really getting hurt. I had nothing to say and just looked at him while trying to understand what had happened and what he was saying. I didn't remember any stairs or falling on them.

The doctor said to rest, and he'd be back later to follow up, but the nurses were the best, and they'd keep taking care of me. As he was at the door to leave, he turned and said, "Oh, the police want to talk to you. So if you are up to it, I can let them know you're doing better. Maybe in the morning?"

The police? What was that about? I was confused, worried about Mother, and not sure what was going on. I didn't remember what had happened, so I closed my eyes and fell asleep without realizing it. As I slept, I kept seeing Crazy's face. It was so close to mine, and I heard that whispering in a gruff sound like a warning but without words. I was remembering a warning, but of what?

The sounds faded into the background, and I slipped into a deep, peacefully quiet sleep, but for how long, I can't say.

Yanked from that peacefulness, I was pulled back into reality in the time it took to simply open my eyes. The warning sound I'd been trying to figure out was back. This time it came with the moist heat and dampness of the person carrying the message. "You better not tell anyone what happened, or else!" It all came flooding back in an instant. Crazy was so close to my ear I could smell his unbrushed teeth. The smell of machine oil filled the air just before his nasty breath clung to my ear like frost on the corners of a window in the dead of winter.

I snapped my head and neck to get away from his face, which sent a shock wave of pain down my spine, across my shoulders, and throughout my head. As the jolt of both remembering and the newly forming pain rushed throughout my existence, Crazy pulled back and raised his crooked smile as if he cared I was in pain but needed to pretend to be a concerned parent tending to his injured child. Mother was at his side. She held her eyebrows high in a look of surprise, like the joker in a deck of cards. A distressed mouth was plastered to a face that had several shades of blue, black, and pink lines and marks, like she had been to a clown store and only washed off half the makeup in her hurry to leave for an unknown urgent appointment.

As I looked closer, I saw it wasn't a raised eyebrow. It was a bandage taped to her forehead causing her other eyebrow to remain stuck in the upright position. The rest of her face tried to show compassion and empathy while fear was dripping off her like she was an oversoaked sponge being wrung out in the sink.

Crazy started to speak, forcing Mother to look his way. I tried not to listen, but it was a futile endeavor.

He said the same thing the doctor had said—I had fallen down the stairs. Mother had reached out to stop me from falling only to be dragged down the flight with me, causing the injuries to her face. It was far from the first time this game had been played with the police, the hospital, and the doctors. I had many broken bones, scars, and defacements repaired by a profession locked into an oath to protect, to heal, to help those who were in trouble. Once again I was in the driver's seat, a momentary position of control, knowing if I didn't complete the tale spun by Crazy, harm was promised to my brother, my sisters, or once again to Mother. It is not an enviable position to be caught in the game of life or death for others. Decisions to make that should never need to be made. Regardless, here I was, knee-deep in the insanity of Crazy and his test of wills. A battlefield worse than facing a bullet, far worse.

One time I tried to tell a nurse what really happened, and she did report it to the police. They did come and talk to me, and I told them what had really happened. It was my word against Crazy's. Mother backed his story, and when I got back to that house, it was a painful lesson, one that took a long time to complete. It was a benchmark of things to come if I didn't comply with Crazy's version of events, so from then on, I knew I'd better commit to what he told me to say, or else.

Crazy went so far as to involve the perfect season as the cause of this brutality. I needed to tell the doctors and police I had been complaining of a headache. That I had been telling Mother and him how my vision was out of focus and my eyes hurt to keep them open. I was going upstairs to bed with Mother beside me, helping me along until I'd lost my balance. I "blacked out," he proclaimed, and fell down the stairs. He went deeper into the mythological tundra by claiming, somehow, it was he who had saved both of us, and if not for his actions, it could have been much worse, so much worse. As he rambled on, I wondered how many times I had "fallen" down the stairs and if anyone actually believed his tales.

The doctor entering the room cut his story off midsentence. He stood at the end of the hospital bed and said how lucky I was. My head had taken serious blows, and they had to keep me sedated until the swelling came down. That was the really worrying part, but everything was looking good, and I should be able to go home soon. He said I was a remarkable young man with a great family. The luck part was spot on, but the family part…not so much, unless you were hellhounds and looking to take over as leader of Crazyville!

As those words passed his lips, I turned my face slightly away from everyone and tried to keep from crying, but with little success. Tears rolled and rolled from my eyes without my ability to control the flow. This caused pressure in my head, which caused more pain, which the doctor could see, so he ordered everyone to leave the room so I could get some rest. I think that at that moment, something changed. I think at that moment, the doctor knew something was off.

Once he was alone with me, he put his hand over the back of my hand as it rested on the side of the bed, looked at me, and said, "I believe someone who can survive what you have gone through will survive whatever else comes your way. I've seen many people come and go, but few have the strength I see in you. Take it from me, you are going to be all right. Just hang in there, and you'll find a way to get to the next place you need to be." He patted my hand and, with a sharp smile, turned and walked out of the room, stopping to address Crazy directly. He wagged his finger, poking at Crazy's chest like a knowing figure of authority.

I couldn't hear what he was saying, but it had an effect on Crazy. Maybe not a big one, but one that must have made him think. He didn't react or respond, and Dr. Petrel finished and walked away without looking back. But he stopped just a few feet away and waved his hand, motioning for someone to come forward. As I watched, I could see two cops walk up to the doctor as he pointed toward the room, spoke for a brief moment, and then headed down the hallway as the policemen made their way into the room.

—⟶⟵—

Crazy was fighting with them to let him into the room while they talked to me, but they were having none of it. The cops were as polite and direct as you'd expect, with very little small talk. They asked, "Can you tell us what happened to you, son?"

I looked past them as Crazy and Mother watched from just outside the open door. I stared at Crazy for a few moments and then at the taller policeman asking the questions. He followed with "If you're afraid to talk with your parents outside the door, just tell us, and we can have them moved down the hallway."

I looked into his eyes and without missing a beat said, "I lost my balance and fell down the stairs."

The cop said he wanted to believe me, but "it seems a little far-fetched, and we've been to your house many times before. If you don't tell us what happened, we can't help you."

I stared at the cops, then past them to Crazy, debating my options and playing out scenes if I told the truth. Would they arrest the rat bastard? Maybe! Would he find a way back? The past said yes. What would happen to me, my sisters, and my brother? I clung to the hope of some kind of family to be around, but surely we'd all get split up and sent away like Crazy said we would. My head was pounding as I tried to figure out what to do. God, I just wanted to be a kid, play football, and talk to girls. This was not a fun life.

I wanted to tell them they couldn't help me. Instead, I just followed Crazy's lies because all I wanted was to go back to sleep. The cops pressed a bit, but it wasn't my first time telling a story, a web of deception to cover up and protect the others from Crazy's relentless insanity. The cops said they'd be back tomorrow to talk to me again and get a formal statement, so I'd better be ready to tell the truth. Then they turned and walked out of the room, past the nervous pair awaiting the results, and kept going with only a brief "We'll be back tomorrow."

Mother came into the room while Crazy left, just a few seconds behind the police. I thought about what was happening and decided to see if I could make a deal with my battered mother. I figured it was worth the chance, so I told her that if she moved out with my sisters, I'd keep telling the same story, but if she refused, I'd tell the truth. I didn't think it was going to work, but it was worth an effort. Mother said that the last time she ran and tried to move out, Crazy had beaten her badly, and she was sure he'd kill her if she tried again. With that I gave in and said I'd keep the story going and that I'd sign the statement supporting the version of lies that only a truly demented person would create, let alone believe.

As the words were just past my lips, Mother said something that truly made me wonder who was crazier, her or him. She said, "Someday you'll leave this family, along with your sisters and your brother, and I'll be all alone. He's all I got, and I don't want to be alone for the rest of my life. I love him, and that's that." To this day I've never been able to reconcile that statement. I've never been able to understand or justify how anyone could live in such a way. How someone could feel so alone, so beaten, that it was better to stay in the insanity than do something to change it. It is a haunting tale that begs for an answer but one I wasn't going to figure out from that hospital bed.

I had a fight in my heart that kept wanting to make things better, to change the living conditions, to protect a mother who was hell bent on continuing the same senseless stuff, day after day, year after year, hospital bed after hospital bed. Was the endgame a beating to death? Was Mother a key player in this vicious cycle of abuse? Was she a participant, a victim, or both? Was it possible to be both? Was it possible to be neither and both? Was there a piece I was missing? Cycles of never-ending abuse, or was I to end that cycle of abuse? I just wanted to be a kid, but clearly that was never going to happen for me. Not in this lifetime.

—⟶⟶—

Sometimes it appeared that she needed the abuse, as if it was the attention she craved. It was as if she needed the abuse, the depravity, and shame just to feel alive, to feel she belonged. She would sometimes say, "I want a better life" but do nothing to try to accomplish it, as if it was only a statement meant to be said and not really something of meaning or value.

Now she was clearly admitting to me how she would remain in this environment until the end, whatever method or form that might become. As this played out in my hurting head, it was dawning on me that her mother had been in the same mess and always in a fight to survive. Always in a fight for life, created by her own drama as if it were a scripted program waiting to be filmed decades before the Kardashians made their debut. It made me wonder what was happening here and if this cycle of abuse was in my future as well.

Mother would tell stories about running away as a little girl. About her mother's drinking and never being home. She'd tell about getting beatings by her mother's boyfriends and even worse than beatings. How the "places" the state sent her were more of the same abuse, only protected by the same cops who sent her to those "homes." How she didn't know my brother's father and at seventeen, how difficult it was for her and her firstborn. I never did hear her tell of good times, only sad ones. A reason I wanted to protect her as much as I did.

I was left wondering if I would follow in this dissolute pattern. This trap of creating problems when no problems existed. Was it something you inherited, or was it something you were born with? Was it a sickness or simply a choice? How come it was only happening to Mother and Crazy? Why was such misery following them around and not following everyone else?

Mother kept talking, but I wasn't hearing her, not a single word. I was lost in the thoughts playing out in my mind, and then it hit me. The doctor and the policeman had said the same thing, and I hadn't heard either of them. I had heard the words, but it wasn't getting through to me. They were trying to warn me, but I was lost in the same generational cycle. Maybe it was getting through for the first time. Maybe I listened to what had been said before: "If you don't find a way out, you'll end up dead—or worse, in prison." That was what I was finally hearing. While it wasn't the exact words from the doctor or the cops, it was what they meant.

It wasn't only coming from the cops. It was the same thing I could now hear coming from so many others, like my friends' parents when they would say, "I don't want you hanging around that kid. He's heading for trouble, if not jail." I was staring at my future as I watched Mother's lips keep moving without hearing a sound she was making. I was going to be just like both of them.

At that moment I knew I needed to change. Somehow I needed to find a way out of this mess. I had no idea how or where to start, but I was going to find a way to end this cycle of impoverished ignorance. I would not blame anyone else for my lot in life, and if Coach Perfect had taught me anything, it was *never quit*! If I did nothing else in this world, I was going to find a way forward and not let anything stop me.

I closed my eyes. All the while, Mother kept on keeping on, selling the same sad song, but for once, it wasn't ringing the bell of her protector. The veil of hurt descended over the final hints of Mother's love. A self-protection against the last sharp shards pointed at my heart, the ones that kept me locked in an unwinnable war of broken souls and forgotten dreams. As the silence surrounded my throbbing head, a sense of letting go crept into my chest as if a million tons were slowly lifting off my conscience. The influential noise of Mother's vibrating voice faded down the forked path beside me, as if I were watching the change take hold before I drifted off to sleep.

—m—

The cops came back the next day, and I signed the report and kept to the story. I was released the following day and back in school the day after that. My eyes were open, looking for a way to be different, looking for a way to change my path and my future. I wanted to somehow change the destiny that seemed to be cast in stone unless I could find the courage to make changes even when I had no idea how or where to start. Even though I had no one to help me, no one to turn to, and not a single person who I could ask questions, get advice from, or rely upon.

In the course of those few days, I experienced so much, from learning to be part of a team that achieved a perfect season to seeing that old lady dancing as my life was surely going to end. To carrying out one more lie to protect someone who might not care or need the protection anyway. It was time to find my path and figure out how to live and not just survive.

So many people at school had come to me, worried about what had happened, as if I meant something to them. Even Victor was back in school before I was and, as always, there to be the friend of friends. I told him what had actually happened, and he remains the only person I've ever completely opened up to regarding the postgame family fun.

Victor and I vowed to never let a person put their hands on our bodies ever again, and with that, the die was cast for the showdown between Victor's father and him and Crazy and me. The future was now set by a pledge, a handshake, and a decision. I would never again let *anyone* put their hands on me, or it would be a fight to the death!

Now that Victor and I were patched up, healing, and back together, I needed to square things away with that one special person, Bethany. The one person I could not shake off or block the feelings I had for, those "warm and fuzzies," a phrase I picked up somewhere along the way to describe how she made my insides float and my outside shake, but in a good way. They were feelings that transformed from a confusingly delightful crush in seventh grade to a heart-stopping basket of puppy love, before completing the voyage into my first true romance. The "warm and fuzzies" was the best description I could come up with for what happened when I was around her. My breath would shorten, my palms would sweat, my heart would race uncontrollably, and my dry mouth would prevent me from saying anything more than single-syllable sound bites like "gurp," "mugg," "yerd"…It was magical to me, and Bethany was the only person I'd ever felt that way about, except Ms. Diamond, the most beautiful kindergarten teacher ever, until she stopped me from eating paste and the feelings quickly changed!

Before being released from the hospital, one of the nurses kept telling me about this young lady and her dad that kept coming by, calling the desk and continually checking on me. Since they weren't family, she couldn't say much, but she got the feeling the young girl was "sweet on" me. The other nurses thought it was a secret girlfriend, so they let her know I was doing fine and set to be discharged soon. It was both heartwarming and sad at the same time. Listening to the nurse, I could feel my face flush and my eyes water, and I smiled, reaching for my ears, all at the same time. It was such a mixed bag of emotions added to the world of chaos already playing out, but it left me knowing I needed to do something.

Bethany was standing in the hallway leaning against my locker, waiting with open arms and that smile, a smile so warming it stops you from breathing and charges the air with pure happiness. "I was so worried about you" slipped across her lips with little more than a whisper as we fell into a deep embarrassment. "I was so afraid for you...I'm so glad you're safe." I didn't want to let her go. Her hug pushed away all my pain and recharged my heart with a love I hardly understood. She was the sweetest person I'd ever had in my life. I could no longer keep the truth from her.

I owed Bethany an explanation, but I knew I could only tell her parts of the truth, just like I had done our freshmen when I had to break up with her. That was the hardest thing I ever had to do. Even the beatings from Crazy paled in comparison to the hurt I had to face only a short time ago...a hurt that never left me.

CHAPTER 10

G oing back two years or so, I did manage to find warmth, comfort, and teenage love that brought a light into my heart. A girl came into my life who helped change my path in a way that I never saw coming. Believe it or not, puppy love would intervene at a time and place where making a decision would mean either life in prison or a path to freedom.

Not long after returning from my suspension for knocking down the girl-hitting bully, a young lady smiled at me and changed my heart forever. It was a smile like no other. It came from her eyes, her cheeks, and her mouth all at the same time. It caused me to break out in a sweat; my face burned like a fire was just inches away and ready to melt my cheeks. I was captivated, speechless, and dumbfounded all at the same time, just because of her smile. What the heck is happening? ran through my mind as I shook my head to try to clear myself of this bucket of mixed emotions. This was something new and oddly exciting. Something I'd never felt before. It was a unique combination of lightness, like the fluttering of a butterfly, except there were thousands of them, and they all moved into my stomach. They must have been trying to escape, since my throat was choked closed and I couldn't breathe.

I panicked as I tried to figure out what was happening. While there was fear attached to the choke hold, it wasn't a bad fear but, rather, a new kind that floated alongside happiness and yet more powerful. I appeared to lose control of my mind, my feelings, and my emotions. Somehow that smile captivated me and launched a brand-new set of feelings and a power that mirrored the strongest battle cries I'd dealt with. A tingly sensation that rippled throughout my entire body. I was flooded with a sense of utter happiness and joy.

What the heck was happening to me, and what was in that smile of hers? How the heck was she doing it to me? I'd never felt such a force or such an attraction. It was intoxicating. My mind was no longer my own. It was sharing a smile from this girl I'd only seen once or twice. Frankly, I had no idea who she was. I tried to remember where she was from and how I hadn't seen her smile before, but nothing came to me. It was as if she had materialized out of thin air, placed in the crowded middle school hallway.

As fast as the heart swelling washed over me, she was gone. Maybe she was just in my imagination. Maybe she was just one more of those shadows I saw, but the feelings were real. I searched and searched, but she was gone, and I was going to be late for my next class.

I tried to ask Mother about my feelings, but that was a mistake, so I said it was one of those things I'd see from time to time. Mother and my brother kept telling me to stop seeing things they couldn't see. Maybe she was just another one of those wisps that came by at times.

My heart sank as those thoughts took control over the warm feelings. I wanted her to be real. I went to sleep thinking about her that night. Her smile kept me warm, and in the morning I realized I had actually gotten a restful night's sleep. I was charged with excitement, but I wasn't really sure why.

I got to school earlier than usual. I wanted to find that girl, so I watched carefully as everyone walked into the main entrance. But she was not to be found. Sadness fell across my body like worn-out shoes providing unhappy comfort, one you know so well.

I headed for homeroom, and as I looked toward the lockers just outside the door, there she was. She was talking to another girl as she reached into her locker. Her hair glistened and flowed ever so gently as passersby stirred the air. She was flawlessly dressed in a light-blue blouse, a soft-colored skirt, and the perfect shoes to complete the ensemble. She was the most handsomely dressed person I'd ever seen. Her smile housed the warmest feeling imaginable. A snow-white light coalesced around her, completing the perfect vision and igniting that spark called puppy love.

As I stood awestruck and dumbfounded by her radiating glow, she must have sensed my gaze. She slowly turned her look directly into mine, and once connected, my heart must have stopped along with my breathing. It felt like a stare for an eternity until she broke the gaze with her brilliant smile and a starburst shooting from her eyes before looking back to her locker.

At the same time, Gary hit me on the back, saying, "What's going on, kid? Who you looking at?" His eyes were scanning in the direction of my perplexed line of sight. "Oh, that's Bethany, and I think she likes you," Gary blurted out with his booming voice. Gary never did talk softly, and for a rather small guy, his lungs and voice box made him sound as if he were nine feet tall and as thick as a masonry building. I can't tell you how many people heard him say those words, but it did turn the heads of many who were close at hand and farther than arm's length, many arms' length!

—ɯ—

"Really, Gary? How is that going to help me? You need to learn to be quiet," I said.

He was confirming she was real at the same time as my face re-lit the fire in my cheeks. "Well, Flame, looks to me like you got the warm fuzzies, and from your blushing, I'd say you got it bad." Gary wasn't wasting his boisterous capacity with that statement. He ensured everyone else understood why I had rose-colored cheeks and a fawning look.

Now, two things need unpacking here. First, the name Flame. You'd think it was a nickname because I was a ladies' man, and I'd love to spin that tale, but we'll let Gary handle that part. I actually got that nickname from baseball. You see, I could throw the ball faster than most and harder than everyone. The problem was my aim. It wasn't very good. If you stepped into the batter's box and I was pitching, you stood a good chance of being walked or hit. Not hitting the baseball, but being hit *by* the baseball. When you got hit, it left a mark that stayed with you for quite some time. A red welt would rise like dinner rolls before you baked them. The broiling blisters were so bright and rosy they looked like flame tattoos on your arms, legs, or whatever part of your body you didn't get out of the way. Hence the nickname Flame! I caught on quickly and stuck like Elmer's glue. As for the term "warm and fuzzies," well,

Gary was the one who introduced it to me and, clearly, the rest of the middle school.

—⁓—

"Hey, you're quite a chick magnet since you decked that jerk. The girl's got the hots for you, man." Gary went on to explain how he made sure everyone knew why I had knocked down the bully and his friend. Protecting a girl and paying the price for it. I, of course, was suspended, so I knew little of the aftermath or hallway gossip. Gary, on the other hand, was quite a PR guy and was happy to mingle with the chicks. It brought him into their circles, a place he thoroughly enjoyed. Gary liked the ladies as much as he liked his motorbikes, and he fit right in as a gossip king among the various groups of middle school note passers. Gary made sure he was in on all the happenings as the boy toy of the 1970s. Gary fit in with everyone. I, on the other hand, never fit in or felt like I belonged in any group and felt most comfortable alone. Not so with Gary. You knew where to go if you needed information or if information needed to be spread.

"I'll go tell Bethany you like her and see what she says," he offered. I reached out and grabbed his arm just above the elbow, causing him to bellow, "*Ouch!*"

I pulled him back before his misadventure got off the ground. "Easy, Gary. I don't know who she is," I said, softening my grip.

"Sure you do. We've been in school with her for years. Her father owns the clothing store on Main Street across from the footbridge. They live by Sweeney School in that nice neighborhood uphill from Victor's house—you know, Cameo Gardens, the projects down at the bottom of Sweeney Hill. We could walk from your house to hers in ten or fifteen minutes, right next to Coach Chace's house, right next door. You know where I mean, right?"

I didn't remember, but it wasn't a new thing for me to "not remember" people, names, or places.

The second warning bell signaled we were late, and at the same time, it was a relief. Gary would just keep explaining until he got hungry, so I just made him believe I understood everything he had said.

"Gotta go; I'm late, kid. I'll talk to her and get back to you. See you after school," he said, running off to his class without listening to a word I said.

I headed to my next class, but I couldn't stop thinking about her. It felt like I was floating just above the floor tiles. I had an air about me as if all the heaviness that was stuck to me had been lifted away, sent somewhere else, allowing me to breathe freely and feel happier than any other time I can remember. It was magical. I swear I could see stars, white spots dancing in the space around me, shining brightly as they filled my soul with hope. It was something new, something better than what I was living with. It gave me a new focus, a new place to bring my mind when I was fighting back against the pain caused by Crazy. The picture of her was forever etched into my mind, that smile that changed my life. It was as if hope had a face and a name: Bethany.

Gary didn't waste any time getting into the different circles in a time before mobile phones and Snapchat. In person and handwritten notes were the messengers of the day, yet somehow, by the time the school day was over, everyone seemed to know I was smitten with Bethany, including her.

"I got your back, kid. You're all set. She likes you too. You're welcome" was Gary's parting gift as he headed down the old stone stairs and out the heavy rustic wooden doors with their half-round glass tops. He had a smile on his face, but not like Bethany. His was more of a chest-pumping caveman who had just invented the wheel. A look of pride and accomplishment. On one hand, Gary could keep a secret, like our discussion about Crazy. On the other hand, if someone liked someone else, well, he'd have it printed in the *National Enquirer* before you knew what had happened. Of course, Gary did find out Bethany liked me, which was exciting. I tried to figure out what to do next on that slow walk back to that house.

As the school year dragged on, I tried everything I could think of to get around Bethany, but it just wasn't happening. She was in the smart classes, and her mom picked her up after school. Her friends were forbidden to hang around with people like me. There was little chance of talking with her, let alone finding time for anything except the briefest of a hallway romance. I'd dream of going to the movies or being able to see her without everyone else standing between us. What was the point of her smile if that was all that could happen?

After months and months of disappointment, the school year ended, and we all went our separate ways for the summer. I had all but forgotten about the smile and given up on my hope with Bethany when the start of summer football camp played out a series of events that would lead to a chance meeting that only fate could string together.

—◊◊◊—

Dan Chace ran the local Friendly's Restaurant and was starting a football booster club. I'd heard about it before school ended, but it cost twenty bucks, so there was no way I'd be able to attend. Mr. Chace was our midget football coach and a super nice man. He had a perfect family, and while he'd yell at you in football, he'd hug you just as much. He was excited to coach football and loved helping others. His son, Pete, was a year younger than me, and while we weren't friends yet, we did enjoy hanging out after practice while he waited for his dad to finish up.

One day, Mr. Chace was stomping his feet and dancing around like he was trying to put out a fire. He was stomping his feet in frustration. Seems we just couldn't understand the football plays he was trying to teach us. I said to the few other guys, "We should call him Angry Chief when he throws his clipboard down and dances around like that." Well, the name stuck, and from that day forward, our coach was known as Chief. Little did I know how much Chief and his family would take hold in my life or our future with those football players.

When Chief found out I wasn't attending the club camp, he stopped by the house and told me, "It's all set, so I'll pick you up tomorrow at five thirty p.m. Just have your mother sign this form, and bring it with you."

I never told them, and I signed the paper myself. I think Chief knew I did by the look he gave me, but he tucked it into his folder, and that was that. It was the first summer sports camp I ever attended, and I loved every minute of it.

After camp ended, Pete asked a bunch of us to come over for a cookout at his house on Sunday. I was excited and made sure Crazy didn't know about it. I sneaked out of the house when Crazy fell asleep in his chair, his brown bottle dangling at his fingertips. I got to their house early. It was such a different world, and I wished life could be like theirs. The party was a blast.

The house next door had a pool. Finally, Chief said we could use the pool, but only for a short while, and only if we behaved. We filtered around the stockade fence and started jumping, diving, and having fun.

Standing poolside, someone said, "Hey, Bethany."

My heart stopped, and with a twist of my neck, that smile walked across the pavers and within seventeen feet of me. In an instant I was cast back to that day in school with her standing at her locker. Those feelings returned as if they'd never left, never skipped a beat, or faded a single pit. It was the most beautiful smile I had ever seen, and it was walking in my direction carrying a bunch of towels. It was Bethany's house and her pool I was standing next to.

You could have knocked me over with a Wiffle ball. My knees almost buckled as she drew near, her eyes facing down, watching where she was going, and then she took a short glance at me from just a few yards away. My heart pounded and my breath stilled as I gave her a tiny wave with my right hand, raised just above my waist. My mouth was open, but I didn't know it. I just kept watching her walk across her lawn and place the towels on a chair. As she turned to head back, she took a second look, this one a bit longer, with a short "hello" mouthed toward me and a wrinkle in her eye as that smile flashed its emotionally charged shine directly into my chest.

"Hey, close your mouth and stop drooling," shouted one friend, breaking the tension and the sound waves as my ears seemed to zone out when we locked eyes ever so briefly. I looked at the pool and then back toward Bethany, who passed a man as she headed back inside the house. The man was staring directly at me, the warm fuzzies clearly not on his agenda. He was giving me a cold, stern look, one that only a father can give. A father looking to watch out for his daughter from the wolf pack of boys playing pool tag and trying to show off. He was sending me a message with his lengthy eye contact, which was confirmed by him pointing a finger in my direction.

We had a great time in their pool, and a bit later I got some time with Bethany. It was the first since the briefest of hellos in the hallways as seventh grade closed into summer break. I would find excuses to visit Pete over the next week and managed to get a few more brief moments with Bethany before my full-time summer job took hold, tobacco picking.

It was four thirty in the morning when the alarm clock sounded. The bus would be at the Barker's Discount Department Store parking lot in less than an hour, so we needed to get moving. We slapped a bologna sandwich together, meat we had bought the night before so we'd have lunch this coming week, grabbed a jug of water, and we were off for the walk downhill to wait for the start of the hour-long trip to the tobacco fields of Windsor Locks. World-class cigar wrappers were in high demand, and the Connecticut "tobacco" valley produced the best-quality leaf in the world.

There were tobacco fields lining so many farms in that area, and they were so common, it looked like today's version of Iowa cornfields, except with huge white nets covering the tops of the fields, which extended for miles and miles. The bus dumped us off as the straw boss barked out each name on his list and sent each of us to a field for the day. Our job involved scrambling under the eight-foot-tall stalks of broad-leaved tobacco and picking four leaves from the bottom. We placed them in a high-rimmed pan and dragged it along behind us.

Gary took the bus, and he and I worked side by side each summer until about ten days before the next school year started. We worked until almost 4:00 p.m. and then returned to the bus for a trip that got us back to Barker's parking lot by 5:30 p.m., then off to deliver papers for a short two hours, back to the house, bed, and repeat. Saturdays were half days and optional to work, but it paid time and a half. The $2.35 made it just over $3.50 an hour, too much for Gary and me to pass up.

The bus was only half-full on Saturdays, but Gary and I still sat together and talked about all the things we were going to do in life. He asked about Bethany, but I didn't say much. All summer long I thought about Bethany and wondered why those warm fuzzies hadn't faded away. I really liked her, and I didn't understand why. I wanted to buy her something, flowers or a card, but Crazy took all the money I made—"rent and food," as he called it.

The tobacco-picking season ended just before school started, and I got to see Bethany almost every day. For the next year, we'd spend some time together, but I'm not sure her father approved. However, her parents treated me with such kindness. Her father gave me work at his clothing store and gave me pants and a few shirts he claimed were a "problem" and he needed to get rid of them. If they fit and I wanted them, they were mine. The funny thing was they always fit. They were the right waist size and the right length, and the shirts seemed to be just a bit bigger than I needed. To me, there wasn't a thing wrong with them.

"Keep this between us," he would say. "No need for anyone else to know our business."

He'd find things that needed fixing or cleaning at his store and pay me more than I made anywhere else. Bethany's mother tried to teach me to read and do math, but it wasn't very successful. I read at a second-grade level, so the hour or two a week was more hopeful than helpful.

Bethany never looked down on me the way so many others had and did. She kept telling me, "You're going to make it" and offered any support she could. Her parents would take us to Boston Red Sox games—my first trip to a ballpark—and in general treat me like a son, but always from a few steps away. To me, their acts of kindness showed a caring and tenderness little known in my life. In some ways, it was lifesaving; in others, life changing.

It was a time when I got to see how a family worked without screaming, fighting, or beatings. I would tell Bethany how lucky she was, but it's hard to see the forest for the trees, and if you don't live in a mud puddle of darkness, well, you can empathize but never really understand the message. And honestly, I'd never want anyone to fully understand.

I could see the hurt in Bethany's eyes when the bruises appeared. The black eyes or the cuts were not easy to explain. She'd ask, "What happened?" But I'd just shake my head and ask her to "let it be, please." Feeling the pain in her heart and seeing her angry tears welling up and slide down her lightly freckled cheeks honestly hurt more than breaking my bones. She would try to help, but just knowing she was worried about me was enough. Besides, what else could she do! I'd never talk about it, but she knew all the same. Maybe it's better to say she had an idea of what was happening, as there was no way to really understand Crazy. I'm not sure there are actual words that can be used. Aside from dodging the beating questions, the time Bethany and I spent was heaven sent. As someone once wrote something about the best of times and the worst of times, the best times in my young life were those far-too-few days spent with Bethany.

Then one day, just like the writer predicted, it all came crashing down. All that I loved, happiness and excitement, was thrown into a gutter, just like everything else once Crazy figured out I had something good in my life. My youngest sister, without knowing she was opening the door to hell, let Crazy know I had a friend, a girlfriend. The path to destroy anything good in my life was quickly unfolding.

It was such a beautiful day. The sun was shining against a soft, blue, cloudless sky. The air was a combination of late-summer brilliance and a brisk early-fall nip. That uniquely southern New England sensation as the season shifts from slumbering summer into the months-long march of leaves and lanterns. A time when that magical glow of Mother Nature kindles the twisted winds and mixed emotions of new teenagers' wide-eyed romance. The special time in everyone's life when the fears and joys of that first kiss fans that amber spark, igniting the fires within.

Each day with Bethany was like our first kiss, captured in this season of mystical moments. Knowing not the steps or rites of passage yet following our hearts as the inspirations struck and stars sparkled when our lips would meet. The quiet whispers of young love sharing a tense and tender touch before the call from her mother separated our cheeks. I was lost in her arms, freeing me of wounds and worries.

"Hey, where are you two?" sounded her mom. She was calling us from the side door. We broke the embrace with a bounce and a bet as we raced with excitement toward her mother's beckon. We chased each other as only young teen love will do. Bethany slipped inside the full-length storm door and tried to pull it shut as we laughed and tugged in opposite directions. Her smile dropped away in an instant as I pushed on the pane of glass separating the two of us. I simply pushed too hard, and the glass shattered. Bethany covered her open mouth with all her fingers. My hand and forearm were now inside her kitchen with the rest of me still outside on the concrete porch. Large pieces of glass were hanging on as other pieces fell, adding to the crashes that sounded an alarm.

Something was terribly wrong, and it wasn't just a broken window. Her mom came running in from the living room with her father right behind just as the largest piece started to fall. It leaned in her direction as it quickly gained speed. I reached with both hands to try to pull it away from her. The giant piece tumbled like a perfectly tossed spear pointing directly at my arm, my wrist, and hand.

The attempt to catch the falling glass and prevent it from sticking Bethany was successful, but not so much for me. It stuck into my hand and twisted into my arm before landing on the kitchen floor with a crash. I was so worried she was hurt I never paid attention to my arm or my well-being.

I was certain her dad would explode in anger over breaking his glass door. "I'm so sorry, sir. I'm so sorry; it was my fault, my fault. Bethany had nothing to do with this. It was all my fault," I said as I tried to get ahead of things so she wouldn't get into trouble. "*I'm so sorry!* I'll pay for the door. Please don't be mad at her. It's not her fault; it was me; I did this," I kept repeating as I tried to catch more pieces that were slipping out of their rubber holding strip. Several more pieces were now dangling halfway down the broken opening.

Bethany, who was desperate to protect me from the hanging shards, started to reach for yet another dangling chunk aiming for my arm. Before she could reach it, it fell, ripping another gash out of the underside of my forearm a few inches above my palm and thumb.

Her dad gently escorted her away from the scattered slivers and into her mother's arms. Not a word came from either of them as I kept apologizing. "*I'm so sorry.* I'll fix it; I can pay for the glass. Please don't be mad at Bethany. It wasn't her fault; it was my fault." Thoughts raced through my mind of being banished from her life. Never allowed to return and having no idea how to fix the door.

What I didn't realize was the amount of blood pouring out of me. Bethany had turned her face and planted it into her mother's shoulder as if she was afraid to look. At first I feared she was going to be hit by her father, but then I realized she was hiding from the river of blood flowing out of my wrist and pouring all over their porch. Her dad still wasn't saying a single word but moved about with a clear plan as he grabbed a dish towel and wrapped it around my arm and the chunks of glass poking from my flesh.

In a calm, composed tone, her dad began with "Okay...it's okay." He made eye contact and offered an unknown smile. Is it a good one or a dangerous one? I wondered. "I need to look at your arm to see how bad it is." He ushered me over to the kitchen sink and peeled back the towel to reveal a huge gash in my wrist and deep cuts in my hand and my arm. The blood-soaked towel quickly lost its ability to help, and the sink was rapidly becoming more of a butcher's wash station than a place for dish duty.

"It was an accident. I'm not mad, so please stop apologizing. It was just an accident," he said, trying to comfort me. "We need to get you looked at. I'll drive, but we'll need to call your parents."

Oh, dear God, please…Don't call them. That would be worse than anything else. Please, no…please, no! In a matter of seconds, my heart went from amazing happiness to bloody terror, and the glass had nothing to do with it.

He wrapped a couple of fresh towels around my hand, wrist, and forearm as he talked. The thought of having to deal with Crazy was too much. "They don't know I'm here, and if they find out…" I started. "I can take myself to the ER. I've been there before, so I know what to do." My protests and efforts at self-service were falling short, very short.

"I'm taking him to the hospital. Have his parents meet us there," Bethany's dad instructed his wife as he quickly moved us over the shattered remains and into the car. "I'm not going to sugarcoat this. You're losing a lot of blood. Those cuts are very deep, and you'll need to be sewn up. The hospital will need your parents' permission. Does Bethany have your home number? I'm sure your parents will head to the hospital just as soon as they know."

I didn't want to answer because I didn't want them to be involved. "Can't you just sign for me, please? Can't we do this without them finding out?" My plea was in vain.

"Look, your parents will want to be there with you, and I'm sure they will be very worried. You didn't do anything wrong, so you're not in any trouble," he tried to reassure me, but I knew better.

"It's bowling night, and Mother is at work" was the best I could offer. My arm was throbbing, and the old familiar pains returned, but for the first time, it wasn't from a beating by Crazy. So what would I tell them at the hospital?

Pulling up at the ER, Bethany's dad hustled around his gray Mercedes with its red leather interior. He opened the door and reached inside to help me out.

"I didn't get any blood on your seat," I said as he closed the door.

"Don't worry about it," he responded, shaking his head as if to discharge my fears. Once inside, he called out, "*We need help here!*" with a sense of profound concern and authority. Without waiting for an escort, he led me down the hallway to the emergency room doctors' station, where they take you after you do all the paperwork.

A doctor and nurse quickly came to answer his call, and he told them, "He has several deep cuts from a big glass pane that shattered on top of him, a storm door window, and he has glass inside him. The cuts I saw were very deep, and a lot of blood was lost. It happened no more than ten or fifteen minutes ago. One towel already was used before we got here," he explained.

They rushed me into the back as he stood there watching. Several others in green and blue matching scrubs gathered around as they took off the towels, cleaned the wounds, and evaluated the damage.

"You are going to need a lot of stitches, young man. You did a real number on yourself, but we'll patch you up, so don't be worried. It doesn't look like tendons were damaged. It's a miracle the glass missed all the really important stuff. You must have someone watching over you," one of the nurses said. "We'll need your parents' permission before we can proceed, and we need to take care of this so we can stop the bleeding. Are they coming, or can we call them?"

The questions poured out of the doctors and nurses like the blood spurting out of me just a short time ago. I not only didn't want to answer their questions, I also didn't know how to answer. It hadn't been that long ago I was there when the clock radio—I mean the baseball—broke my nose in the middle of the night. I did the best I could to tell them where to find someone to sign off so I could get this done. No one could find Crazy or Mother.

After two hours, a nurse asked me if the man who brought me could come back to see me. I was surprised he was still there. "Please, I'd like to see him," I said.

Bethany's dad walked into the room asking, "How you feeling, son?" After some small talk, he said, "It seems you've been here before. The nurses remember you, and they have a long file in their records."

"I've fallen a few times," I offered.

He just shook his head a bit, not buying what I was selling. He let it be, and I was grateful for that.

"You don't need to hang around here. Mother works until after midnight, and I know Crazy has bowling tonight across town until after ten p.m."

His face darkened as the words sank in but quickly shifted to a less frustrated look. "Well, I've got no place to be, so mind if I sit with you for a bit?" he asked.

It was late afternoon at this point, and I knew I'd be there for a long time.

"My daughter wanted to come to see you—"

I cut him off as quickly as I could. "*No*, please, no. I don't want her to be here when…Well, it's best she not meet…I mean…" My voice trailed off.

"Don't worry; I understand. Let me go call home so Bethany knows you're going to be okay."

He and I talked about different things for a few hours before he said he needed to leave. He told me he wanted to help, so if I needed anything, just ask. I was so hungry, but I didn't want him there if Crazy showed up, so I thanked him for all his help, and off he went before stopping a few steps down the hall. After a measured pause, he turned back, pointed at his heart, and, with a deeply meaningful tone just loud enough for me to hear, said, "Keep the faith." Then he turned and walked away.

I fell asleep but woke up when the throbbing pain reminded me where I was. It was just after midnight, and the next shift was talking about what to do with me. Then two cops came down the hall, and panic started to race through me. Oh God, what fresh hell was coming my way? One of the cops I knew. He'd pulled Crazy off me a few months back. The nurse pointed the cops toward my curtain. They both looked at me with hands on their belts as cops do when standing still. As they started to move closer, I took a deep breath to prepare for the questioning about to take place.

"Sir, we got a call from the head of the ER, concerned about your welfare. He said they needed to sew you up but couldn't find your parents. We're here to help. Can you tell us how to contact one or both of your parents?" the senior patrol officer asked.

"Sarge, I know this kid. Give me a minute…"

The two walked a few feet away from my earshot. After their quiet reflections, the sergeant stepped back, saying, "Look, we're not here for anything else. We know what happened, so don't think you're in trouble. We're just trying to help get you patched up. In fact, our boss is friends with the man who brought you here. He told us you were a good kid and you did nothing wrong. We just need to get a parent to sign a release so they can stitch you up. Can you tell us where your parents are? We went to your house, and your sister wouldn't open the door."

I responded with "My mother's at work, and Crazy's at the bowling alley by the airport. The lady at the desk said she remembers me, so you should have a work phone for her. That's all I can tell you."

The cops told me, "We'll see what we can do," and they turned and walked back to the nurses station. A short discussion followed, with the sergeant picking up the phone and calling someone. Moments later and after a very brief decision with a few looks in my direction, he handed the phone to the doctor, who had been watching the proceedings. The doctor had some brief words, then handed the phone back to the nurse, thanked the cops, and signed a paper, followed by the sergeant doing the same. The cops gave me a brief tip of the cap as they turned away and walked down the hallway and out the door, and they were gone…at least for now!

Two nurses prepped the room with trays, paper-covered tools, bottles of liquid, needles, and other surgical tools lining the bright, shiny metal counter on wheels. I was surrounded by that cold atmosphere only present in the cement block walls encasing the pure white environment of sterilization. That infamous setting of an emergency room hospital. If you've ever had the displeasure of being in one of these rooms in the 1970s and been all alone to boot, it was as unfriendly a place as you can imagine. There was no one to comfort me, no one to walk me through the process or tell me a story. No one to ease the fears or help me look away from the sliced openings deep in my flesh as they peeled back the skin, muscle, and tissue to clean the wounds. Blood was reflowing as a doctor practiced calling out medical terms like he was preparing for a test. "It'll only hurt for a minute. The needle is the worst part." Just the cold, methodical machine of professionals doing what they had trained for with such precision. Their confidence locked onto me like a vise grip holding my consciousness in lonely reassurance. If you've ever been in a place like this, all alone, you know what it feels like. If you haven't, I pray you never have to, at least before you have to grow up.

Sitting there, it hit me: I was on my own. There wasn't a single person to care for me or worry about my outcome. As that thought began to sink in and the Novocain needles started to push deep into the soft, fleshy parts of the open wounds, the pain and the reality, my existence and the cold truth of life struck me just like the needle pricks. Sharp, to the point, painful, and isolated. It sucked to be all alone, and it hurt more than the open wounds with glass being dug out of them. Sadness had its grip on me once again.

Mother came walking down the hallway, purse slung over her arm, hands crossed in front of her midsection. She was smiling as if all was well, but the folks at the nurses station were not showing her any courtesies but rather polite discord.

A brief encounter before we walked out of the ER and started heading uphill the quarter mile or so to that house. Mother was less concerned with my injuries than she was with what Crazy was going to do when we got there. "He's pissed. That man showed up at the bowling alley confronting him, and the police showed up too. I had to leave work and pay for a ride to get you," she said, scolding.

"Why did you do this to me? He said you were fighting with someone and breaking windows. The police came to the house a few times. What's wrong with you? Are you going to be arrested *again!*" Mother clearly had her views and was determined I was in the wrong, so it was pointless to try to set the record straight.

"I can lose my job, and those kids at that facility need me there," she continued, referring to the state facility for the mentally ill, the criminally insane, and those with disabilities and no place else to go. Her job was her sanctuary, and while she never said those words, it was clear to me. She'd leave sometimes on a Saturday before noon and not come back for days on end. She'd make short phone calls to check in but not much more.

She and Crazy spent less and less time at the house, which for the most part was fine. Ninety-eight, ninety-seven, ninety-six... She just kept talking and was now sweating from the uphill climb. Or was it from the tongue-lashing she was giving me? Fourteen, thirteen, twelve…"Listen to me." She stopped us just steps before the broken concrete leading to the pathway. "Your father—"

"He's *not* my father," I snapped back.

She continued, "He's madder than I've ever seen, and whoever this girl and her family you've been hanging around are, he's going to make them pay for embarrassing him in the bowling alley and having the cops come to the house. Hell, that man even came here last night before the police did. There is going to be hell to pay, so just be careful. Don't antagonize him, don't push him the way you do, and most of all, tell him you're sorry, and maybe, just maybe, we'll survive this one."

It was a plea I'd heard before, but this time it had some mustard on it. Mother was pointing, shaking her finger at me, and berating me as if I had intentionally cut myself and planned this entire event just to cause Crazy problems. Without saying another word, we turned to finish the steps and went into that house.

Crazy sat in his usual chair at the table and just stared as we walked into the kitchen. A beating was an absolute. The old leather strap was on the table, his rifle was behind him, and his favorite knife was stuck into the wood block he used to test the edge of his blades. His sharpening stone was oiled. A larger-than-usual bottle of stamina sat two-thirds empty, just an arm's reach if he leaned forward a bit.

"*What the fuck have you done now?*" And so it began…

The beating was one sided. I just stood there taking the lashings, ducking to protect my face and stepping in between Crazy's efforts to hit Mother. Blood soaked through the gauze wrapped around my freshly sewn wounds. The leather strap was swinging in all directions, striking my legs, back, and neck. I would block many shots with almost a calm "never mind." His blows stung my unstrapped arm, leaving welts to bubble up like a prehistoric bee sting, one the size of a sparrow.

Crazy finally tired and sat down to take a puff of his cigarette as he tried to catch his breath. I wondered how much longer I'd have to wait before fighting back and putting us all out of this misery. His physical work was done for now; his verbal tirade was only beginning. It was going to be a long day. Crazy went over his intentions, what he was going to do to me for "disrespecting" him as I had by ordering Bethany's family to a confrontation, sending the police, and making the hospital calls, as if I had that ability, that power. He made it clear I was "never to see that family again."

Silence was the day's best approach—not my known approach, but it had been a long day. Finally he tired enough that he needed to take a break. Once he climbed into the reclining chair, I knew the day was over. When he passed out, I made my way upstairs. My thoughts started to circle around his threats to "settle things my way" regarding Bethany's dad. It was a horrifying statement and one I was sure he'd follow through on.

I closed my eyes, and it didn't take long before my exhausted body and mind fell into darkness and a form of sleep known only to those who can keep their mind alive, alert, at the same time as they get some sleep. My last thoughts were of Bethany and how heartbroken she was going to be. I could feel the new level of pain darting in my chest as I faded away, the tunnel closing as a soft breeze blew across my face.

—◊—

Time dragged on as I recovered from the glass incident and the beatings that had followed. I never stopped thinking about Bethany or her dad. That part of my life was the only form of happiness I had. I hadn't been looking for it, but it had found me, and I can honestly say I had never felt so much love, even though it was young love.

The cops came to the house several more times while I stayed in my room healing. I could hear them arguing with Crazy over broken windows at a storefront. Someone had been repeatedly vandalizing the clothing shop Bethany's dad owned. It had to be him. He had threatened that if I didn't stop seeing "that family," he'd make them pay. It seemed as though his threats had materialized. The crazy bastard was making good on his word, "terrorizing that clothing store owner and his whore of a daughter," the last part being the most hurtful of all statements. If I didn't end things with Bethany, Crazy would make life miserable for them just like he did for me.

I had to do something. While it made my stomach turn into a knot just thinking about it, I had to do what I could to stop Crazy. I slipped out the back window and went down the neighbor's driveway and headed toward Bethany's house.

How many steps was this going to take? I hated every one of them and dreaded each pace as I slowly walked the distance, closing the gap with ever-growing regret over what was about to happen. I gently knocked on the newly replaced glass door. Bethany's mom looked out the side window and shouted, "*Bethany! Your boyfriend is here!*" as only a good mom can, with a ring of love and a smile from the heart.

A hug greeted me, followed by how worried she was and how many times she wanted to call or stop by, but her dad thought better of it. She talked and talked. All the while I just listened, sadness pouring out of me, but still not tipping the hand I had come to play. Her face had that smile, with her perfectly lined-up teeth and rose-colored cheeks showing off her beautiful features. Her hair shone and gently moved as the breeze drifted across her porch.

"I missed you so much. I was so worried about you..." she continued until finally something dawned on her. Something was wrong, and it started to take hold of her. She pulled back just a bit before asking, "What's wrong? What's the matter?"

I didn't respond right away, as I was gathering courage and fighting the urge to tell her the truth. "Did I do something wrong? *Tell me!* What's going on?...Are you all right?" A tear formed in the corner of her eye. Hurt started to overshadow the radiant glow surrounding her.

I couldn't let it go on any longer. Finally, with my heart feeling like it was going to fall out of my chest, I let out, "I have to break up with you."

Her face shattered as the shock shook her to her core. "Why?" was the only word before the shock closed her throat. The swelling in her eyes was more than I could bear.

"I don't want to lie to you, but that's all I can say. I just have to break up with you." If I told her more, danger would follow; that I was certain of.

As her face absorbed my words, my deed, I could feel her pain roll over the warming affection and into sheer hurt. Not the beating kind, but the worst kind. The breaking of a wonderful person's heart. It felt as if I had crushed her spirit and stolen her happiness. I was hurting the only person who had shown me affection, love, and true caring. It was the toughest thing I'd ever done and the most painful experience of my life.

My heart was screaming, *Stop it! Tell her how you feel!* while my mind was telling me Crazy would cause her and her family so much more pain than what I was delivering. It was something I knew had no good outcome, and it was a bad decision no matter which way I played it.

She turned and ran into her house. I got up and slowly started that long walk back.

When I got inside, I told Crazy I had ended it with that family, and I promised never to see her or any of them ever again.

"It's about time. Seems the clothing salesman's been having window troubles. You don't need that whore anyway."

He kept on barking as I walked up the stairs and into my room, sadness stuck to every part of my soul.

Doing the right thing never felt so wrong, but at least it would stop Crazy from further retaliation. It was the saddest time I could remember. I had to find a way out of this place before it killed me or changed me into what I hated most. Folding myself onto the sunken mattress, the springs poking into my ribs, I closed my eyes and fought to bury the hurt of love lost. I tried to forget the pain I had caused Bethany, but it was impossible. It felt like a hurt that would linger for the rest of my life. I was so sorry to have hurt her. Then my thoughts turned darker as I started turning the pain toward someone. Someday, someday soon, I'd make Crazy pay for what he had forced me to do. The more I thought about it the angrier I grew.

Then, something else happened, something I'd fought against since he first slithered into our lives. I was starting to sense the same shadowy bubbles that lived with Crazy; they were surrounding me. It felt like darkness was beginning to take hold of my insides. It was fast becoming a powerful urge. An overwhelming force to accept evil. To become someone that wanted to destroy and kill rather than someone with hope. I was starting to feel like Crazy…Dear God, was I becoming Crazy?

CHAPTER 11

"*Oh my god! You killed him!*" screamed my sister, the older of the two.

The city police burst through the door just moments after her declaration. The banging at the door finally stopped when the dead bolt was unlocked by the youngest sibling. She was in a frantic scramble to get help before someone died, before a killer was cast into the concrete and steel cell where society keeps its murderers. The final punishment—or was it a final lesson?

How did it get to this point? Why didn't someone step in to prevent this outcome? What was going to become of my sisters... my brother? Why didn't God help us!

My sisters, my brother, and Mother were all saying the same thing. The situation was becoming the most intense, the most hostile, and the most dangerous we'd ever experienced. It had become a daily battle, at least on those days Crazy showed up. We all knew something was coming to a head. Even my aunt worried it would go too far.

I had no place to go, and if I left, my brother and Mother would be at the mercy of Crazy. At least he knew I'd step in between him

301

and Mother, and he knew I was big enough to cause him concern. I could see it in his eyes when he tried to get around me and hit Mother. At this point in the game, the game of survival, Crazy knew he'd have his hands full should he hurt Mother again. I had made that clear. That left me as the only target of his physical rage. Even I could sense the end game was coming, a fight that would leave someone hurting so badly the dynamics of this war would be changed forever. Even the darkness around Crazy seemed different, as if he, too, knew an ending was near.

In my view, it was Crazy who would be the loser. I had spent my entire life preparing for this battle. Wishing—praying, really— for enough size and physical power to ensure the right outcome with me standing and Crazy finally in his place, knocked off the hill, his perch of a decade or so. At the same time, it was as if he was planning for the same thing, but only if he could ensure his victory. He'd tuck knives under cushions or hide them under his favorite chair. He kept a shotgun next to his bed, and he carried an old straight razor in his pocket. He had a fear growing inside him, but only when his eyes weren't bloodshot with brown-bottle liquid courage, which wasn't very often yet enough so I could tell the difference.

The flowing ripples of evil coating him seemed to shift as well. They consolidated into powerfully packed bunches, awaiting their feast. It was a terrifying tell.

This final battle started a week earlier, when I was named the starting outside linebacker for the varsity football team. The school called the house to invite the parents to a pregame event. That was the starting point, but it quickly blew up every single good thing that ever happened to me. Crazy was determined to make sure I lost this latest good thing as well as my life or my freedom. It was a week that changed all our lives forever.

—⁓—

It was autumn of my sophomore year of high school. We had moved into a house on Mansfield Avenue a few years ago. It was the longest time spent in one place, and we'd settled into the neighborhood. It was a common middle-class area within the city limits of Willimantic, which was part of the larger town of Windham. We lived in residential cluster housing that had small yards in tightly packed communities. The three-bedroom house had windows facing directly into our neighbors' rooms. If the shade wasn't pulled down, you'd get some interesting views from time to time. Most of the houses were built in the early 1900s, and this one was no exception. Its stone foundation and dirt basement floor was the cleanest part of the house. While Crazy refused to allow any of us to have friends over, between the shamble living and the everyday dangers, inviting friends over wasn't a thought.

The house was a gabled front-box colonial, a two-story building with a mudroom off the kitchen that housed a washing machine and had a clothesline secured to the small covered porch just two steps outside the side entrance. The living room was open and connected to the dining room. Stairs led to the three bedrooms above and to the only bathroom in the house. We had a tub but no shower and a sink with hot and cold water taps at each end. Wood paneling along with 1930s wallpaper showed the age of the house. Glue, tacks, and tape were unsuccessfully used to control the peeling process. The wallpaper kept trying to free itself from its confinement on the plaster. It looked like it was trying to run away, just like I wanted to do, to be free of that house.

I ran away so many times I honestly can't remember them all. The cops would find me, eventually, and return me to that house, or I would just walk back and start the game all over again. Have you ever fought a mental war deep inside your mind over leaving a place that you know will kill you—a place you are 100 percent positive you need to leave, yet you just can't find what you need to finally put that part of your life behind you and never look back? If you've lived that mental nightmare, then you understand what I'm talking about. If not, try to imagine having everything ripped from your life in the blink of an eye. Imagine walking away from everything you know, everything. Imagine trying to figure out a new starting point without a single reference point or a single person to help you along the way. You have no money and no place to go. If you run away, you lose your connection to school and football, the one thing you know you love. Imagine having no place to put your head at night, not even a car to call a place to live or to get out of the rain or the snow. Imagine having doors shut in your face and hearing, "This hoodlum isn't coming in this house, and you're not hanging out with him"—a common phrase slapped across my face many, many times as I tried to find comfort in any place possible. Imagine being able to hear the whispers or see the pointed gestures when they don't think you're looking. The unkind pushing away, creating distance from people you've never met or seen before. Yet you know exactly what they're saying, exactly what they're doing as they try to avoid the invisible force field they secure around themselves to ensure you don't touch them or the air around them. It's like you have smallpox or the plague and you're the cause of the outbreak. Imagine no one willing to open their arms to offer a hug, or everyone turning their faces, unwilling to offer even a smile. A warm meal is your biggest goal of the day, or even half a sandwich. Imagine you can feel what they're thinking: "Get this bum away from me." Those looks that tell you more than the sender has the courage to voice. Eye rolls, snickers, chins poked upward with a slight head bob of disapproval. Its effects garnish your decision-making process and cause deep internal divides. That's the life facing a runaway.

—⟋⟍—

"You are off the team! No more football!" came from the screaming mouth of an increasingly unpredictable tyrant. I was named the starting outside linebacker early in the season of my sophomore year, which was an honor not many had achieved, and candidly, it made me feel great. I had built up to 170 pounds, and while I wasn't all that fast, I made up for it in hitting force, and God knows how I loved to hit on the field.

Off the field it wasn't a treasure to hit others but rather a concern. I never put my hands on anyone who didn't start something, force the issue, or pick on someone unable to protect themselves. I didn't like to fight, despite the local myths and legends told by prosecutors or the gossip mill. The why never really made it into the reports, just the legal terms for "fisticuffs." I never saw myself as a "bad boy," but it surely seemed everyone else did. I was just trying to survive the best way I knew how.

One week before my first start on a varsity team, Crazy was already searching for a way to take this away from me as he'd done with most everything else. No matter what good came to me, no matter how I tried to make a life, he took it away. He forced me to give him the money I made and ripped up any clothes he determined to have come from anywhere he didn't approve of or have a receipt to prove where I'd gotten the apparel. Those pants and shirts from Bethany's dad? Well, those were set on fire in the backyard when Crazy found them hanging on the clothesline. New clothes were a red flag, so you learned to keep the nice stuff hidden or outside the house whenever possible. Now he was coming for football. It was about all I could take, and something had changed deep inside me.

Just before being named starting outside linebacker, I was in a fight with three guys who had been picking on my sister. Two were brothers and older than me, and one was in the same grade as my sister. He had put his hand on her, hurt her arm, and grabbed her face while shoving her against her locker. They left a couple marks on her; one was more than I needed. If Crazy had found out, I would have had to go to their house. But my sister kept it quiet and asked me to stop them. She was so scared and didn't want to go back to school.

The older two were in the grade ahead of me and had an older friend. I found them after practice, just down the street from the upper school parking lot. I put a hurting on all three of them, and my sister never had another problem with any of her schoolmates. However, someone called the police, and before I could get away, the cops grabbed everyone and hauled us in—jail time.

I was released, but it was hanging out there, and Crazy was determined to make sure it was a tool he could use to stop me from playing football. I felt something coming, and it wasn't all that good. While I couldn't figure out what it was, it felt like an ending, or maybe it was a new beginning.

—m—

I worked harder than ever to make the starting lineup. I went in early to watch games on eight-millimeter black-and-white film. I stayed after practice to work out and ran extra sprints before showering and walking those steps back to that house.

I wanted to play so badly it was crushing to hear Crazy say I was "off the team." I had to find a way to stop Crazy, but how? Maybe he'd enjoyed too many brown bottles and had forgotten about it. That wish quickly dissolved when I was called to the principal's office a few days before my first varsity start. In the office were Crazy and Mother. My heart sank, and my life felt like it was over. The coach was in the room as well.

"His grades suck, and you have him playing games" popped out of Crazy's mouth. "What kind of a school system you running here?" he hammered away. "He's been arrested, and he causes trouble wherever he goes. He should be expelled and put to work digging ditches. That's all he'll be good for. He's a bum, a punk, and will never amount to nothing." Crazy just kept peppering away, his bold move determined to get me removed from the only thing left in my life that gave me any joy. He was pissing all over it. "If you don't remove him from that team and put him into special classes *today*, I will sue this shithole after withdrawing him from high school," he said, storming out of the office with Mother in tow, giving me that "I told you so'" look with a smirk I'd seen so many times before.

The security officers followed just feet behind him. Crazy kept his rant flowing until he was well past earshot.

"Well, son, there isn't much we can do here. It seems you'll need to figure this out with your father."

"He's *not* my father!" I interrupted.

"Okay, you need to figure this out with them, or we'll need to remove you from the team," concluded the principal. "Once he sends the letter withdrawing his authorization for you to play, my hands are tied. You're almost what? Thirteen or fourteen? So there isn't much we can do. You're fourteen now, so you need a parent or guardian to sign for you. If we can help, let us know. Go on back to class for now. Keep out of trouble please, will ya? You're a good kid, and we understand there are issues here. Hang in there, but stay out of trouble and keep the faith…You have a lot of life in front of you."

I walked out of his office and down the hallway with my head hanging and all energy evaporating from my life. What was I going to do now? Maybe I should just quit school and go to work full time. What did he mean "keep the faith"? Whatever it was, it was ringing in my ears like an endless echoing loop but sounding far off.

I felt as lost as I'd ever felt, and Crazy was following through on the only thing he ever kept his word about: destroying my life. The pain started turning into that anger that appeared just before a fight. An energy seemed to flow around me like a tornado, providing the power to destroy whatever was needed. I had a limitless supply of firepower as long as I stayed within that circle of anger, that thunderous force that showed up each and every time I was out of options or at that point of no return. I took that energy to practice and crushed everything in sight, only stopping when a couple of coaches pulled me aside to tell me, "Hey, we're all on the same side. You're killing your own players. We love your aggression, but save some for the game."

After practice, I stayed in the locker room until the head coach forced me to leave, saying, "You can't stay here, kid. I know you got it tough, and I wish I had a place for you, but not here. The janitor is heading in to mop the floors, so you'll need to leave. I can give you ten more minutes. I hope you get it worked out on the home front. We really need you on the field."

The janitor had already started mopping up and had heard the head coach's "pep talk." It was the same janitor who had found me sleeping outside a year or so back. After a few minutes of mopping, he stopped and leaned on the handle. "You know, the boiler room is a pretty warm place. I take a nap in there from time to time. If you ever find you're stuck in the cold, come find me. If I'm able, I'll see what I can do."

I was outside in the cold autumn air once again. It was the same place I'd stood before, 2,442 steps to that house. The parking lot was empty, it was dark, and my thin jacket wasn't keeping the cold from biting at me. The wind was bitter and snapping at my body. A hand on my shoulder told me it was time to move forward, take that step, and keep moving. I could feel something beside me, something I'd felt before, but this time it was different. It felt like something was changing or maybe about to change. The feeling was stronger than ever before, a kind of winding-up feeling. Or maybe a geared-up feeling. Either way, it was very different.

I felt like these steps were going to be the last ones I'd take, almost like the feeling when eighth grade ended and I took that final walk, putting middle school behind me, but without the hope and promise of a new adventure.

It was an oddly airy quiet. I have no idea how long I stood there, thinking, wondering, before a gust of wind hit my face and broke the lost concentration. I took a deep breath, exhaled, looked down at my feet, and prepared to take that first step, one more time. Where was this step taking me? It was time to find out. I looked down and watched as my foot moved forward, and it hit me: I really needed a new pair of shoes. First step complete, and on to the second step…Keep the faith; keep moving forward! A calming mantra taking shape.

Two thousand four hundred forty-two, 2,441, 2,440, 2,439… Focus on the steps, and you'll get anywhere you set your mind to. Looking back as I got to the top of the hill overlooking the school and the football field, I wondered if this was the last time I'd ever see this place. Another exhale, and the next step. Two thousand three hundred eighty-eight, 2,387, 2,386. Just keep moving. That hand on my shoulder giving a comforting, almost reassuring squeeze and then a nudge. One that felt like I needed to get moving. A sense that timing was important.

I turned in that unhappy direction, and I was a bit startled by an image. The old man with the round face. That white hair and red plaid jacket. It was like he was in a bubble, or maybe a bubble was in front of him. The air distorted, as if I were looking through water or a magnifying glass. The distortion circled him for several feet. He looked down at his feet and then back at me, but I didn't understand the meaning. He seemed like he wanted to lead the way, but it felt more like he needed me to hurry up and keep moving. It wasn't normal for me to hurry these steps, but tonight, that was exactly what I did.

When I got to the place where the plaid-clad old man stood, a shining reflection on the ground caught my eye. I didn't give it a second thought as I paced past it. Then, for some inexplicable reason, I felt the urge to stop. I turned to look back toward the shiny object just as a light bounced off its surface. I stepped back and reached down to pick it up. It was an oversize coin of some sort. Nothing like I'd ever seen. It was heavy with odd markings and a relief of some kind etched into the center. I placed it in my right front pants pocket and turned back to my steps to Crazy.

Before I knew it, I was at the side door. The screaming was already in full force when I opened the door and counted that final step to Crazy. Once inside, all eyes cast upon my face. All the anger and rage boiling in the air was instantly directed at me. It struck with such force that it felt like an invisible hand slapping both cheeks and flicking the tip of my nose. The cold, bitter sting woke all my senses as I felt that animalistic alert pumping from within.

The entire house was awash with a firestorm of hate, and everyone was present, including the shadows. I didn't have a second to adjust my eyes from the moonless night outside to the shadeless lightbulbs illuminating the kitchen before I heard, "*Where the fuck have you been, you good-for-nothing rat bastard?*"

The rooms were filled with former flying objects that had soiled the walls and been smashed to bits. Whatever dinner had been now covered the stove, the wall above the stove, the floor, and part of the ceiling. My sisters were scurrying about to clean up the endless maze of broken dishes, groceries, and flying cookware. A grouping of green beans was glued to one sister's snarled hair. The other sister's shirt was soaked with the fluids flung by the beastly bastard. I must have just missed the main event that started the dinnertime bedlam, but I knew this drill far too well. I now understood the spirited message to quicken my steps.

My brother was lifting the overturned table and putting it back in place as if to reset everything for another round of demented Jenga. As my three siblings put back all the parts and pieces of the kitchen, Mother stood in the pantry with a cloth over her face. I couldn't quite tell if she was crying, wiping her face, or nursing her nose. Crazy must have exhausted himself just before I arrived. He was heading for the living room and walking out of the battle zone so his minions could clean up his handiwork, his favorite bottle of liquid courage in his hand as he pushed back on the easy chair to stretch out and recoup. That smug grin curled up in the corners of his mouth. A gratifying glow circling him like flies ready to dive-bomb cow droppings.

My sisters were both crying, sobbing mostly, and I figured the hard crying had ended a short time ago. There didn't seem to be any dents in those two, so I looked to my brother to check his markings. He had a cut above his eye, and his hair was matted with bits of food. He looked like a modern day poster child of neglect and abuse, the Trick-or-Treat for UNICEF kind with the sad, soaked face from some third world place.

His leg was hurt, by the signs of a limp as he shuffled the table leaf back into place, closing the section that had flipped open after being tossed 180 degrees. It was a scene right out of the funny farm. It would have been insanity for normal people, but for us it was commonplace. How wrong was it to live a life where beatings were normal, terror was customary, and turning the inside of a house upside down was commonplace?

My older sister let out a yelp, recoiling in shock and pain as she lifted her finger. It had a deep cut from the pointy remains of a dinner plate that had slid under the stove. The blood quickly dropped spots on the greasy floor, which was stained with a brown mixture of supper's carcass. I handed her a napkin. Her tear-filled eyes caught mine, and she silently mouthed "thank you" as she knelt in place. Her other hand went back to work cleaning up the mess. She looked back at me and said without sound, "He said he'll kill you… You should go." She nudged her bloody finger toward the door.

I gave her a smile and with a soft breath said, "I'll be all right… Keep the faith!" I had no idea why I said what I said, but as I did my thoughts went to Bethany and her dad.

"I told you to get in here!" commanded the master, this time with all his authority. It did nothing to change my mindset, a growing focus on a plan I could not understand but was willing to execute. Something was urging me forward, something other than my own willingness. I was beginning to feel like I did after Crazy made me break up with Bethany.

Mother was still holding her face under the cloth, a towel darkened with something, water maybe. Was she trying to cool off her face or wipe her tears? I moved toward her and put my left hand on her shoulder. Lifting the towel with my right hand revealed the cloth's secrets. She was crying, all right. The towel was blood soaked, and so was her face. She had a cut over the bridge of her nose and another one on her ear. Looking a bit closer, I saw her fine strands of hair, normally delicate and soft, matted with her own blood. An open wound carved deep into her scalp told the story and reminded me of so many nights just like this one. Something had to change. That urging within me was growing, that one I felt post breaking Bethany's heart.

The scene was so horrific I knew then and there it would never leave my memory. Mother touched my arm and cried even more deeply, more soulfully. Her tears cried out for mercy, begging God for a warrior. Someone to save her children, yet it seemed to be a personal call. It was as if her prayers were hitting me like a drumbeat, commanding I stop this psychotic plague that just kept returning time after time, with no hope of ending or changing unless a warrior materialized. As Mother looked into my eyes, I saw one of her eyes no longer had any white remaining. The red-blood-filled socket with all but a pinprick of brown darted past my gaze and pierced my soul. The clash of pain and fire swelled within me like floodwater stressing the confines of its mighty container. The blink of her swollen, bloody eye broke the bond just before she covered her face and winced from the pain. Her agony added to the growing pyramid of power pumping and pounding its irrepressible potency.

Flashes of our life, times when we were happy, flipped across my mind like a picture show. A slow-motion version of past events played out, mixing the pre-Crazy happy times before being overtaken by the insanity of a life forced to live. An image of a shield mixed in; a horse, a rider, a spear all took part in the flashes, a collage of images showing me this life. A call started to echo inside my head, a whoop and then a screech like that of a large winged creature, a hawk with its mighty talons pointing like knives toward its enemy became clearly visible in my mind.

The images were broken by Mother's words. "Leave before he kills you…He will kill you…Leave, son, before it's too late."

At the same time, Crazy bellowed out his command with every ounce of his professed authority. His demand only strengthened my resolve, and I could feel that power ever growing within, churning like stoking the coals of a fire built to tame steel in a blacksmith's forge.

There had to be an end to this medieval molestation of our minds. The brutalizing of our bodies. The shattering of our spirits. The catastrophic assault on our emotional makeup. It all must come to an end. This cycle of insanity must be stopped.

I turned away from Mother and headed past my siblings right into the wolf's lair. As I crossed the threshold of his kingdom, he was well on his way to rising to his feet to meet my oncoming temperament. The force of wills met with a brief pause, allowing only enough time for Crazy to dip his shoulder and load up his left fist with his infamous hook shot. It was the same swing that had shattered my face in Scotland, as well as my legs. A thousand hate-filled memories crashed across my cranium as he looked to unload his lethal blow.

Without thought, I moved away from his powerful punch by simply sliding to my left and letting his landing hit nothing but air. The follow-through from missing his mark found him falling down like a child after his first step. He landed on his face, sliding on the greasy floor, the sticky mess of supper still not completely cleaned. I wanted to chuckle, but something held it back and readied me for the next round as he rolled himself into a kneeling rethink.

A stunned silence hovered in the heavy night air. Crazy held his position and looked at the rip in his pants. His thigh was bleeding slightly. A knife in his right hand caught my attention. It must have made the cut when he hit the floor, but I never saw it in his grip.

My sisters scramble toward the kitchenette and cradled around Mother's hips, the younger one pressing snugly between the cabinets and the limited space the three corralled.

The bubbles of spiraling black circled him as if to formulate his plan and recharge his batteries. It felt like they were calling in reinforcements. As I stood there, hands by my sides, a reflection in the window behind him cast the image of a horse and rider. Its front hooves rose while its mighty muscles flexed to show the power of the magnificent animal, its feathered rider clutching his spear, holding the reins in his other hand with a shield locked on his forearm. The image cleared when the neighbor pulled her face back and closed the curtains. I couldn't make out if it was the old woman who lived there or if it was the young girl who was friends with my brother and recently moved in.

Crazy's eyes looked down at my pants, below my waistline, that smirk gleaning its hate-filled glare. A cut in almost the same place as his, the midsection of my thigh. Perfectly carving a two-inch slice in the worn-out blue denim jeans. No blood and no pain. Was it that deep and hadn't started to hurt yet? Like the gashes from the glass door at Bethany's home, when nothing hurt for a short while, and then, well, it was incredibly painful? Was this the same kind of cut? Was the pain and blood seconds from claiming its place on the battlefield?

I pushed my fingers into the gash and opened it to see how badly I'd been stabbed. The oversize coin broke free from my pocket and fell to the floor. It landed upright with a *ting* before balancing on its edge. It rolled slowly across the hardwood floor as if blessing the place where my head had been beaten into the boards so many times in the past.

Crazy cast his nastiness with all his might onto that coin as it dared to close the gap and enter his sphere. The roll completed as it touched his toe. It hung for a moment on its rounded edge before falling like a spinning top with that whirling circular noise metal makes as it dances itself to sleep. The faced relief on that coin stared back at Crazy as if to warn him of an ending of his reign.

A crackle and grinding sound emanated from his surroundings. A yellow tinge blossomed about Crazy like a frail flower struggling to open in a warm, tainted mist of a false spring day. A whiff of stove gas tacked across my face with that foul odor of old eggs sitting in the summer sun. Was it a gas leak or something far worse? It felt far worse.

Crazy rose with a slow, dominant demeanor, his arms holding white-knuckled fists formed for the fight. The yellow-black flow darting around him sucked into his shoulders as if on command from his wide-mouthed inhale. His chest bumped forward. His forearm flexed in a forgone warning as his feet charged at me like a demented bull full of green apples.

The thoughts of his prior assaults raced through my mind as I braced for his charge. I bent my knees as if readying for the tackle. The sounds of Coach Perfect hardened the scene as his teachings were heard deep in my mind. A quiet confidence took hold from within before spreading just behind the rage filling my every muscle. It seemed like a slow-motion charge, yet my mind was in full gear. I could see my moves and knew what to do without really knowing how I knew.

Rage and raw power tightened my entire outer self. I sidestepped his charge and hammered his back, knocking him onto the arm of his favorite chair. He wasn't on the floor long before whipping around for his next assault, this one knee level. I moved backward, but my feet caught on scattered debris. His rush crashed us over the TV stand. I kicked him off me and drove him back into Mother's gifted antique mahogany display case. Crazy crashed through the glass door, smashing the family heirlooms. His anger destroyed the remaining cherished pieces to ensure complete devastation of the limited inheritances and shattering any remaining value.

I regrouped and awaited his next move while he picked glass from his upper arm. My sisters were screaming for mercy and begging for help. I heard one on the phone as she'd done before after dialing that number she knew without a reminder. Her terror clearly alarmed the operator, "going to kill him" repeated between the tears and the shrieks. Mother was still standing by the sink, her face buried in the bloody rag, lost in it as if it was her protector. My brother slipped out the side door and hopefully away from the dangers and likely death to follow.

Crazy eyed the shotgun he had concealed behind the now busted cabinet. We both know instantly the one who controls that gun will win this war.

A light flickers from the moving curtains next door and catches both our attention. A pretty face seen through the window pasted behind the glass. Her freckles standing out against her ocean-blue eyes. My attention lost by her beautiful look. For a moment that face charged the air with a hint of happiness and a feeling of hope. My heart smiled a bit as her eyes caught mine, when a flashing sound of "tomorrow" racked my senses. I didn't know why, but I knew I would see her again. As that sweet feeling set in, a sight of that white-laced lady jumped into view.

A crack filled my head, and I saw the floor racing toward my face.

Crazy had hit me with the butt end of the shotgun. Then, in the muffled distance, I heard that sound, one so uniquely metallic it can only be the racking of a round into the chamber. A sickening *click* followed, but there was no *bang*. He tried to reload, but the gun was jammed.

My sisters are screaming with all they have. Begging Crazy to stop and yelling at God, "Don't let my brother die." One sister pleading into the phone, tears streaking down her face.

Crazy tried to hit me again with the butt of the shotgun. I moved just enough to avoid the hit. The gun slammed into the floor with the barrel pointing at the ceiling, when—*bang!*—it went off, sending steel balls into the plaster and cascading a powdery mix into the air. The jolt sent the weapon into its own orbit before stopping once it hit the wall across the room.

He pounced on me and pounded with all he had. The rage and anger pumped throughout my body and my being. *"No more!"* I shouted with a thunderous roar. I flipped his body like a rag doll into the doorjamb. I reached for him with my fingers on fire and gripped his chest, tossing him against the dining room chairs.

Blood was splashing from us both. His mouth was spitting red sauce as flashes of lessons past danced across my mind's eye. Without hesitation, I pulled him from the crumpled mess, lifted him off his feet, and slammed his existence into the hardwood flooring, a place where I'd spent so much time with him above me beating my life away. It was now my turn to teach him the lesson. Burning hatred and evil anger creeping ever so close to controlling my soul.

My weight was on his stomach, my feet locking his legs in place. My fists hammered past the futile protection offered by his weakening limbs, those hands of abuse no longer a threat, his poking steel fingers helpless against the lifetime of praying and plotting the turn of tides; the day of reckoning was raining on Crazy. The pure power I felt as the images of my mother's beatings snapped out like a documentary from the horrors of war. That pure power had a limitless supply of raw anger and rage feeding it fixation and vengeance.

His hands reached for my face. One grabbed my throat, his thumbnail pressing deep into my skin. I shook off his weak effort with a shoulder snap, knocking loose his grip. It was enough to change my focus to ending this evil bastard once and for all. Both hands slid around his neck. The web of my thumbs lodged securely under his protruding Adam's apple. My fingers squeezed like a vise grip of death so tightly I could have popped off his head. It felt like I held the force of thunder and the power of lightning in my fingertips and I alone controlled destiny!

His chest settled a bit. His hands weakened. His arms dangled slightly. His legs yelled in a frantic shaking and then stiffened, rigidly pointing like wooden arrows locked in flight. Froth foamed in the corners of his smirk-lacking mug. The dark light of his eyes stepped back with a pause before fading down that same tunnel I had faced so many times before. He gasped and spit as I rested my grip. Blood shot from his mouth onto my face. Free-floating red mist flung through the air like confetti at the Macy's Day Parade. The slow-motion fall of the blood spatter changed my focus as I watched it drift downward like the fine spray of an ocean wave.

His great hatred was lifting out of the center of his chest, rising like smoke drifting skyward. A clammy calm claimed the room. The utter silence inside me was one I'd never known. It was like walking among the stars, surrounded by vast open space and billions of miles of calm, peaceful silence. The quiet was so great I no longer felt my body or my hands as they fought to finish their work. My heart felt free of all my pain. It was as if my prayers had been answered.

In the distance I saw the white-laced lady, her flowing grace captivating and warming. She pointed at me as if to suggest some meaning, something within. She seemed to be giving me options, but I didn't understand...or did I!

The feeling of being caught between the world of Crazy and the peaceful presence of the white-lace lady was momentarily broken by his entire body shaking beneath me. The sight of a shadow walking out of Crazy created a clear image just inches in front of me. The feeling of a life force surrendering the will to exist. As I watched the life leave his being, I could feel sadness begin from an unlikely place. A picture of Bethany as she mouthed the words, "Let it go...Let it go." Her smile reclaimed the fog hanging over my heart. The darkness that seemed to be transferring me was broken. The picture of Bethany's smile, her voice, her loving warmth reopened my senses. I released my grip around his lifeline and pushed myself off his beaten remains.

The sweet sound of Bethany's voice and her heartwarming image yielded to the noise all around me. My sister's screaming, the banging on the door. The knuckles rapping on the window behind me. The yelling. "Open the door *now*" coming from outside. Standing over Crazy, looking down at my life's mission as the cops filled the rooms. "*Step back*...Step away from him," commanded someone with actual authority.

Two officers grabbed ahold of my arms and escorted me outside. My sisters were crying hysterically. Screams of "He's dead" slowly withdrew into bellows of sad, hurtful sobs. Paramedics rushed into the house. The street was lined with cruisers flashing red and blue lights. More authorities entered the scene. Cops crowded the small front lawn. Neighbors watched from all directions, pointing, talking, shaking their heads. Kids on bikes raced to see what was happening. I knew most of the people in the growing crowd, and they knew me.

Mother was pulled from the house, resisting the order to leave, the order to get to the ambulance. Her bloody face was clear to all watching, her blouse caked in dark-red batter, her hair stuck in all directions. My sisters were taken out of that house ahead of me and were now standing beside a cruiser a few yards down the street. As I passed my sisters, I saw the old man in red plaid standing across the street. His round face offered nothing of things to come. Just a stoic stare of quiet reflection.

The entire scene had settled down, with each of us being questioned as to what had happened. Then, without warning, one of the EMTs bolted from the house, a look of total fear strapped to his face. He cleared the front door and smacked square into the cops on the porch. Without so much as a by-your-leave, the seasoned paramedic jumped from the porch to the sidewalk below and ran straight to the street. He didn't stop running until he was corralled by several cops as if he was fleeing a crime. "I'm *not* going back in there. Now *let me go!*" yelled the uniformed figure.

A startling concern gathered with an unknown wondering. Questions abounded as we all turned back to that house. The rising tones were followed by a commotion, and then it was as if there was an all-out fight happening inside, but how and with whom?

Radios crackled with codes and calls for assistance from inside that house. Several cops rushed from the crowded street and lawn. Up the steps, past the front door, and into the fray. After a few tense minutes, it settled down as one of the cops walked out the door. "We've got it under control."

It must have been my brother, but he'd never resist. Maybe he had lost his mind and given in to the ways of Crazy! As thoughts raced through my mind, several cops crossed the threshold with someone in tow. Surrounded by a half dozen dark-blue uniforms was a figure, facedown and being carried out the door, hands cuffed from behind, ankles shackled and chained to the cuffs on both wrists. His body was bent like an inverted human U. The six burly officers shuffled past the door and headed down the steps before his head lifted as he passed me by. The flashing colored lights and limited visibility on the street or from the porch made it hard to see who it was. That all changed the second the sound blasted from his mouth. "*This isn't over.*" It was Crazy! He was alive!

My heart sank in sheer disbelief, and at the same time, it filled me with respite, the strangest mix of feelings anyone could experience. Like the Wicked Witch before the house fell on her, he blew a storm of warning. "I'll get you for this. This ain't over...I'll fix you!"

The threats were real, but the impact landed with little if any meaningful punch. The vile vomit he was shouting as he was tossed onto the back of the cruiser had far more impact on the neighbors and law enforcement than it did on me. I would never again be beaten, by him or anyone else, ever. That was the feeling that levied on me as he was driven away.

The next officer to come talk to me was one I'd engaged with in the past. This wasn't going to be much fun. "We'll be placing you under arrest for the time being, or until we can figure out what happened here. Your sisters said your father—"

I cut him off midsentence. "He's not my father."

"Whatever the case may be, we still need to sort this out, and until we do, you're being detained. If your—if *he* presses charges, well, you'll have to deal with that once it happens."

What the hell did that mean? "If he presses charges"? Sweet Jesus! This was going to be an even longer night! "Son, officers saw you on top of him through the window; we need to figure this out, and jail is the safest place for now," said the cop.

I was taken to the hospital to be looked over and patched up, as need be, before completing the journey to lockup. By the time I got to the police station, it was well past midnight. The shift change had the tales of a crazed man coming back "from the dead" with a fire and vengeance never seen by the local force. They told a story of an EMT so terrified he had to be admitted into the hospital. Apparently this EMT, and a few others, had seen something no one could understand or explain. It would make an interesting tale if only they knew "the rest of the story," to steal a phrase from Paul Harvey.

It was a long night, but I never did end up in a cell. Instead I was offered a cot in a back room, given a sandwich and a soda, and told to get some sleep. They'd need to talk to me in the morning. For now, they wanted me to be safe. Crazy found his way into the rooms with the bars.

I kept it simple in the morning. I didn't really say much except that I was protecting myself, my sisters, and my mother. For now I was being charged with breach of peace, and unless Crazy pressed assault charges, that would be the end of it. Unless, of course, the prosecutor had other ideas.

One of the young cops told me his boss, the police chief, had gotten a visit from a friend of mine. That friend had spoken highly of me and asked the chief to go easy on me. The only friend I knew with that kind of pull was Bethany's dad. I was released with a promise to show up for a court date, as my unknown benefactor had also vouched and assured the prosecutor I wouldn't miss the date and that I'd "stay out of trouble."

When I got back to that house, it was cold and quiet. No one had returned, and the mess was displayed in all its unbelievable glory. As I stood surveying the damage, I thought about the question from the lead detective: "What will you do from here?"

"I was wondering the same thing, and honestly, I have no idea. Any chance you're looking to adopt a teenager?"

My comment made him smile before he said, "*Nope.*"

I checked the window to see if I was going to get any help from the reflection, but nothing happened in the glass. However, the lady next door was watching, and she pulled her curtains shut when she saw me look in her direction. Standing in the broken remains of the kitchen, with rotting food splashed across the floor and walls, I pondered what was next for me. What would I do? What could I do? Where could I go? How would I live or even survive? I had no place to turn to and no direction to pick! What were my options?…Did I even have any options? One thing was certain: I was all alone, and I needed to figure out a life away from this insanity.

First I needed to clean up this mess. My sisters had no options either, and I knew they'd be back here sooner or later. So I set myself to cleaning and fixing everything I could. It took a few hours, but when I was done, at the very least, my sisters wouldn't have to deal with it.

I headed to my room to figure out how to complete the only option available. The only choice that seemed to make sense, regardless of how hopeless it felt. I brought along a trash bag and a length of rope as part of the plan. As I passed the front door just before the stairs, I saw a police cruiser parked on the street. The cop was just sitting there. I waited and watched him for a little bit before heading upstairs. Maybe the cops were just giving the neighbors comfort. Who knows? As long as he didn't bother me.

As I moved up the stairs, I wondered aloud how many steps it would take to actually complete my unknown plan. Was the first one going to be the toughest, or would it be the last one, the final step? Maybe the final step would be the best one ever. Either way, I had to bring this to an end; of this I was certain.

I wondered what would happen to my sisters when I wasn't there anymore. I wondered if my brother would miss me or if he'd just say, "It is what it is" and keep moving forward in his distinctive way. Maybe it would be better for everyone once I was gone. Maybe Crazy would leave them alone, finally. Once I was gone, I'd bet he'd be happy. He'd have succeeded in his decade-plus-long plan to get rid of me. I'd bet he wouldn't even know I was gone or that I had ever really been there after a few days passed without me. Then my thoughts turned to Mother.

Mother...oh, my mother. That one and only person a child has to look to for that special bond. That unique feeling known universally as a mother's love. There was no other way on earth to replicate that feeling, and no matter how badly a mother treats her child, that bond remains.

Of course, something changes when you reach this point and you're forced to make a choice, a decision like I had to. I wondered what had happened in her life that caused her to make the decisions she did. Was she simply following in her mother's footsteps? Was it that simple? Would my sisters follow in hers?

One thing was for sure—I wasn't going to follow in her steps, and I had a plan to make sure it never happened. Would I miss her when I was gone? Was it possible to miss her? So many questions ran through my head. Here I sat as a brand-new teenager wondering what would happen once I was gone. I just wanted to be a kid, have fun, play baseball and football, and chase girls! How I wished I could talk to Bethany. I missed her so much and wished I'd never hurt her. I wondered what she would think of my plan. Thinking about her reaction had me worried, and the more I thought about Bethany, the more sadness gripped my throat and squeezed my heart.

I'd better stop thinking about all this before I changed my mind. I sat down with my face in my hands, tears pouring from my eyes. My insides hurt so much; I just wanted all the pain to stop. I was so confused and so alone...What would I do?

After a short while sitting on the edge of my bed, I took a deep breath and opened the heavy-duty black plastic trash bag, snapping and popping it a couple of times so it would open fully. I looked inside its vast emptiness with a pausing stare, thinking out my final decision, the last one I'd ever make in this house. The end game! I placed the rope on my pillow and stood up. Just as I did, I heard the front door close and the sound of Mother's voice calling from below.

—✺—

"I'm up here," I shouted, and she started climbing the stairs. She reached the bedroom door and stopped in the hallway. Her face was patched, bandages covering the markings of her choices in life. "Who cleaned up downstairs?" she asked.

"The cops did. They showed up with guns, badges, and buckets with mops. They brought their own paper towels and Windex too!"—my response with a bit of attitude.

She tilted her head as if debating if it really happened.

"Really, Mother, who do you think cleaned the mess?"

"Well, it all happened because of you," she responded.

Silence followed as we looked at each other, caught between the remains of that mother's love and brutal reality. The wall grew a little taller, protecting against the pain from within this house. The walls we create to protect our emotions from people like Crazy.

I snapped the trash bag back to life, and with pointed indifference, my eyes moved from her broken face. "I'm leaving." I started to put the few clothes I had into the black garbage bag. I searched for socks and that secret stash of money I had hidden under the radiator.

Mother said nothing as she watched me pack. I felt a huge sense of relief, but I wasn't sure whether it was coming from inside me or from Mother.

By the time I had the plastic bag filled with my belongings, she still hadn't said a word or moved from her perch just outside the door.

"Where will you go?" she finally asked.

"I have no idea," I said. "But I need to get out of here, Mother, before this place kills me. And I'd tell you to do the same, but I know that won't happen."

"I won't stop you, but I am worried about you and where you'll be."

Now she wanted to worry about me. I was puzzled. In my heart I still loved her as deeply as I could ever remember, like those happy days before Crazy crept into our lives. I felt sad for her and, at the same time, oddly happy for me. It was time to move on and find a life, a real life.

I walked past her and down the stairs and opened the front door. Mother was a step or two behind me. I turned to look over my cleanup work and get a last memory of this hellish household. My jacket was still in the kitchen, so I dropped the bag and headed to grab it. I stuffed it into the bag, tied the rope around the top and under the bag, and slung it over my shoulder. My right arm reached out and pulled Mother to me for a last embrace. I gave her a kiss on her forehead, a smile, and a soft "Goodbye, Mother."

As I crossed the threshold onto the porch, I almost thought I heard her start to cry, but I was unwilling to turn back ever again. I went down the last steps from Crazy's house and onto the sidewalk's path to freedom. I looked to my left and then to my right, not sure which direction to turn. This was as far as I had thought out my plan. At the sound of a shutting door, I looked to my left at the police cruiser. Its uniformed officer was walking toward me.

Just past the cop was that old man in plaid, his white hair standing out against his red checked jacket. He had a crinkle across his mouth like the makings of a smile forcing its limited presentation. To his right turned his face. Standing beside him was a young woman a foot or so taller than he was. She had long, flowing blond hair with deep-blue eyes that felt like they touched my soul. His arm reached behind her back as if to gesture her forward in some kind of handoff. No words came forward. Not a sound was heard, but I had a feeling of something I'd been told many times before entering my mind. "You'll be okay...keep moving forward." There seemed to be something more, but I couldn't clearly get it in my mind. Just as I thought I was about to understand…

"*Son*…you all right?" broke through from the officer. "What are you looking at?" he asked as he turned and looked toward the old man. It was best not to answer; I had enough issues in my life without having to explain seeing people no one else could see.

"The prosecutor wants to see you. Seems you might be in more trouble than my boss could deflect. You should get a lawyer. I think you're going to need one. Officer Winkler started a collection fund for you. Said you helped catch the guys who robbed his home last year, and he wants to try to help if he can."

With that, the officer handed me an envelope. "Where will you go?" he asked.

"Honestly, sir, I have no idea. But I need to find a way to end this cycle of insanity before I end up in prison or worse. All I have is a feeling of hope, a vision of a life outside this place, and a garbage bag of dirty clothes. I need to figure it out."

"Some big guy with an accent came by the station looking for you. Said you'd know who he was and that he left something in your locker. He said you were starting on the varsity team this weekend, and he was here to watch you play. He said you have a future and we should keep an eye on you. Anyway, I have to get back to the station.

"One more thing. The chief said to let you know your mother signed a statement saying you were the cause of the fight and your fath—her husband—didn't do anything but try to protect himself. Seems she's blaming you for everything."

It was a heartbreaking statement but not a surprising one.

As he turned to walk back to his cruiser, the old man and young woman were still standing there, watching, waiting. He opened the car door and said with a commanding voice, "Keep the faith…Keep moving forward." Then,\ a look of confusion covered his face, as if he was wondering what had caused him to say those words.

Behind him, the old man pointed with his left arm as if telling me which direction to head.

I looked up the road and then back toward the place where my two friends were standing, but they were gone. The cruiser drove off, and I turned to my right for a short glance at Mother as she leaned in the doorway. Her arms were folded across her chest before she offered a single curt wave with one hand and a melancholic "Gooood luuuck…"

My customary inhale, this one deeper than ever before. I let it loose as I looked down to my feet and then took that first step toward hope as a new feeling of freedom washed over my entire existence. This first step was going to be easy, and I wondered how many steps it would take to get to that unknown place in front of me.

In the distance, the sounds of police sirens started their winding noise. My heart and my step quickened in unison as the sounds behind me gained in volume and proximity. A huge smile splashed across my face at the same moment I heard clearly in my ears the sharp whisper of that voice I'd come to trust: "*Keep the faith…Keep moving forward…* Just do it a bit quicker!"

Made in the USA
Columbia, SC
12 May 2023